Settling the Canadian-American West, 1890–1915

Settling the Canadian-American West, 1890–1915

Pioneer Adaptation and Community Building

An Anthropological History

John W. Bennett

and

Seena B. Kohl

University of Nebraska Press

Lincoln and London

♾ The paper in this book meets the minimum requirements of American National Standard for Information Sciences—Permanence of Paper for Printed Library Materials, ANSI Z39.48-1984.

Library of Congress Cataloging-in-Publication Data
Bennett, John William, 1915–
Settling the Canadian-American West, 1890–1915: pioneer adaptation and community building / John W. Bennett and Seena B. Kohl.
p. cm.
Includes bibliographical references and index.
ISBN 0-8032-1254-2
1. Frontier and pioneer life—Northwestern States. 2. Land settlement—Northwestern States—History. 3. Northwestern States—History. 4. Frontier and pioneer life—Prairie Provinces. 5. Land settlement—Prairie Provinces—History. 6. Prairie Provinces—History. I. Kohl, Seena B. II. Title.
F597.B456 1996
979.5—dc20 95-1826
CIP

When we think about the Virgin Prairie
when those dedicated people came and all the
hours of hard work, heartache, and sacrifices
that made it what it is today;
it almost seems like a cake baked by God
and frosted by these hardworking pioneers.
Perhaps this is why some of us still hang on to this land
our fathers worked so hard to own.

Vera Johnson Kuenzel,
from a reminiscence of her childhood
on a homestead in northern Montana

Contents

Illustrations

Figures

Table

Photographic Portfolio

Acknowledgments

The book was a collaborative venture, with the authors jointly responsible for the project planning and fieldwork and the basic design and first drafts of the manuscript. Rose Passalacqua served as editorial assistant for several versions of the manuscript. However, the final version was produced mainly by John Bennett, assisted by Charu Malik. Judith Anderson read the final manuscript and offered many useful suggestions.

Dan S. Sherburne was responsible for collecting and analyzing data on migration and demography, a project that was initiated by Niki Clark; Christine Hensley was responsible for the historiographic analysis and bibliography of the local history books. Niki Clark developed the early computer bibliographic referencing procedures to record source materials, later expanded by Hensley. Washington University undergraduates Martha Kohl and Julie Zimmerman Holt analyzed documents and built collections of relevant topics. Artwork was supplied by Jeff Kaufman and Jason Shapiro. Dan Sherburne, Martha Kohl, and Kathryn Bennett assisted the authors in the field and contributed to the search for documents.

Major financial support for the project from 1985 through 1989 was supplied by two successive grants from the National Endowment for the Humanities. The Department of Anthropology at Washington University provided various secretarial and financial services; special thanks go to Marcella Waddell, Carol Pettus, Stephen Molnar, and Robert Canfield. The Faculty Development Leave program at Webster University freed Seena Kohl from a portion of her teaching responsibilities. Curators and librarians in the following historical societies and archives provided help in locating materials: in Montana, the Montana Historical Society, the Blaine County Historical Society, the H. Earl Clack Memorial Museum, the Mansfield Archives at the Montana State University Library at Bozeman, and the University of Montana at Missoula; in North Dakota, the State Historical Heritage Society, Bismark; in Alberta, the Provincial Archives, the Medicine Hat Museum, the Glenbow Library and Archives, and the Sir Alexander Galt Museum and Archives of Lethbridge; in Saskatchewan, the Provincial Archives, the Saskatchewan Folklore Society, the Canadian Plains Research Center, and the Regina Public Library; and in the Midwest, the Minnesota Historical Society, the Wisconsin Historical Society, the Westerheim Museum in Decorah, Iowa, and the Norwegian American Historical Association.

Among many of the persons who responded to our requests for searches, we mention the following as especially helpful: Dave Walter of the Montana Historical Society, Donny White of the Medicine Hat Museum, Ian and Ruth Wilson, formerly of the Saskatchewan Archives, Jean Dryden of the Provincial Archives of Alberta, Darrell Henning of the Westerheim Museum, Jack Holzheuter of the Wisconsin Historical Society, Douglass Cass of the Glenbow Museum and Archives, and Kenneth Aitken of the Regina Public Library. Throughout the study Glenda Bradshaw of Helena, Montana, played an important role in archival research for Montana. Judy Sterner of Calgary, Alberta, and Stuart Mein and Herb and Alice Gruning of Regina, Saskatchewan, also provided research support. Mein compiled a bibliography of the special corporate settlements (sectarian and secular) in Saskatchewan and Alberta, in preparation for a special study we were not able to complete, because of lack of time and funds.

Local historians and librarians in Saskatchewan, Alberta, and Montana provided cordial and interested help. In particular we thank Joel Overholser of Fort Benton, Montana, Alex Johnston (now deceased) of Lethbridge, Alberta, Conrad K. Warren of Deerlodge, Montana, and Eleanor Clack of Havre, Montana.

The work of academic historians David C. Jones, Henry Klassen, Ian MacPherson, Clyde Milner, Howard Palmer, Ralph Roeder, Eliane Silverman, and Paul Voisey provided important ideas and perspectives. We are indebted to all the local history book compilers and writers, in particular Ruby Langel of Chester, Montana, who assembled most of the materials used for the chapter on the railroad-homestead town. We also thank the editors of the local history books who agreed to be interviewed and the many more who responded to our survey. The remarkable historical consciousness displayed by the heirs of the pioneers of this region is in part due to the efforts of local historians and the major historical institutions in encouraging their writing.

Settling the Canadian-American West, 1890–1915

Chapter 1

Locale and Approach

This book is based on the use of remembered experience for understanding how people adapt to new environments and create communities. The setting is the Canadian-American West during its final period of agrarian settlement, from approximately 1890 to 1920. This settlement of the northern U.S. states and the Canadian prairie provinces was fed by migrations from Europe and eastern North America and represents the last great westward population movement in the history of the continent.

The people involved in this population movement and their descendants have produced autobiographical materials of many kinds, and the communities they formed have compiled histories of growth and development. By the 1980s, several hundred published local histories existed. Our interest in these materials was awakened during our earlier research in the region, which was governed by objectives more aligned toward social structure and economic development and could not fully utilize documents of this type.[1]

The reminiscences and works of history cited in the book are presented in three sections of the bibliography. The general section contains all published sources referred to in the text by an author's name and date. The second section comprises local history sources and includes a map of our "Heartland Collection" of community history books; each local history book (LHB) is given a number, which appears at the end of any quotation taken from that book. Archival documents and privately printed manuscripts make up the final section.

Most of this literature does not adhere to accepted academic standards, and it has been criticized for this by professional historians (Bowsfield 1969; Orser 1988; Voisey 1985), although some have begun to appreciate its usefulness.[2] The chief problem in analyzing the material is familiar to all scholars who work with personal documents: the interplay between authenticity and veracity. The first term concerns the "ring of truth"; the latter concerns the facts—details of dates, persons, and events. Although in our research we were concerned with both, we were perhaps more sensitive to authenticity than the academic historian would be. We looked for insights into the process of behavioral adaptation and therefore focused on what the writers emphasized, repeated, rationalized, glossed over, or obsessively dwelt upon. These interpretive vectors suggested which aspects of their experiences were important to the first settlers and their descendants. They represent for us the experience of settlement and community as it has become translated into cultural heritage. At the same time, we were able to verify the details of much of this material; for example, accounts of events and experiences could be checked against news items and detailed local histories.

The book has a binational perspective; the term "Canadian-American West" pertains to Canada and the United States. This perspective is established in historical writings (e.g., Sharp 1955) acknowledging that for the century preceding the decisive settlement of the region, human traffic moved freely north and south across what eventually became the international boundary. For the most part, the people who settled the region were from similar ethnic and national backgrounds, and criss-crossed the boundary in search of ideal locations. Even today, the international boundary crossings in the vast sweep of northern plains country between western Ontario and North Dakota in the east and Alberta and Montana in the west are often routine and perfunctory affairs, when one may spend more time visiting and gossiping with the customs officials than proving one's nationality or submitting to luggage searches.[3] The process of settlement was, in both countries, mediated by powerful federal government programs, facilitated by private railroad interests, and supplied from the same eastern sources. The strategies of obtaining land, establishing homes and farms, and creating towns were virtually identical on both sides of the

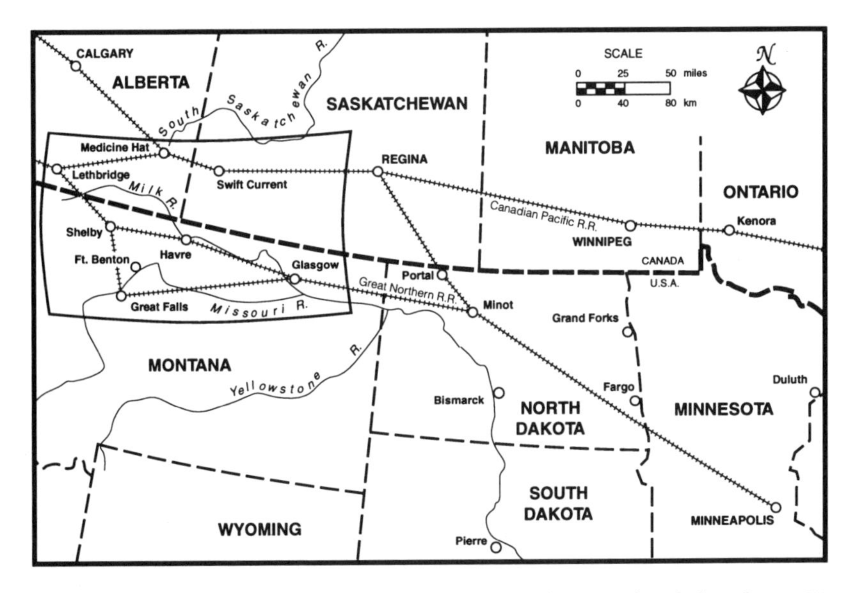

Figure 1. The Northern Great Plains (box refers to the area detailed in figure 2). Principal provinces, states, towns, and cities circa 1900. Portions of Ontario and Minnesota are included to suggest the important staging areas for emigrant movement. The two major railroads—the Canadian Pacific and the Great Northern—are shown, plus the two principal north-south connecting lines in the east and west.

fence and, in fact, were a matter of joint planning in some cases and deliberate imitation in others.

The region we studied can be defined as a rectangle within a larger region extending north and south of the international boundary (see figures 1 and 2). The larger area (figure 1), which we call the Northern Great Plains, includes portions of western Minnesota, North Dakota, and Montana on the U.S. side and southern portions of the provinces of Ontario, Manitoba, Saskatchewan, and Alberta on the Canadian. The smaller region (figure 2) we call the Canadian-American West Heartland. It is equivalent to the "Whoop-up Country" described by Paul Sharp (1955)—the area where Indians, fur traders, settlers, Mounties, and the U.S. Cavalry interacted vigorously in the last half of the nineteenth century and the early twentieth century. Another familiar name for the U.S. side is the "Montana Hi-Line," which refers to the row of counties across the northern rim of the state and their linking transportation routes.

The northern plains region has a twinned appearance: On the Canadian side, runs the Canadian-Pacific Railroad; on the U.S. side, the Great

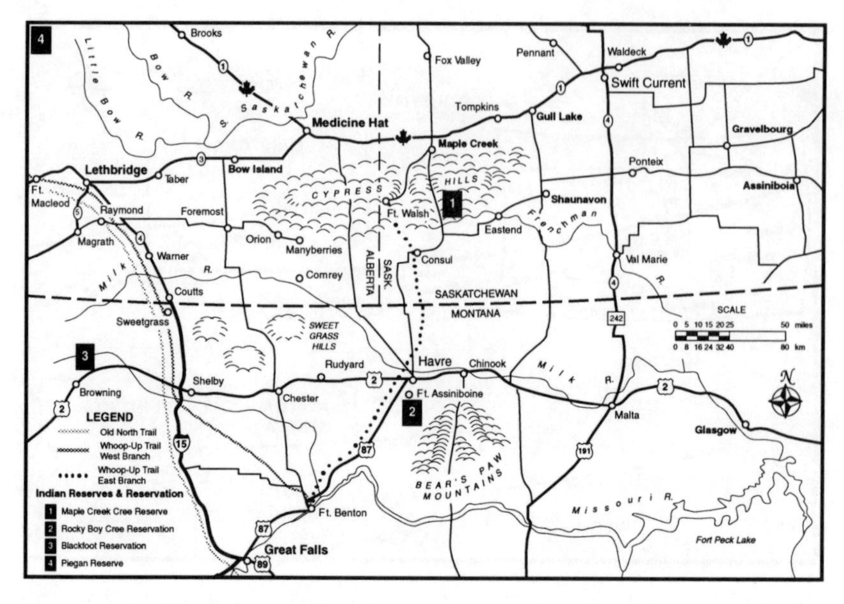

Figure 2. The Canadian-American West Heartland. This figure continues the mapping of transportation arteries by showing the major east-west and north-south automobile highways. The map does not describe any specific time period; it includes old trails as well as modern highways. (See figure 1 for the major rail lines.)

Northern; Route 1, the Trans-Canada Highway, roughly parallels U.S. 2; there is a balance between major cities, like Medicine Hat, Alberta, and Great Falls, Montana, and secondary centers, like Swift Current, Saskatchewan, and Havre, Montana. This mirror-imaging is of course the result of the similarity of settlement and development policies on both sides of the boundary, operating in a region with parallel geographical features.

It is a sparsely settled region, a land of great open spaces, relatively few towns and villages, and modest networks of roads. The rural population, never dense, hit its peak around 1910, when settlement programs on both sides attained their apex. Population declined steadily thereafter but may have reached stability in most districts by the late 1980s.

The open character of the terrain does not mean that there is an absence of physical resources that would attract settlement but rather that its resources are few and specialized—production for the markets of agriculture and extractive industries such as oil, potash, coal—and are manipulated by the larger society with speculative commodity pricing. This causes the local socioeconomic system to undergo continual fluctuation, making investment risky or scarce. The combination of the basic resources—land, water, soil, minerals, and climate—and the way our economic system uses them has produced the vast "empty" territory A. B. Guthrie Jr. called "big sky" country.

It is also rough country, country not beautiful as landscape beauty is generally defined by North American and European civilization. Mountains become visible on the horizon if you go far enough west. Inside the region occasional islands of hills or plateaus rise two thousand to three thousand feet above the plain. The ground is sometimes level but more often rolling and lacking conspicuous vegetation; there are few trees in the prairie (as the Canadians call it) or plains (the term depends on the country or which geographer you read). Early explorers called it a desert because of its aridity, its variable temperatures (which often span forty degrees in twenty-four hours), its violent thunderstorms and blizzards, and its almost constant wind, blowing cold from the northwest or hot and dry from the south. These conditions were not inviting for prospective settlers who wanted to remain in the region. It was especially hard country to farm, and physical discomfort, combined with disappointment and anxiety, was a major cause of the steady exodus of settlers.

The region was known as "man's country" to the early ranchers, cowhands, trail bosses, and fur traders, and this attitude may be one reason for the exaggerated courtesy shown to women as the weaker sex, which persists in the northern plains even though it has been abandoned in more urbanized parts of western North America. However, the attitude was also accompanied by a contrasting image: the rugged frontier woman and homestead housewife who weathered the storms, raised her family, and guided her husband.

Does the sparseness of settlement imply failure of some kind? Well, yes, in terms of the hopes and expectations of those settlers who wanted to build the legendary "City on a Hill" or find what Harry McClintock and later Wallace Stegner called the Big Rock Candy Mountain. However, the rugged few who managed to carve out a living in spite of, or because of, the challenges of climate and economic insecurity found the country and sparse settlement rewarding. They were the stayers, and it is their experiences on the whole that are featured in the writings produced by the third and fourth generations away from settlement at the end of the twentieth century.

These writings, plus material in the locally published history books and letters, diaries, and anecdotes sequestered in regional archives, are our primary sources of data. They feature two main kinds of memory, corresponding to the individual and group levels of adaptation to the frontier. The first kind includes the reminiscence and autobiographical materials, written by people who had the experiences or who learned about them from parents or grandparents. The second kind consists of the collective memories of community life in the local history books, which contain stories about the forging of bonds between people, or the key events in the life of a town or country neighborhood. The influences that shape or modify memory differ for the two types of literature, but the distinction is hard to make because the community history writings are often highly individualistic; that is, the writers identify the community with their own experiences and those of immediate associates and family members. This was inevitable in the pioneer situation, owing to the very small population, the prevalent mutual aid and shared experiences and hardships, and the need to work together to create a community. But the memories, however individualistic they may be, are still part of the shared or collective memory of the community, and the basic rationale for writing the local history books is to reproduce, gather, and inscribe this shared memory for the ages.[4]

The genre contains certain constraints. As one grandson of a pioneer rancher observed, "I can think of a lot of things to say, but I don't dare put them down on paper." The constraints are both formal and informal; people writing about their community in a celebratory spirit are not inclined to recite embarrassing anecdotes, and when the writings are part of official community history projects, the editors often instruct the writers to go easy on such material. Despite these controls, much does come out, often carefully hedged as innuendo or, in a few cases, as poems, jokes, or anonymous anecdotes.

Another set of constraints derives from the nature of the sponsorship of these writings. The recent efflorescence is the result not only of a generational progression in awareness of history but also of direct financial support offered by historical societies and planning commissions associated with political anniversaries. Both Canada and the United States in the 1960s, '70s, and '80s had a plethora of anniversaries of "foundings"—of neighborhoods, towns, provinces, states, even nations, events associated with the migration to the Canadian-American West and its aftermath of political consolidation. The editors and sponsors of the local history books and reminiscences series have local agendas and responsibilities not always associated with the impartial reconstruction of history or social analysis. As anthropologists interested in culturally shaped interpretations of experience, we can appreciate this spirit and profit from it.

There have been changes in the form and content of local historical writings based on changes in local concepts of history. Early publications were attempts either to write a simple, factual history of the founding of a town or, in the country neighborhoods, to describe the establishment of a community by describing the experiences of a few founders and their interactions with neighbors. The focus is on the locality: its residents and institutions. The later, more comprehensive books tend to emphasize the experiences of families and individual settlers; they are influenced by the concept of heritage, remembered experience.

The Influence of Heritage

The heritage concept implies that the history of a locality becomes a statement about its remembered cultural composition or identity. The Canadian or American nationality of the localities in our region is taken as a given, but within and beyond this ascribed identity are other sources of identification, including the nationality of an individual's forebears, religion, kinship connections, and place of birth, whether as remote as the former homeland or as near as the immediate neighborhood where settlement first occurred. And this latter identification is what leads to the basic format of the large, comprehensive local history books written in the 1970s and '80s: Every person who settled or even wandered through the area deserves inclusion, and so do all the churches, clubs, nationalities, and even the stores. Heritage is therefore a celebration of pluralism. Today the very word "heritage" also connotes an undifferentiated past time when people were special, unique, when life was harder but also more colorful and authentic. Above all, it refers to people and things that *must not be forgotten*. This cherishing and safeguarding of the source is often considered to be more important than telling a chronologically ordered story. Thus, the geological past, Indians, curious features of the landscape, old trails, pioneer ways—all these phenomena can be considered the "heritage" of the people of the present.

Since heritage as a quasi-literary movement is in part the product of specialists—scholars and cultural and commercial promoters interested in tourism, printing contracts, and the construction of museum displays and libraries—it represents to some extent a conception of history imposed on the localities. While local people still write the local history books, they do so in part in a framework given to them by outsiders—sympathetic outsiders, but people nevertheless outside the community culture. From the practical standpoint of the analysis of documents, this means that one must pay close attention to directives and guidance supplied to the editors and writers. As such directives are institutionalized, their content moves upward into national-level literature through museum displays, scholarly histories, accounts of such topics as the role of the frontier woman (and the ties of this topic to the feminist movement), and television specials and films on the West, frontier life, and migration. In turn, this growing incorporation of local history into the national cultural media feeds back into the community and influences local producers of the material.

Veracity, Authenticity, and Enhancement

The problem that must be faced by every analyst of events taking place in the recent past—within the span of, say, three generations—is that professional writers, like novelists, are capable of rendering more colorful and detailed accounts of past events than most people who actually witnessed them. In addition, "true-to-life" accounts of events were often not written by witnesses at the time they occurred but produced years later by those witnesses. In other words, re-created or at least partly fictional memories can appear to be more authentic than true memories (the law of literary authenticity), and, as time passes, people can become capable of writing more persuasively or colorfully about events they experienced some time ago (the law of retrospective enhancement).

These two "laws" suggest that a writer with imagination, working with good data from the past, is capable of recapturing that past more authentically than actual participants who wrote letters or diaries, and that a certain detachment or temporal distance is required before one can realize the importance and meaning of experience—or at least attach such enhanced meanings to the memories. These laws are hardly original; every historian and historical novelist discovers them, sooner or later. A first-class play or motion picture can re-create the meaning or visual imagery of the past better than quickie novels or autobiographies written earlier; historical reconstructions of complex events, taking into account every factor in their interrelationships, may be more accurate than contemporaneous journalistic accounts written by competent observers. Memory, literary capability, imagination, objectivity, time, and reflection are all factors that influence the record of events and experiences in complex ways.

In reading our source materials, we sometimes made comparisons between the two forms of writing in terms of tone and the implicit meaning of the experiences rendered, although we did not use the belles lettres materials to document or validate what we found in the original documents. That is, we tried to choose sources that had reasonable veracity as well as an element of authentic color.

Often early reminiscences and autobiographical materials produced by first-generation settlers are rather austere and factual; feeling tone and meaning must be guessed or interpolated. Later reminiscences, written for the most part by men and women who experienced the frontier as children, are usually more detailed, more "literary" in their use of figures of speech and adjectives, and have more complex sentence structure, all resulting from advanced education. This distinction can be illustrated by juxtaposing two accounts of similar experiences, by different writers, years apart:

> My father had me get up early in the morning to see to it that the stock was watered.
>
> Written about 1926, by a man in his early thirties

> Those cold winter mornings, when the icy fog rose around the barn, and the dairy cows moved around restlessly, will stay in my memory forever.
>
> Written about 1965, by a man in his mid-sixties

Which description is preferable? For what purposes? Should the analyst trust the first statement more than the second because it was written earlier, by a person whose age gives the reader confidence in the possibility that he actually had the experience? Or does the reader feel more inclined to use the second statement, where the chance of fictionalization may be greater but the feeling tone appears to display greater authenticity? We had to make many decisions of this kind, and we often compromised, extracting fact from simpler, perhaps truer accounts but color and meaning from the usually later, more elaborated versions.

Three Terms: "Frontier," "Pioneer," and "Adaptation"

In organizing and interpreting the materials, three terms or concepts gave us difficulty because their usages are inconsistent and vague.

The first term is "frontier." Any frontier, of course, is not so much a place as a moving line; as people enter an unpopulated place, it becomes a frontier, but almost immediately thereafter it becomes a settlement. Only in the *very* dim past were the western lands truly unpopulated, but the invading settlers refused to accept the Native Americans as legitimate inhabitants. Still, the word "frontier" in general connotes an undeveloped place where one had to do one's best in order to survive. Actually, in northwestern North America there were several frontiers in addition to the agricultural one: the fur trade frontier, the mining frontier, the mountaineers' frontier, and the urban frontier (the last referring to the small cities that sprang up along with mining, the buffalo bone industry, and other instant means of capital accumulation, often in advance of permanent rural settlement). "Frontier" can also be used as an explanatory concept, as Frederick J. Turner employed it in his well-known "frontier thesis" on the origins of American democracy (Turner 1920). The Turner approach had enormous influence on the writing and interpretation of American history, and the Canadians and Russians, both with substantial frontier episodes in their histories, have felt compelled to comment (e.g., Wieczynski 1976; Bolkhovitinov 1962; Lobanov-Rostovsky 1965; Wyman and Kroeber 1957; Careless 1989).[5]

"Frontier" can also refer to time periods, and we use such terms as the "frontier period," the "homestead frontier," the "postfrontier period," and so on. Precision in dates and places is impossible because, as noted, the frontier is always moving. Still another familiar meaning of "frontier" is the period of earliest entry into an unpopulated place; therefore "postfrontier" can refer to the period of definitive settlement in which adaptive customs and institutions associated with the earlier frontier period persist. And, conversely, "prefrontier" refers to the period of exploration prior to substantial settlement of any kind.

Another troublesome term is "pioneer." The homesteaders and town business leaders who came to the Canadian-American West around the turn of the century were not pioneers in the sense of first-comers, since other people—American Indians, métis, explorers, travelers, hunters, mapmakers, miners, and railroad engineers—had already been in the region. On the other hand, the incoming settlers considered themselves authentic pioneers since they were the first to settle down and attempt to build an enduring community. Therefore, when we use the term "pioneer" to refer to these settlers we are, on the whole, accepting their own usage.

The third term, "adaptation," is the key word of our basic interpretive approach: how the incoming settlers perceived the hardships and how they managed to cope with them. "Adaptation" is ambiguous, since it can refer to quite different kinds of behavior: tolerating and accepting conditions as they are and making the best of them, attempting to change conditions, or attempting to change one's own habits in response to a challenge. In the broadest sense, "adaptation" is simply living, surviving, carrying on. In a narrow sense, it refers to distinctive combinations of acceptance or tolerance with innovation or change that characterized the coping strategies of settlers. "Coping" is probably the best term to use when referring to adaptation as a behavioral process. If "adaptation" is used to refer to a group or a social process it is, for this book, a matter of establishing the conditions necessary for community life.[6]

The titular authors of this book are also compilers and interpreters; perhaps the true authors are the writers of participant-produced history whose words appear on many of our pages. Our contribution was to comb through this enormous fugitive literature and select the items of greatest scholarly value. We also tried to interpret the materials; that is, to see if some well-tested principles of social and sociopsychological analysis might reveal their meanings. Such analyses appear in our chapters, but we have avoided those excursions into theory that would force the data into molds not intimated or visualized by the original writers.

Chapter 2

Settlement and Environment in the Canadian-American West

We use the term "Old Northwest" for the region including northern California, Oregon, Washington, and perhaps northern Idaho, western Montana, and the southern portions of British Columbia and Alberta. In the 1840s, this region was divided between Spain, Britain, and the United States. Boundaries were vague, violated, or disputed; and by 1818, troubles with the Indians—often stirred up by the fur traders—had become enough of a problem that Britain and the United States agreed to a treaty of "joint occupancy" in areas that would become Montana and parts of Idaho and Wyoming.[1] This meant that the fur traders from either British Canada or the United States could exploit the territory without concern for national affiliations. In fact, Americans of all trades took the treaty as an open invitation to plunder or settle, and traders and pioneer farmers and ranchers began moving in. A similar process took place in California, eventually driving out the Mexican Spanish. Exploration followed the opening of the territory and the early settlement of boundary claims. Much of this early exploration consisted of the travels of individuals, but as the nineteenth century proceeded official expeditions were formed.[2]

The fur trade was an international entrepreneurial impulse that lasted well into the nineteenth century.[3] It left its cultural residues in a frontier spirit of rugged individualism and, from the standpoint of the two emerging nations, a kind of detachment from nationality or origin. Companies could be formed by men of either nation to exploit the furs in either nation. Frequently they betrayed each other, their companies, and their nationalities when the occasion was ripe. Fur traders were the first settlers in the Old Northwest, although their communities consisted only of semipermanent encampments, great annual get-togethers, and forts and "factories" along the rivers, many of which became the sites of western cities.

The internationalism or non-nationalism of the fur trade also had its genesis in the cultural geography of the region (see figure 1). The front range, or eastern slope, of the Rocky Mountains created a natural alignment for movement north and south. The Old North Trail—really a network of trails established by Amerinds beginning in postglacial times—was the basis for a series of major nineteenth-century routes between British-Canadian and U.S. territories and still survives in the form of modern highways.[4] The survey and establishment of the international boundary along the forty-ninth parallel in the early nineteenth century marked the first stage in the demarcation of the western regions of the two nations, but for years—into the 1890s—the border was largely ignored in practice.

The decisive step in the interruption of the north-south alignment of the international society was the building in the 1880s of the two northern transcontinental railroads: the Canadian Pacific (CPR) and, a few years later, the Great Northern (GNR). The same man, American James J. Hill, was active in both projects, especially the Great Northern, but many other American and British-Canadian investors and engineers were involved.

Until the railroads provided an easy route to eastern centers of trade and manufacturing, most of the supplies for the small, early frontier settlements of the Canadian-American West came up the Missouri River from St. Louis to Fort Benton, Montana, then were carried by bull wagon to other U.S. and Canadian locations. From 1875 to 1883 about 20 percent of the total freight shipped through Fort Benton went to Canadian buyers; in 1877, 1,025 tons of freight went to North West Mounted Police posts. In one year alone, 1885, the Canadian "assets" of the I. G. Baker Company (one of the two major trading companies in Fort Benton, along with the T. C. Power Company) were $44,507.96—almost half of the total assets (sales plus inventory) listed on their balance sheet. For the same year, sales to individual customers in Alberta and Saskatchewan who can be identified as pioneer ranchers totaled $24,424, somewhat higher than the total for identified U.S. settlers (more data in Klassen 1991 and Berry 1950). In other words, until the Canadian Pacific took over the supply trade for the Canadians, the Fort Benton companies enjoyed a binational monopoly. The last steamer came up the Missouri to Benton in 1890, and this date can be taken as the decisive onset of the rail-dominated east-west orientation of economic traffic.[5]

Settlement, then, until and into the period of the American Civil War and the latter days of the Hudson's Bay Company in Canada, was a matter for scattered traders, pioneer farmers, and, of course, farther west along the U.S. Rocky Mountain front, the mining camps, many of which eventually became cities and towns. After the Civil War and after about 1870 in Canada came the ranchers—the cattlemen—driving herds up from Texas and other central and southern plains areas where cattle had been multiplying during and after the war. Returning veterans and Eastern and British investors saw these herds as a great resource, and it was not long before the northern ranges, as the northern plains came to be designated by Texans, were populated by practitioners of the range livestock industry. This industry was carried on by ranchers or managers of outside-owned cattle companies, who occupied a small permanent tract for the headquarters but ran their cattle and horse herds over unfenced range land. These people were the first agricultural settlers of the region, and the cultural traditions they introduced persist everywhere.[6]

In the beginning, ranchers welcomed the appearance of farmer-settlers—"nesters"—since they could use their sons as ranch hands and their daughters as housekeepers (or wives). This kind of employment was the most common type for young farmers and their children in areas of the Dakotas, Montana, Alberta, and Saskatchewan, where older, established ranching industries preceded the homestead openings. In time this developed into a kind of paternalistic social system in which the farmer-derived employees became clients to their rancher patrons. The "western" cultural activities and symbols associated with ranching became prestige markers, and as former homesteaders moved into cattle production they adopted the hats and boots and engaged in the horse hobby. But as time passed, these class distinctions became marginal; ranchers' children began marrying farmers' children, and many farmers developed into substantial cattlemen. And since the number of farmers associated with homesteading was far greater than the number of ranchers, farmer society began taking over political control of communities, states, and provinces.

As settlement proceeded, differences between the Canadian and U.S. national cultures began to emerge. The basic legal arrangements for homesteading were substantially similar in the two nations, but the way the whole affair was managed and the extent of preparation for receiving immigrants were quite different.[7] We should note that the Canadians incorporated the settlement areas of Alberta and Saskatchewan into the Northwest Territorial government after 1871, which meant that regulatory laws and assistance programs concerning the expansion and development of livestock, farming, and dairying were in place before anything like this appeared in Montana and North Dakota, even though settlement of the Canadian area lagged. And the Canadians brought the North West Mounted Police (NWMP)—later the Royal Canadian Mounted Police (RCMP)—to the frontier to handle both the Indians and the affairs of the settlers. This advanced state of preparation on the part of the Canadians was in part due to what they perceived as frontier disorder across the line.

Such distrust was grounded in a series of occurrences that created the international folklore of the Canadian-American West. There were three major incidents: in Canada, the Cypress Hills Massacre of 1873 and the Riel Rebellion of 1885, and in the United States, the Nez Percé War of 1887. In each case the old north-south alignment was reasserted by bands of refugees fleeing across the border to safety.

The Cypress Hills Massacre (see Archer 1980; Peterson 1986; Goldring 1973) was actually a small incident in which a band of Canadian and American renegades shot up an encampment of Assiniboine Indians near a whiskey-trading post in the Cypress Hills of southwest Saskatchewan. However, its symbolic value was considerable, since it seemed to validate growing Canadian suspicions of the dangers posed by the lawless Americans. Both Ottawa and Washington got into the act before the matter was finally settled in a couple of court trials in the United States and Canada.

Both the Nez Percé War and the Riel Rebellion, a revolt by the métis (persons of mixed Indian and European descent), were late-frontier episodes caused in large part by governments taking over land held in unrecognized title by indigenous peoples—Indians in Idaho and Montana, and mainly métis in Canada. By abrogating their informal and traditional tenures, the governments permitted settlers to pour in, with armed rebellion as the inevitable result. Louis Riel and Chief Joseph of the Nez Percé were men of exceptional charisma and ability whose defeats and punishments eventually became symbols of government duplicity and cruelty.[8]

These events, which received a certain amount of attention from Ottawa and Washington, were simply the most famous episodes of border crossing. More frequent were the adventures of people of varied ethnic and national origin—Indian, métis, American, or Canadian—who engaged in whiskey-trading and horse-stealing until the Mounted Police managed to get the situation under control in the late 1870s. The second major NWMP post, Fort Walsh, had been established in the Cypress Hills expressly to control these depredations. The American forces were never as efficient as the Mounties, and contemporary documents make it clear that the invention of the NWMP in 1873 was a deliberate action taken by the Canadians to install a competent, colonial-type constabulary on the frontier to curb the activities of both Canadian and American renegades and to compensate for the bungling of the U.S. Cavalry and other officials.[9]

The presence of the Mounted Police and the existence of the Northwest Territories Administration provided an efficient basis for Canadian organized settlement. While homestead facilities and settlement on the U.S. side had begun earlier, their procedures were less well organized. It was not until there were enough homesteaders, with locally created town and county governments, that the American territory could be considered to have achieved a state of political order enjoyed by the Canadians a decade or more earlier.

Homesteading Policies and Procedures

Land for settlement in both Canada and the United States was available from several sources: government-offered homesteads, railroad land-grant tracts, and, in Canada, those Hudson's Bay Company lands exempted in the cession of the company to the new Canadian government in the 1870s. The great majority of land consisted of the homestead tracts offered by the U.S. and Canadian authorities. Homestead laws had been passed by the Americans as early as the 1860s and in Canada about a decade later; but in both countries they were utilized initially by only a handful of settlers because of the lack of transportation and the lag in land surveying. Intensive settlement began when the government and railroads decided to provide transportation and land surveys in earnest, around the turn of the century. Thus in the end the majority of settlers in the Canadian-American West in the final decade of the nineteenth century and the first decade of the twentieth century were homesteaders, because homesteading was the main concern of the settlement programs of both the United States and Canada. People came for other reasons—trapping, lumbering, mining, commerce, real estate speculation, ranching—and some of them, particularly the ranchers, did take out homesteads when the land had been surveyed and opened for claims. With a base in these "home ranch quarters," they subsequently acquired large spreads by purchase and grazing lease. Some town businessmen acquired homesteads in lieu of cash for payment of bills.

By emphasizing homesteading and homesteaders we display a bias toward those emigrants who had serious intentions of permanent residence. However, only a minority of those who attempted homestead farming in the northern plains—perhaps 25 percent in the better-soil districts and as few as 10 percent in many if not most areas—actually stayed to establish long-lasting agricultural enterprises. The remainder departed, found better farms, went back to their original homes, or wound up as townspeople in businesses and services. Many of the farriers, mechanics, carpenters, and store clerks in the little towns had been homesteaders or had combined homesteading with trade in order to take advantage of the equity of land ownership.

Homesteading was a convenient way to get out West. By declaring the intent to homestead, prospective settlers were entitled to make use of various facilities for transportation, land claims, loans, and other services provided by government and private agencies. Whether or not emigrants really intended to farm their homesteads, they had something they could use as a springboard for whatever they decided to do to make a living. And by taking out a homestead, settlers automatically established a connection with the authorities, since they were then on official notice to "prove up," that is, to show that they were serious about farming and living there.

Both the U.S. and Canadian authorities established rules requiring homesteaders to demonstrate that they were genuinely interested in settlement. While the rules differed somewhat, the essentials were the same: the homesteader was expected to construct a dwelling on the property, to begin to farm the land, and to reside on it for a specified period. A homesteader filed for a particular tract, paid a small registration fee, and, if no one had already taken it, received a confirmed right to occupy it, provided he could demonstrate his intention to develop it. Meeting the requirements was referred to as "proving up" in the United States and doing "homestead duties" in Canada.

The regulations for both countries, after some initial experiments (especially in Canada), set 160 acres as the official individual allotment, but the limited productivity of much of the area for cultivated crops soon made it necessary to increase this amount. Both countries eventually created ways to add land to the homestead at nominal cost and called the procedure "pre-emption," but the definition of the term varied. In general, similar terminology for homesteading was used by the two countries, but the details are confusing because frequently the same term was used for different procedures or legalities. The rules changed with experience and as the railroads and governments discovered that permanent settlement in this region required as much help or indirect subsidy as it was possible to provide.

In the United States, all adult members of a family could take out a homestead; in Canada, regulations barred adult women who were not heads of households. The authorities knew that it was difficult to prove up or do duties when the homesteader lacked funds and equipment, and therefore the validation procedure was often relaxed in individual cases; however, the rules were just strict enough, or enforced just often enough, to make it difficult for an individual to assemble a collection of homestead tracts and go through the means of proof on each one. Here large families had an advantage because they included enough mature members to take out numerous homesteads.

Many settlers understood that the homestead was a gamble or an investment that could be sold for a profit after they had proved up. In one southern Alberta district we researched, over half the original homesteads taken out between 1908 and 1912 were eventually sold to neighbors or to land speculators who came in late, knowing that after two or three years a large proportion of the original settlers would be ready to leave, having discovered that even 320 acres were not really enough to provide a living and pay the increasing costs of farming.

In the broadest sense, the homesteading period in the Canadian-American West—roughly 1890 to 1920, to give it its full extent—was an episode of intense disposal of land by government, railroads, private land companies, speculators, and individual owners. Town merchants, for example, often managed to assemble considerable private holdings by taking over the homesteads of settler customers who went broke and were unable to pay their bills for equipment and food. Many who left the region tried homesteads elsewhere or returned to their original homes. Some who remained found nonagricultural opportunities.

While the railroads and the governments had separate lands to dispense, in fact the two agencies worked together in order to bring the settlers to the land. Both the Canadian Pacific and the Great Northern developed a remarkable network of main and branch lines all through the northern plains. We counted, from route maps for the peak years (1895–1911), a total of thirty small branch lines (often old private ventures) heading north or south to bring settlers and their effects across the international boundary to the main east-west lines. Along the main lines alone, the number of stops was impressive. The GNR, from Grand Forks, North Dakota, to Shelby, Montana, a stretch of about 750 miles, had ninety-three stops on the timetables. The CPR had ninety-nine stops between Winnipeg, Manitoba, and Calgary, Alberta, a stretch of 840 miles. Many stops were merely flag downs, but even so the totals suggest the extent to which the railroads were serving the homesteaders and businessmen.

Fares and shipping rates were low. An emigrant could rent a whole freight car to get from St. Paul, Minnesota, to Chinook, Montana, for sixty-four dollars; the second-class fare was fifteen dollars per person, and one hundred pounds of baggage went for sixty-four cents. This and other facilities and inducements provided by the railroads were not simply altruistic: The lines had to recoup their investments by populating the countryside and towns to create a market and acquire goods to ship back east.

Considerable competition for settlers existed between the United States and Canada, and each copied the other's slogans and inducements. The GNR archive in the Minnesota Historical Society has an advertisement the CPR published in U.S. newspapers, reading in part:

> Get Your Canadian Home
> FROM THE CANADIAN PACIFIC
>
> The Home Maker
>
> We will make you a long-time loan—
> you will have 20 years to pay for the
> land and repay the loan—you can
> move on the land at once—and your
> Canadian farm will *make you independent*.

The clipping was accompanied by a letter from one GNR official to another: "I enclose clipping of the Canadian Pacific ad in the Saturday Evening Post. This novel scheme of the Canadian Pacific's in actually lending settlers money, in addition to giving them time and easy payments is going to be a great benefit to them and make our work just that much harder."

The Great Northern, of course, had its own promotional literature. One ad, printed in eastern Canadian papers, read:

> YOUR CHANCE IS WEST
>
> You can get a 160 or 320 acre farm free in Montana but you'll have to hurry. Along the Great Northern Railway are several million acres of government land available under the homestead laws. . .

Clifford Sifton, the flamboyant Canadian immigration commissioner, opened recruitment offices all over the northern United States, and Americans sent recruitment agents up into Canada. The effect of these activities was to augment the population mixing on both sides, although the data seem to show that more Americans went up into Canada than Canadians into the United States. Although his census data are not entirely reliable owing to problems of definition of national origin, Karel Bicha found that large numbers of Americans returned from their Canadian venture within a decade or so. Specifically, he states that between 1896 and 1914 about 600,000 residents of the United States moved into Saskatchewan and Alberta (Bicha 1965:9–10), but by the 1920 census only 200,000 Americans were counted in these two provinces.

The Resource Picture

Before the incursion of white settlers into the northern plains, most of the inhabitants—various groups of Cree, Sioux, Nez Percé, and Blackfoot—did not farm, although they were generally aware of crop-raising since they had farming relatives and were in contact with Pueblo agriculturalists in the Southwest. The irregular distribution of groundwater, rainfall, and suitable soils in the plains inhibited attempts to retain or develop tribal-level agriculture (Dale 1967; Crowe 1936; Schlesier 1993; Wedel 1979; Bennett 1990, Hildebrand and Scott 1987, Weaver and Albertson 1956). Bison and other animals were in plentiful supply, and the Indians built a technological adaptation and a whole way of life around the pursuit and exploitation of these animals. This adaptation required them to move from place to place on a seasonal or even daily basis dependent on native resources: grasses and forbs, natural streams and ponds, brush vegetation for shelter.[10]

While resources for grazing animals were reasonably adequate, the variability of rainfall and soils and marginal supply of all resources made

600	1100	1100	1000	950	900	550	800	450	450	550	450
600	900	850	850	1050	950	550	500	550	700	800	450
700	750	500	500	1100	900	500	500	500	800	750	600
600	500	500	500	850	1100	500	550	500	550	550	700
500	700	950	500	500	1150	1300	550	850	600	1050	1050
600	500	600	500	500	1300	1000	1150	600	500	550	1000
400	400	260	400	400	420	450	450	450	500	500	1050
400	420	500	400	420	420	460	420	450	500	500	650

Figure 3. Soil variability as indicated by tax valuation. Soils vary greatly in the northern plains as a result of glacial runoff. This diagram shows the tax valuation, in dollars, for each quarter-section of a 24-square-mile district. The higher the value, the more friable the soil, or the more humus content it has. Crops would vary accordingly: hay and grass crops on the low-valued tracts, wheat and other "cash grains" on the higher-valued land.

successful crop farming difficult. However, ranchers were not entirely immune from such problems since they had to raise forage crops once their lands were surveyed and fenced. The farmers' lack of knowledge of the periodicity of resource variability meant that farmers could not be certain of whether they could survive a year of experimental cropping and still obtain a saleable (or edible) harvest (see figure 3 for an illustration of soil quality variability). Generally speaking, the typical homestead farmer had a fifty-fifty chance of getting through the first year on the basis of what he could make in cash or barter from field crops. While wheat, barley, and rye—the dry-field grains—are well adapted to drought conditions, they still require minimal moisture in the growing season, and sometimes in the northern plains this fails to occur (see Myrick 1941; McGinnies and Laycock 1988). One resource or another was likely to trip up a beginning farmer: the soils might be too poor for a new crop, the rainfall too meager, or the storms full of damaging hail; late frosts might stunt early growth, or heavy fall rains rot the harvest. If farmers had some livestock, they might do better, although many homesteaders who had to sell a cow, horse, or goats to raise enough cash to get through the winter regretted it the next spring, when the animals had to be replaced by purchase. In general, homesteaders were continually beset by trade-offs between raising crops for sale on the market and raising food-stuffs for family use.

Environmental dangers to the rancher's operation were intermittent drought and bitter winters. Severe winters could do great damage. As long as the stock were roaming across largely unfenced range and foraging for themselves they were vulnerable to cold. An occasional fence, especially along the railroad tracks, could cause the animals, drifting with the winds and blizzards, to pile up and freeze to death. Prolonged droughts meant the dying back of the native grasses and the drying up of water holes. But the disastrous seasons were infrequent enough that the ranchers had an opportunity to do well for a considerable run of years. If drought or a bad winter did come, a man could always sell some of his stock, eat some, and also retain a small start-up breeding herd.

The Great Winter of 1886–87 wiped out more than half of all the cattle in the northern plains, and the disaster triggered a basic change in the technology and procedures of cattle production. Instead of relying on native supplies of grass and water, the new settled-down ranchers began to add cultivated plants to native grasses for forage, and then to irrigate these crops, which at a minimum entailed the husbanding and impounding of snowmelt waters and directing the runoff onto pasture areas. This trend toward intensive ranching was encouraged by the land survey. It forced the ranchers to fence off portions of the range they owned or leased, which in turn demanded carefully controlled grazing and constant monitoring of the movement of the stock.

Farming also involved a specialized "cultural ecology." Sod had to be broken, the soil tilled, the stones removed, rough areas smoothed over, the crops seeded, weeded, and harvested. Domestic animals had to be fed and suitable fields reserved for their pasturage. Fencing was necessary not only to demarcate ownership but also to control land use. The farmer was required to plan, experiment, and take calculated risks from the outset; he could not rely on native resources but had to improve and fit them to his production regime.[11]

By the 1890s, the privately sponsored emigration promotion and guidebook literature on western expansion had passed into the stewardship of the governments and railroads, where it was turned into vigorous propaganda. In a substantial pamphlet entitled *Western Canada: How to Get There, How to Select Lands, and, How to Make a Home,* published by the Canadian Pacific in 1902, the reader is introduced to the subject with the following:

> The record of the growth of this portion of Canada [i.e., the early versions of the Prairie Provinces and newly opened portions of western Ontario] is a tale of marvelous progress and advancement, of vacant lands being peopled, of thriving towns and villages arising where a few years ago the red Indian camped, of exports changing in one generation from bales of fur to thousands of train loads of golden grain.

In dealing with the winters, the pamphlet, quoting another CPR publication, sounds like a tourist blurb for a modern ski resort:

> The bright, clear cold of an ordinary winter day of Manitoba is most enjoyable. With little or no thawing and no sea or uncongealed great freshwater lake to supply dampness, the air is crisp and dry, and where in England or on the seacoast, with a few degrees of frost the air is chill and raw, many more degrees of cold in the Canadian Northwest is only enjoyable and stimulating.

And, of course, the scenery and the farming opportunities always sounded simply splendid, as in this description of the Cypress Hills:

> The Cypress Hills, which may be dimly seen in the south from the railway, are especially adapted for stock raising, and as general farming is not extensively followed, the grass land that nature has so bountifully provided will not be disturbed by the plow, thus giving to the farmer on the plains adjoining never-failing hay meadows and unlimited pasture ground for his stock. The snowfall is light, the climate is tempered by the Chinook winds, and water and shelter is everywhere abundant.

The description has a certain degree of accuracy: the Cypress Hills (like the Bear's Paw Mountains in Montana, just across the border) *are* good for stock-raising, but the ranchers took over the pasture and the farmers down below had little chance to use it for grazing until the 1960s, when they managed to persuade the Provincial Cooperative Commonwealth Federation government to create grazing cooperatives out of excessive leased grazing land assigned to ranchers. And, of course, winters were longer, colder, and snowier than the description implies, although the warm Chinook winds coming down off the Rocky Mountains at intervals could spread out over the plains and relieve the cold and frost in a matter of minutes. High-altitude parts of the Cypress Hills were eventually opened for homestead farming, but all these settlements failed by 1920 because of the short growing season and have since reverted to ranching. In general, detailed knowledge regarding the variability and marginality of physical resources was omitted from the settlement promotion literature. The prospective settlers were in no significant way prepared to cope with such conditions.

The farmers were required to learn by doing. The difficulties were such that many gave up after a few months or years. Some things, however, became known or available quite early. The Canadian settlements in the Red River Valley of Manitoba had existed for a generation prior to the migrations further west, and there empirical plant breeders had created particular strains of grain crops—notably Red Fife wheat—that grew fast and matured early. These became generally available by at least the first decade of the twentieth century. Special shallow tillage methods designed to promote moisture retention and discourage soil-blowing and weed growth developed rapidly, along with the summer fallow method of strip cropping, which allows alternate fields to rest and accumulate moisture.

Scientific agricultural experimentation really began with the railroads, which used it to entice settlers westward. Some of this work was sound, some was defective or dishonest; but the pioneer work of both the Great Northern and the Canadian Pacific established a basis for new government experiment stations in the states and provinces. A network was well under way by 1915. Research still proceeds, and new information about resources and their uses is provided annually; but it is a slow process, since the cycles and patterns of the environment change over generations, or at least decades.

Although western Europeans and eastern North Americans lacked experience with semiarid northern lands, emigrants from various parts of Russia and northern Europe, especially Scandinavia, were more accustomed to difficult growing conditions, seasonal variability, and hard winters. And settlers who had lived for months or even years in the Dakotas, Nebraska, or other Great Plains locations before moving further west or northwest were already acclimated. But all prospective settlers had to face the fact that permanent residence and the establishment of a viable economy in the environment of the northern plains took more work, more fortitude, and usually more money than in more fortunately endowed regions. "This is no place for them that wants an easy time of it," remarked an Anglo-Irish emigrant to Saskatchewan, quoted by a biographer in a local history book.

The country landscape of the northern plains today is punctuated with rectangular alignments of trees that constitute windbreaks around farm houses, gardens, and even fields. The planting of these windbreaks became a fad in the 1930s and '40s, something like the irrigation craze around the turn of the century. In addition to blocking wind and catching snow, they were said to provide shade in hot summers, reduce excessive evaporation, and create places for picnics and shelter for pheasants and other small animals for sport and pleasure. The labor expended on these tree belts was enormous in the early years, since it required continual tillage of the soil around the trees to prevent dry-outs and soil baking. Trees had to be planted in successive rows of different varieties, the types more vulnerable to drought and cold in the inner strips. In periods of drought, farmers determined to grow shelter belts had to carry water to them. In the dryer parts of the region, like the Palliser Triangle in southeastern Alberta and southwestern Saskatchewan or parts of eastern Montana, many farmers gave it up as a time- and energy-consuming task, but in the districts with somewhat higher and more reliable rainfall the tree belts have prospered and have evolved into small, rectilinear forests with wild undergrowth. With houses and outbuildings tucked inside, the belts provide a manmade physical environment utterly alien to the native vegetation but productive of serenity and comfort for the inhabitants.

The most serious consequence of breaking the old plains sod for cultivation was its exposure to wind and water erosion. The Dust Bowl of the 1930s, recalled as the "Dirty Thirties" by residents, was a major event in North American environmental and cultural history, and, on a more local scale, little dust bowls have been recurring ever since. While the drought-and-depression years were certainly catastrophic, in the view of many of our document writers it was simply one more source of the perennial hardships associated with settlement in the northern plains. You either "adapted or died," in a phrase that became popular during the period and was picked up by some of the scholars who wrote the history of the West in the 1940s and '50s. Actually, periods of drought are recurrent, often lasting a year or two, and even the earliest accounts of settlement, prior to the 1930s, mention the consequences of lack of moisture. Women often refer to the "dust problem": No matter what you did to keep it out, it managed to seep in. Soil-blowing, which created the dust, will continue to be a problem in the Great Plains as long as the sod is broken. New tillage methods help to stabilize the soil, but the basic cause of blowing—loosening the soil in the first place—continues.

Weeds were the other serious consequence of the sod breaking. The normal competition between various wild plants of the plains had kept any species from dominating, but many vigorous plants introduced from other parts of the continent spread rapidly. Homesteaders first took the whole family out and simply pulled weeds out of the rows. Later they used chemical agents, then, as the dangers of chemical saturation became known, special tillage methods.

The cultural significance of the environment of the northern plains lies in the determination of the settlers to overcome its constraints on permanent, sedentary residence. The recurrent themes in the local history and reminiscence literature express this determination and the relative success of the stayers. They honor the pioneers who fought the first battles with the environment and "won"; they celebrate the success, against all odds, of constructing viable human communities in a kind of Siberia. The experience not only produced a remarkable folk literature but also a remarkable type of human being: hard-working, able to take defeat and carry on, and, above all, in possession of a sense of self-detachment and the ability to laugh at one's foolishness in putting up with the hardships.

Chapter 3

Settlement Patterns and Ethnicity

Research on migration by demographers and sociologists has produced a technical vocabulary and theory that we avoid, since it is based on specialized mathematical analysis. Much of the theory is concerned with motivations for or causes of movement. We had no particular need to determine causes of the migration to the Canadian-American West since the data speak for themselves: the explanations of cause and motivation given by the writers of our source documents. The basic issues were the desire for land and personal autonomy, supplemented by inducements emanating from kin and community. And once the movement began, its momentum was sustained through processes like "chain migration," in which immigrants moved westward in a series of stages, using homes of friends and relatives as intermediate stopover points. They perpetuated the process by writing letters back home encouraging people to come out, and even sending prepaid tickets (see Macdonald and Macdonald 1964).

The assembling in one location of settlers from a particular ethnic group, village, or religious sect is called either "cluster settlement," an informal process, or "bloc settlement," in which whole population units formed up in the home country and traveled to a predetermined frontier location. In this brief discussion we will refer to all cases of concentration of settlers of common origins as "cluster." Clusters could be formed by chain migration, but in special cases entire communities or congregations might immigrate as a corporate group, facilitated by agents who provided the location for the colony. "Sheet settlement" refers to a more or less even distribution of settlers of particular origins across a geographical area.

The rapidity of migration and settlement in the northern plains tended to encourage sheet distribution, and the clustered concentrations so common in the U.S. Midwest and central plains for earlier migrations were not as frequently formed. Saskatchewan probably had more clustered settlements than other states and provinces as a result of a series of colonizing or corporate community ventures in which capitalists, philanthropists, or religious sects acquired particular tracts. It was also facilitated by the policies of Clifford Sifton, the Canadian commissioner of immigration, who was determined to fit particular groups and populations to particular environments.

Settlers from the British Isles were uniformly spread throughout the prairie provinces; as the dominant settler population they apparently felt no need to aggregate on the basis of ethnic or religious allegiance. Scandinavians, on the other hand, while fairly well distributed, did form a few concentrations created for the most part by chain migration processes. Ukrainians show marked clustering along the northern Park Belt area of the provinces. The Ukrainians were channeled into these areas by immigration agents, but in addition they possessed a distinct Russian-derived culture that tended to encourage aggregation.

Figure 4 illustrates dispersal and clustering of settlers in western Canada, in this case, those from Scandinavian countries. Dispersal of individuals and families was encouraged by rapid settlement, or the "land rush" pattern—vigorously promoted campaigns to settle various areas of available land over short periods of time. Subsequent movement from location to location, in search of better facilities, soil, or water, accentuated the dispersal pattern. Clustered settlement could be brought about by organized group migration schemes and ventures, but also by subsequent movement when a particular locality would function as a magnet for lonely or dissatisfied individual settlers.

Scandinavian settlement has been studied extensively with reference

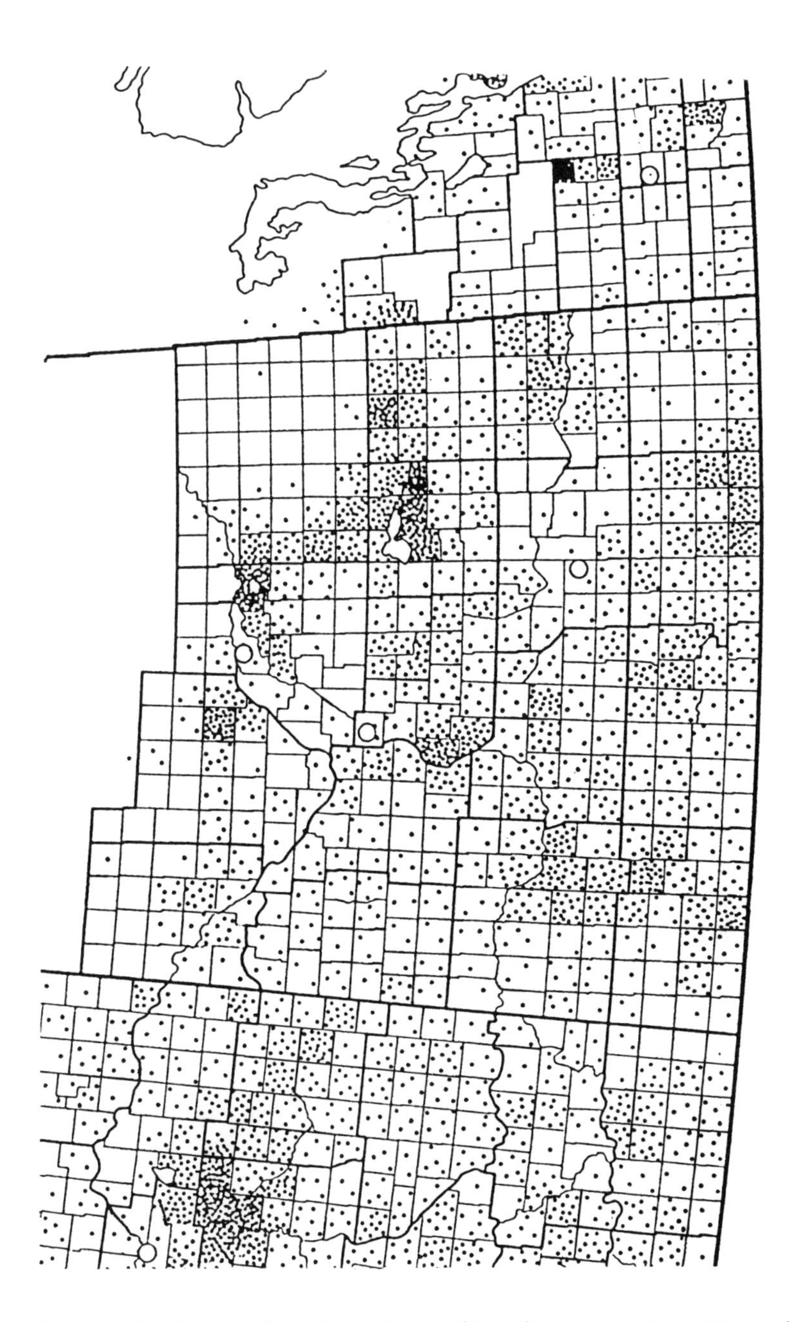

Figure 4. Distribution of rural population of Scandinavian origin, 1921, southern Saskatchewan and adjoining portions of Manitoba and Alberta. Each dot represents 25 persons. Source: Canadian Census Data.

to settlement patterning and origins. Two studies traced the movement from "parent" regions in Norway and Sweden to destinations in the upper Midwest (Gjerde 1985; Ostergren 1988). Both authors show considerable differences among various communities and regions in terms of participation in emigration. In both cases, the problems precipitating emigration concerned changes in inheritance and household formation (due to changes in production and increasing population), and the earliest emigrants tended to be those who had some resources but were anxious about their children's opportunities. Gjerde writes that in Norway, U.S. shipping companies had thirteen agencies registered in Oslo and 6,254 representatives spread throughout the country in 1881 (Gjerde 1985:130). As a result of "America letters" (letters written by settled immigrants in America to the folks at home in Norway) and prepaid tickets, the volume of emigration from these communities quickly increased and was directed toward New World sister communities. Over time, the kinds of emigrants changed. Landed farmers were succeeded by landless (but not necessarily destitute) laborers, and nuclear families by single men. But throughout, emigrants took advantage of the experience and familiarity offered by kinsmen and neighbors who had preceded them to North America.

Settler Demography and Origins

The northern plains were the most deliberately promoted and organized of all western North American settlement areas. Immigration began in earnest in the 1890s and was over by 1920; 1910 to 1912 were the peak years. The prairie provinces experienced rapid growth immediately after the turn of the century, with a fivefold increase in population from 1900 to 1910; an eightfold increase between 1900 and 1920 reflects the birth of children in the emigrant settlements. For North Dakota and Montana, where sporadic immigration started as early as the 1870s, the influx was sufficient to double their populations between 1900 and 1920. The increase for North Dakota was heavily concentrated in the 1890s, reflecting its position on the migration path from the Midwest to Montana and eventually north into the prairie provinces. The Midwestern states—Minnesota, Wisconsin, Iowa, Illinois, and Missouri—functioned for the northern plains much as the New England states in the earlier nineteenth century had served the Ohio Valley region: as a source of settlers. The difference, of course, was that these Midwestern states were mostly populated by recent immigrants from Europe or the eastern United States, while the earlier New England immigrants were third- or fourth-generation Americans before they moved west. As for Canada, Ontario furnished both indigenous and foreign-born immigrants for the western provinces.

But as the Canadian-American West developed its own demographic base, the movement increasingly became a matter of north-south travel across the international boundary. An inspection of North Dakota local history books reveals that by 1910 the state had become a major source of Canada-bound emigrants. A swath of counties on a diagonal Southeast-to-Northwest line had suffered considerable economic difficulty in the decade from 1900 to 1910, and the community and family histories for these counties provide details of migration north to Canada.

Canadian and U.S. census reports for the peak settlement period—1900–1920—provide information on the numbers of settlers and their countries of origin, although the census categories are rather vague and it is not always possible to come up with precise figures. For example, table 1 can be used to estimate the number of settlers by birthplace for three censuses—1900, 1910, 1920—in two U.S. states and two Canadian provinces. Ambiguities are particularly evident in the category "Foreign-Born," which is not specific as to country of origin. A person born in Canada who moved back and forth across the border in search of a suitable home could have been counted as either "foreign" or "native," depending on where he and his family happened to be during the enumeration. Such ambiguous national identity was common.

However, for all three censuses, residents of Saskatchewan, Montana, and North Dakota who were born in their respective native lands—Canada or the United States—outnumber the "foreign born." This suggests what other historical and biographical data confirm: A plurality of settlers in these political entities came from North America, although an unknown proportion might be young second-generation offspring of earlier European immigrants. Alberta stands out as having a large proportion of "foreign born," and we shall assume that many of these were people born in the United States.

For the U.S. states, Montana had the largest proportion of "natives," reflecting that settlement in Montana began early, along the Rocky Mountain front in the context of the mining, lumbering, and ranching frontiers. People from this early Montana settlement moved north into southern Alberta and adjacent parts of Saskatchewan in the late 1870s and '80s to create the first Canadian ranching frontier.

Canadian and U.S. census data for 1910 indicate a plurality of the

Table 1. Percentages of native and foreign-born residents of states and provinces in the northern Great Plains, 1900–1920

Census Year	Alberta		Saskatchewan		Montana		North Dakota	
	N	F	N	F	N	F	N	F
1900	57%	43%	60%	40%	72%	28%	65%	35%
1910	43%	57%	51%	49%	75%	25%	73%	27%
1920	54%	46%	60%	40%	80%	17%	79%	20%

N = native-born (by nation)

F = foreign-born

Sources: U.S. and Canadian census data.

Note: U.S. censuses are dated from the year of enumeration (e.g., 1900); Canadian, from the following year of data release (e.g., 1901). We have used the U.S. dating for both.

Canadian-born settlers in western Canada came from Ontario, Canada's Midwest. Other provinces furnished fewer, but their percentages increased slightly by 1920. Initially the majority of U.S.-born residents of North Dakota and Montana came from the Midwest states, from Minnesota to Iowa, but all U.S. states were represented in small numbers. By 1920 Montana and North Dakota increasingly became the most frequently cited birthplaces, as the settlement population began to reproduce itself. In general, the U.S. and Canadian census data suggest a westward shift in the parentage of residents and the development of an indigenous western population as emigration tapered off around 1920.

Overall, the British Isles and Scandinavia furnished the lion's share of European-born residents of the northern plains during the three census decades, but particular countries and settlement areas developed specific patterns. For example, Norwegians were especially numerous in North Dakota but not in Montana. Individuals born in the United States were the biggest category of immigrants to Alberta in all three censuses, but not to Saskatchewan (although they increased in 1910–11 in connection with Clifford Sifton's "Last Best West" promotional campaign). Russia and Poland furnished sizeable numbers for Saskatchewan but not Alberta, and so on. These irregular distributions reflect the differentials of chain migration, special recruitment campaigns, and other factors tending to channel settlement of particular nationalities.

What Is Ethnicity?

Everyone is an "ethnic," in that every human being is shaped in part by ideas communicated to him or her by parents who felt they were passing on the proper way to live. Such concepts and behavior patterns are influenced by religion, language, communities, nations, tribes, or neighborhoods, and any one of these or many other sources of early experience can be the source of ethnicity. But ethnicity is also to some extent a voluntary, self-conscious affair: something you create, defend, neglect, ignore. That is, one can level or sharpen behavioral and cultural characteristics. Leveling implies a disposition to ignore or make light of ethnic distinctiveness or peculiarities; sharpening is the tendency to focus on those traits as key aspects of a person's identity.

The homestead frontier was characterized by a remarkable disposition to level differences between neighbors and friends, even when the population was polyglot. The reminiscences and history books are full of passages mentioning the origins of the incoming settlers: "no matter what the nationality, and we had many from different parts"; "There were the German settlers and the Swedes and the Dutch and a few Norwegians"; "the English, Scottish, and Irish and a number of Eastern Canadians." The passages usually go on to describe the way these people "from different parts" cooperated and helped one another. And there was a willingness to manage differences even when they caused problems: "In a new country the people came from different countries and problems were sometimes perplexing. It took a keen sense of humor, as well as a steadfast faith to be a help in such cases" (Mrs. Andrew Skauge, in her family history, LHB 45:36).

The reasons for tolerance of cultural difference are embedded in the circumstances of the frontier, where nearly everyone came from a rural background, was poor, and was beset with problems of sheer survival. In such extreme circumstances people usually—but of course not always—tend to assist one another. So in the early years of the century American sociologists perceived the immigrant population as a melting pot in which ethnic traits were dissolving and a uniform, generic "American" culture was forming (see Glazer and Moynihan 1975). Both country people and immigrants in the big northern cities shared this experience: All found it necessary to learn the ways of the host country as fast as possible. Perhaps the key factor was linguistic. Settlers from foreign communities were required to learn the language in order to cope with the exigencies of life (see Schach 1980). The process gave the appearance of full and rapid assimilation into the majority or at least dominant culture.

By the 1950s it had become apparent to sociologists that the melting-pot thesis was out of date, since strong ethnic revivals were under way.[1] Such revivals, for the most part, focused on the benign aspects of the original homelands: their songs and costumes, literature, food habits, historical achievements. The heritage movement was not a challenge to the majority culture; on the contrary, some of the most vigorous proponents of Old Country heritage were among the most loyal and "assimilated" Americans and Canadians. Of course there were exceptions: the oppressed, or suppressed indigenous groups, such as blacks and Indians, who mounted vigorous and sometimes militant campaigns to change their subordinate status and eliminate discrimination. The European-derived groups had found it necessary in the early years of the twentieth century to assert themselves, but on the whole they did it though securing occupational niches open during an expanding industrializing society, acquiring education, and moving upward in the political and social hierarchy—possible for them because discrimination on the basis of race, while widespread in North America, nevertheless was not severe enough to forbid all social movement or achievement.

There is an impression of quick and easy transition from immigrant to assimilated citizen, assuming that one generation, which is all it required in a majority of cases, can be considered a short time. However, in particular communities, and for particular immigrant groups, the experience could be difficult. The documents contain anecdotes of the hardships associated with an inability to speak English, of incidents of discrimination on the basis of religion (Catholics were often discriminated against by the Protestant majority), and especially of problems experienced by settlers from Eastern Europe, who entered late in most parts of the northern plains and thereby got the poorest land. Many of these people settled in blocs or clusters, so they could indulge in their own culture and be free of possible embarrassment or discrimination. Sometimes the melting pot worked in a single human generation, as the children of all immigrant groups became Americanized or Canadianized and began to marry outside the ethnic cluster. In two generations, Ukrainians, once a bloc-settled "peasant" group in Saskatchewan subject to discrimination, became prominent in academic and political affairs in the province and elsewhere (see Petryshyn 1985; Lehr 1982).

And while discriminatory behavior among the immigrants was apparent in many places, it diminished quickly under the pressure to adapt and to share the tasks and hardships of early settlement. The documents contain remarks suggesting this process: "We didn't have much to do with those people at first because they didn't think like us, but later we became real good neighbors." As the mutual-aid networks proliferated and people learned each other's languages and customs, the frontier rapidly, and by necessity, developed its own distinctive culture: an egalitarian system conforming on the whole to the majority cultures of Canada and the United States, but which also possessed distinctive habits and values associated with the problems of adaptation on an undeveloped frontier. Ethnic sharpening was diminished in such an environment.

Differences in occupational skills could be more productive of discrimination or even exclusion than national origin or language. Religion could also be important.[2] Catholic settlers, especially if they were served by a chauvinistic priest, were encouraged to avoid contact with Protestants, a pattern that lasted into the 1950s and '60s, when a marked change took place. The Vatican II decrees instructed the rural dioceses to participate ecumenically, but intermarriage between the various religious and ethnic groups had become a common occurrence by the third generation.

There is little question that the Canadian-American Northern European Protestant majority exerted subtle pressure on the other groups to conform, or even to remain apart. Ethnic clustering was reinforced by the cultural distinctiveness of various groups and by the tendency of the majority population to avoid close contact. But in the end there was substantial conformity to the North American institutional template, since this was the majority culture. And it was the loss of original cultural forms that stimulated the third and fourth generations to begin to recover what they considered to be their heritage. The modern heritage movement takes place within the context of the majority culture, and now it is really a way of celebrating diversity as the dominant theme of that culture. In effect, by reconstructing and articulating, usually in English, the colorful customs of the Old Country, the heritage proponents tend to blur the differences between these patterns even while seeming to enhance or sharpen them.[3]

Ethnicity and Nationality

The retention of ethnic cultural patterns on the homestead frontier was influenced more by the immediate social environment than by patriotism or legal and political factors. However, there were some national factors at work. Canada, for example, has always shown a somewhat greater tolerance for cultural differences in its population than the United States, despite the fact that the accepted democratic and pluralistic ideology of both countries holds that a person's culture and religion are his own business. During the settlement period the Canadian authorities deliberately facilitated bloc settlement of particular nationalities or religious groups; the United States was less interested, though such settlements were not opposed if the immigrants were well organized and financed.

In addition, Canada's immigration regulations recognize the status of the "landed immigrant." This made it possible for an immigrant to retain his nationality for a period while he was also, for most purposes, a provisional Canadian citizen. This probably fostered cultural retention and ethnic clustering, but the effect appears to have been greater in Canadian cities than in the country.

The métis people provide a different lesson: that ethnicity without nationality can place a group in social and political limbo. In the past, the métis were neither Canadians nor Americans in the sense of nationality (although legally they could have citizenship), since they deviated from the accepted cultural symbols and occupations. The métis are descendants of the offspring of Euro-American men, mainly French, and Native American women. Originally they inhabited lands in the central and northern parts of Manitoba and Saskatchewan, from which they were gradually excluded after confederation. The land issue led to the final unsuccessful rebellion in the 1880s, after which they became a landless, marginalized people, wandering on both sides of the border. To become Canadian or American in the ethnic-nationality sense a métis had to deny his hybrid ethnic background. This led to some paradoxes: although métis could have been in a particular region for generations, and so represented indigenes, the European settlers could immediately assert kinship with the national populations since their nationality status was clear. (In recent years, the métis, taking their cue from the successes of Indian groups, are asserting their ethnicity and cultural heritage. And some families who had for years concealed métis background have begun openly to claim their identity [see, Clifton 1989; Harrison 1985; Peterson and Brown 1985].)

Aside from problems of ethnicity and nationality, there is the question of just how Canadians and Americans conceive of their own identity as citizens. We have noted that the settlement period in the Canadian-American West opened with minimal national consciousness on the part of the settlers (with some exceptions, perhaps like those Americans who tried out Canada during the "Last Best West" episode and then returned to the United States). But the majority of settlers from humble origins in North America or Europe were only vaguely connected with nationality.

They were settlers who crisscrossed the international boundary looking for the ideal place, renegades of mixed or ambiguous nationality who preyed on Indians and settlers, and traders who had posts and businesses without regard for national sovereignty or even customs regulations. These settlers regarded national identity as something for city folks or politicians, and in place of ethnic or national identity were concerned with land, personal autonomy, or security. National identification with either country came slowly to the Canadian-American West, not as a single act of Congress or Parliament but as a slow accumulation of responsibilities and benefits, of political customs, and above all from long-term residence on one side or the other.

Ethnicity and Heritage

Religious worship and identification is related to the development of the concepts of heritage and ethnicity in the Canadian-American West. Freedom of religious belief and worship was probably never in human history so fully accepted as it was here—so fully accepted that by the 1950s residents of the little towns were complaining that there were simply too many churches, too many beliefs, and that they were fragmenting civic effort. A culture dominated by egalitarian values produced a form of heritage in which although all members of the community are North Americans, they go to the church of their choice and have an ethnicity of choice. The heritage movement offers a compromise between sharpening and leveling ethnic identity. To prefer some of one's ethnic symbols as a part of personal life style over those of other groups is to preserve a sense of difference; but this kind of sharpening has no social bite, for it is a manifestation of generally accepted, personal-choice-oriented cultural pluralism.

The second prominent feature of the new ethnicity—the ethnicity-as-heritage concept—is the ethnocultural organization, to use a Canadian term. Zenon Pohorecky (1978:213–26) compiled a list of over 1,000 such groups for Saskatchewan alone, but on close examination only about 440 fit our notion of such organizations (that is, organizations formed by descendants of emigrants based on former nationality, language, or religious persuasion). Heritage organizations focus on local histories of former homesteaded districts, small towns, church parishes or congregations, school districts, or counties, and family histories and genealogies. By constructing descent and affinal trees and filling in the history of particular families in particular communities, a sense of heritage is created. Locality histories and genealogical compilations eventually find their way into the archives of nationality associations (e.g., the Ukrainian-Canadian Association or Norwegian-American Association). These organizations successfully operate across the international boundary, since many of the settlers developed and maintained kinship and friendship networks over large areas as a result of the wanderings of the first comers. They have also resumed Old Country proximity and kinship ties overseas. In creating and documenting an ethnic heritage, they provide the means for people born in North America to have a revitalization experience, discovering an identity they had neglected or ignored. The identity is not entirely a matter of resurrecting one's own memories, but includes—perhaps even features—fictitious or re-created memories through a reading of the heritage literature and participation in heritage activities.

Along with the heritage associations there are the local historical museums and societies—one in every town in the Canadian-American West with a population of at least two thousand or three thousand. These organizations live by anniversaries, and the local history books are frequently the products of their activities, accounts of the founding of towns, the initial settlement of country districts, the establishment of provinces and states, and on up to the national level (confederation and the bicentennial). The local museums typically have a three-layered collection. The earliest is simply the local experiential attic—artifacts and souvenirs donated by aging first- and second-generation survivors of the settlement period. The second, and more recent, is the heritage collection—the reminiscences, family histories, and the committee activity associated with the compilation of local history books. The third layer, just emerging in many localities in the Dakotas, Montana, Alberta, and Saskatchewan, is the cultural program, in which the different ethnic groups, or their appointed representatives, are persuaded to sponsor exhibits, special days, new collections, festivals, and so on. Some of the museums rename themselves; "cultural heritage center" is a favorite label, the modern successor to the "old timers' museum."

The paradox of western settlement in North America is that it had a major influence on two partly contradictory social processes: cultural pluralism, or the recognition of differences as politically and morally appropriate, and communal mutualism, or the willingness to lend assistance to one's neighbors, regardless of cultural differences. Ethnic differences can be either sharpened or leveled, depending on the nature of the pressures emanating from the majority society and also on local circumstances, providing, of course, that such factors are permitted free play. In the earlier great western migrations, as one might expect, ethnic cultural differences were leveled. There was little choice in the matter if one recognized that the welfare of the individual settler was part of the welfare of the whole community.

But later, in the second and third generations, with their growing linkage to the larger societies of province, state, or nation, tendencies toward ethnic sharpening—and the correlatives, exclusion and a degree of discrimination—began to appear. This was tied to the larger, and awakening, definitions of the majority culture, based on a fusion of North American and Northern European political-cultural-religious criteria. These were always implicit in the system from the beginning, but they did not become significant in social relations until the postfrontier period. And this period overlapped with the last hours of settlement, when people from homelands in Eastern Europe, viewed as "exotic" by British-American settlers, entered in large numbers. They were not Protestants, and even if they were, it was often an exotic branch (Pentecostal, Anabaptist, Pietistic). If they were Catholic, their Catholicism was, in the early days, colored by a sense of exclusion and difference, often fostered by local priests. And if the community existed as a cluster or bloc settlement, as it did frequently in Canada, the sense of exclusion was accentuated.

This in turn fed pressures, often quiet and indirect, to conform to the majority pattern—that pattern informed and structured by the basic institutions of free public education, local tax- or rate-paying, doing good works in the community, participating in local government, and so on. All things, more or less foreign to the "exotic" groups, that have to develop slowly, through two generations. The pressures to conform to a majority template were more insistent on the U.S. side of the border, and so assimilation, in the broader sense of the word, proceeded more rapidly there. In Canada the pressures to conform existed, but the pressures to make that conformity effective in a short period of time were weaker than in the States. Thus the number of ethnocultural organizations seems to be greater in Canada—not at the national level, where the big immigrant-based nationality associations are as well represented as they are in the United States, but at the local level, in the form of particular communities and sections of these communities.

Chapter 4

Setting Out: Emigration as a Social Process

Demographers and sociologists have spent years attempting to discover why people migrate and how they make the decision to do so. But people who move—like the emigrants to the Canadian-American West—come from various countries, cultures, and walks of life, with different kinds and quantities of resources to bring to the experience, and they decide to migrate for varied personal reasons. So much individual variability makes migration theory difficult to formulate.

"Decision to migrate" suggests a single, one-time action. It characterizes only those migrants who did not *experiment* with movement: trying it out, coming back, extending the period of migration over years, and involving a number of relatives or friends; movement, that is, in the form of planned and phased changes of location and life-style. We prefer "emigration" to "migration" because it suggests such deliberate action.

There were incentives to move. To leave home—especially from places where one's forbears had lived for generations—required considerable motivation. Since the people who chose to emigrate came from many places and walks of life, certain incentives must have been influential across the board. In the case of western homestead settlement, these are not hard to find. Demographers usually distinguish between "pushes," things that people dislike or cannot tolerate in the homeland, and "pulls," things that are attractive in the chosen destination. In the case of perhaps a majority of our emigrants, the push of economic depression and political tyranny in rural areas in North America and Europe in the 1890s and into the twentieth century, combined with the pull of "free land" in the West, provided the major incentives to move (Hatton and Williamson 1994). Everyone was responsive, to some degree, to these incentives.

However, this kind of broad sociological generalization is not our objective. We are more concerned with the details and the complicated activity of moving as these were described in the source materials. When we assembled the data, we were struck by the relative paucity of lengthy or detailed accounts. A representative example, taken from a family history written by a child of an American family that homesteaded in Canada, follows: "Liking the sound of all that open land in Canada, and having a growing family, they sold out and brought what they could with them" (LHB 41:585). This tells us that the universal free land pull and the universal economic difficulty push (i.e., the growing-family theme) furnished incentives, but the statement lacks information on how the family came to the decision, what they took, who went, who stayed home, or how they felt about leaving home. Why are so many accounts, followed by full detail and description of making a new home after arrival, so brief? Our best answer has already been suggested: For many emigrants, there was no single point in time when an irrevocable decision to move was made. For many, emigration was a drawn-out affair involving back-and-forth movement, help from and to kin and neighbors—emigration as kind of experiment. Hence the tendency for the second- and third-generation writers to focus on experiences after arrival and not on the relatively brief and highly instrumentalized episode of deciding to move. In order to obtain a reasonably detailed picture of the onset of the emigration experience, it is necessary to make full use of the longer accounts we were able to locate in the sources.

The Emigration Process

Emigration for nearly everyone involved numbers of people: relatives, friends, neighbors. The agricultural homesteading population, including many of the small-town businesspeople, was dominated by family and neighbor groups: young families from the same homeland locus; parents, children, and grandparents, with a few uncles and aunts; children traveling with neighbors, en route to their parents' homestead established the year before; a pastor and part of his flock. Even when an individual or couple came along, they often did so by pre-arrangement with friends or relatives who had preceded them. It is impossible to give statistics here, since that would involve a separate project requiring a search of many kinds of old records and tabulations of what information exists in the family histories (which are notoriously uneven with respect to particular details). But it seems clear from the materials we found that emigration to the Canadian-American West during the period of intensive settlement frequently, even usually, involved several persons in any emigration unit.[1]

Even where individuals did constitute the units—as in the case of the single young men who came West for adventure or jobs—they became involved with settlers immediately on arrival, or even on the trip out, as was the case of N. K. Neilson, a homestead farmer in southwest Saskatchewan:

> In the Spring of 1910 I landed in Maple Creek. I was just twenty-three years old. After I served eighteen months in the Danish Army I decided to try my luck over the ocean. On the liner there were lots of emigrants who went to all parts of America. I got acquainted with people from the States. It didn't take long to persuade me to come along to Valley City, North Dakota. I had nothing to lose and one place was just as good as the next. When a person is young and full of ambition everything looks bright and rosy. . . . One day I met lots of Danes. . . . they were very enthusiastic about going to Canada, take up land and get rich in no time. That's just what we all thought. (LHB 45:43)

There were more men than women on the settlement frontier. The history books are full of anecdotes about these young men vying for the attention of unmarried girls, and how at community dances with a shortage of women, a young man might tie a scarf on his arm and take turns at being a dance partner. A trial demographic study we made of two typical homesteader districts in southern Alberta near the Montana boundary records two men for each woman between 1905 and 1912. The predominance of men did not mean that women were subordinated or neglected; on the contrary, in the new homestead districts and small towns women played a vital role.

It was common in this period for prospective emigrants, living in eastern and midwestern Canada and the United States, to send out young men, older sons, nephews, or neighbor boys as "scouts" to size up the situation and locate some land. These young men frequently found jobs with the resident ranchers, in town, or on the railroad, as in the case of the Morehouse sons, who came to Alberta from Illinois in 1913. Their letters are among the few documents that give details on the vicissitudes of experimental settlement and include instructions on the kinds of equipment the family members are to bring out with them at the time of the final move.

Kent Morehouse, the scouting 28-year-old son of Lewis Cass Morehouse, wrote his father in Normal, Illinois, from Athabasca, Alberta, in February 1913:

> Send your freight on to Edmonton at once. Mark it for K. W. Morehouse, Edmonton, Alberta Canada (if not already sent) and mark it also: "Settler's Effects". Put the same on the bill of lading, mailing the original to me at once, also a complete list of the goods. Athabasca is not a port of entry. If I leave here before the goods arrive I'll arrange for one of my friends to tend to clearing the stuff, for me. . . . As per my last letter to you. I will make no move toward getting a team until you all get up here and we talk it over and see how things look by then. . . . Now please don't you worry about our scheme of all living together working. Why of course it will. The government literature expressly so states and settlers are doing it right along. So lets put our energies on planning constructive work, ways and means. I have decided that if we do not get a team at first then we will go pretty slow on these things which require hauling out. We can use our axes to make a lot of things. In fact, I know of houses that have no sawn wood in them save the table top and the window sash. But I hardly think we'll go that far.

He wrote another set of instructions on 27 February 1914:

> I have several things of importance to write you about. I advise getting your seeds there, for they come from south anyhow and are cheaper. Buy several root vegetables in abundance and enough alfalfa seed for one acre. I figure our main crop this year will be oats and potatoes. I want to see, also, on the farm, one ox team, one cow, chickens, and, if possible, several pigs. We shall need in tools, one wagon, one plow, a harrow.

Since these emigrants were North Americans, they could handle emigration as a planned and staged operation. Kent Morehouse and his brothers could send for tools or seeds when they needed them. Many emigrants from Europe did not have this opportunity, especially if they came directly to the West. However, those Europeans who made intermediate stops with relatives or friends along the way in Eastern states and provinces were in a similar position to the North Americans. The quantity of baggage varied, depending on the length of the journey, the mode of transporation, and the amount of ready cash, or at least convertible possessions. But every emigrant came with effects, including the basic tools and supplies considered necessary to start a new life, and also habits, ideas, social skills, and proficiency in carpentry, music, or medicine. Perhaps the most effective capability was behavioral flexibility and openness to new experiences.

If the emigrants were Canadian- or American-born and started from a convenient railhead, they were able to rent one of the "settler cars"—whole boxcars they could fill with a complete household inventory. Others packed their household goods in wagons.

Possibly a majority of the emigrants tried several places before they decided to stay put, and many came and went more than once. The Alstad family, as recorded in the Toole County, Montana, local history book (LHB 95:172–73), tried out locations in both Canada and the United States before making a final choice. Joe Alstad's father came from Norway in 1878 and first went to Philadelphia, where he had relatives. He then went back to Norway after a year or so to collect relatives and next went to Minnesota to join Norwegian settler communities. After homesteading there, the family went to North Dakota, where they stayed a few years. Next, around 1900, they moved into Saskatchewan in the first Canadian land rush. After a few years they "sold their land at a good price and returned to the United States—to the country they were so proud of." This meant Montana. By 1919, because of the drought in Montana, they went back to Canada, this time to Alberta. Since conditions there were not much better, after seven years they moved back to Montana. Finally, on retirement they went to Idaho to live near relatives. This family's hegira is somewhat extended but not really unusual, and it is interesting to speculate as to just what ethnic identity they might have possessed: Norwegian, Canadian, and American, all three, or none? Whatever else they were, they were certainly professional settlers, familiar with the frontier and settlement cultures of Minnesota, Montana, North Dakota, Saskatchewan, and Alberta.

For many if not most emigrants, the trip overseas or westward was not their first extended journey. The search for work required leaving the family household even before the westward migration. Edna Tyson Parson, the daughter of Anthony Tyson, a homesteader in Neidpath, Saskatchewan, begins the Tyson family history with the search for work by her father and his brothers in England in the late 1800s. Anthony Tyson worked for ten years, periodically visiting his mother. At the age of twenty-two he left for Canada, joining his homesteading brothers nearby. The family of mother, siblings, and their wives was reunited when he and his brothers obtained sufficient cash resources to bring them to Canada (LHB 57). However, for many people the journey out was not a simple one-way ticket like Anthony Tyson's, but meant a long period of movement, earning money, making contacts, trying out one area, and then moving again.

Deciding to Go

> I had just turned 15 years old when the government opened a track [sic] of land in Montana for homesteading. I came from a family of 10 children, 4 girls and 6 boys. Two of my older brothers were past 21 years, the legal age for filing on land. I remember one evening when Dad came home, and at the supper table it was mentioned as to the possibility of going West. Dad was very casual and diplomatic with the subject and would glance at Mother to see what reaction she was taking. I knew right then that Dad was ready to try it. He had always been an adventurer and had made several trips to western South Dakota and Nebraska. Mother had always held him down and I am sure that in many cases it was for the best. This Montana deal though seemed different, free land, all one had to do was just live on the land and improve it a little, and in a few years it was yours. Finally, after many days of careful consideration, it was decided to go. My two older brothers and Dad were the lucky ones to make the trip. The distance they were to travel was about 1200 miles and this seemed a long way to me.
>
> Lewis Anderson, opening paragraph of a reminiscence of his experiences as an adolescent on a homestead in Montana (LHB 104:26)

This document is one of the few that actually describes a decision-making process at the intimate level: how the topic of emigration and settlement was raised and discussed in the family unit—diplomatically, it seems, in this case. It provides another example of the scouting process. The emigration or move of one family member often started the homestead "itch" or "fever"—the urge to emigrate and to find opportunity at the end of the trail. In making the decision to emigrate, family obligations and personal opportunity tend to be balanced.

We have another example of the decision-making process in a set of letters written by David Christie to various family members. Christie tried out Montana as a potential place to move from Minnesota, while his wife, Emma, and their children remained in Minnesota. During this trial period (October and November of 1883) he was homesick and saw the country as "desolate" and "cursed." He wrote to Emma in October of 1883 from Bozeman, where he had been looking for land:

> I feel just about played out and thoroughly disgusted with this Damned desolate country. No Sir I will never settle in this cursed country where they only have about 3 months of pleasant weather.

Four letters after his return to Minnesota, written in the spring of 1884, illustrate the complex and often agonizing balancing of personal goals and family responsibilities. In a letter to his older brother Alexander, 16 March 1884, David Christie wrote:

> I am still in favor of going to Montana for it seems to me there is a better chance for one with small means to get a start for work can be had at good wages. . . . Now if we go South and east of course we would have a milder climate . . . but it would take lots of money to buy land . . . and as to schools for the children I think there would be no better chance in North Carolina than there would be in Montana and then there would be no freedom to a northern man for that same feeling of hatred still exists there [the Christie family were strong Union advocates]. To a great extent of course it might be better for Father and Mother but there is no use talking if I should move south the problem would be no nearer solved as to them for they seem bound to stick where they are Father would go any where I think but Mother will never leave the place she is just so mulish. . . . It would be on their account only that I would give up going to Montana. So you had best write to them and find what they are willing to do because if they are bound to stay where they are I shall go to Montana. I am willing to do anything that is for the best and that will keep the family together.

By the end of March the decision to move to Montana had been made, despite the fact that his parents remained in Minnesota. On 21 April he wrote that he had a good job in Montana for six months. He planned to look for a homestead, put up a log cabin and then send for his wife and children. But letters written during the next six months in Montana reveal second thoughts. On 12 June 1884, he wrote to his wife, Emma, about his hesitation:

> Dear could you stand it to live here where you would have no neighbors and there be no school for the children it seems like sinking oneself in a well I will think it over and you let me know just what you think about it.

On 18 June 1884 Emma wrote that David must decide and he should decide quickly. The same day, he sent a letter telling her that he was thinking about going to look for land in Oregon, Washington Territory, and California, where there were better climates and where it was "more sivilized." In her letter of 20 June 1884, Emma responded to his ideas about looking farther afield:

> It is getting about time there was something settled on. . . . I don't think you know what a unpleasant life i have to live this way . . . i don't feel i shall bea willing to live this way very much longer. . . . i want you to settel on what you are going to do and let me know. . . . I am opposed to go where our children can't go to school but i think that we should stop and think that we have not very much.

David Christie, pushed by his wife and desiring to reunite his family (many of his letters describe his loneliness), finally decided on Montana. Despite the weather, the terrain was familiar, and friends and kin were in the area. Thus there was a disposition to trade off the advantages against the disadvantages, to weigh the opportunities on the frontier against the welfare of the children and one's own needs. The Christies finally settled in Bridger Canyon, northeast of Bozeman; his brother Alexander (Sandy) later homesteaded closer to the Montana-Canada border.

Reviewing the letters, reminiscences, and autobiographies, we find that some writers emphasized the adventure, others, the lack of alternatives and the poverty at home; some recalled their decision to emigrate with feelings of loss at leaving their kin, whereas others merely recalled the availability of what they called free land: "They read so much about the wonderful free homesteads in Alberta, that they loaded a boxcar with horses, machinery, and some household goods, and came to Warner, Alberta, early in the spring of 1909" (written by the son of Michael John Nicholson, a homestead farmer in southeast Alberta; LHB 1:21).

Virtually all accounts emphasize economic opportunity. For example, Roy Benson, a homesteader near Munson, Alberta, wrote to his father in May 1909:

> There is lots of money coming in here from the states farmers and men who never saw a farm and a good many of them will plant their little wad right here in this country and then go out and curse the place because they didn't get rich but one meets that class of people every place. I think there is a chance for a man to make money here if he will only stick some say they can't grow anything in this country—one has only to ride along on the train to see about that—of course where the ranchers have their bases one don't see anything but cattle but where they are farming one can see big straw stacks. . . . Wages are good farm labor $30 the month teamsters $30–45, engineers from $3 to $6 a day carpenters $40 to $50 masons $60 to $70 and one can get good board for $5 a week and men are scarse.

Leaving Home: Benefits and Costs

"Leaving home" is a phrase full of symbols of sadness, renunciation, nostalgia. Certainly leaving familiar sights and sounds, friends and relatives is a complicated business, whatever the emotions. But leaving home can also be a purposeful act, a solution to a problem, a welcome renewal. The massive public response to the inducements offered by the two governments and the many private agents and brokers suggests that the emigrants had good reasons for accepting, and that parting was not always a matter of sweet sorrow. Consider the following, from a reminiscence by Annie Lacore King:

> So when, in the Spring of 1906, the thot was somehow implanted in the Noble County [Minnesota] Press that land in the province of Saskatchewan, Canada, was rich and tillable, and that both homesteads and land at low prices was attainable, it caused much comment among the family. It was becoming clear that the King family had an oversupply of laborers—in that brother Tom, now 26, and brother James, 22, and thot of "hiring out," as the work at home could be well

> managed by the remaining Johnny, 20, and little Pat, 13.—Now, here was an opening, and a project worthy of their attention! Tom was first to leave for Saskatchewan, accompanied by a few of the neighbor boys. . . . They remained till cold weather and came back with tales of good wages, good crops, and easy acquisition of farm land.

Eventually the whole family followed, along with some of the neighbors.

Most of the emigrants came from places where land was scarce, taxes high, economic conditions poor, or the landlords grasping or tyrannical. The move to the West was not taken lightly, but at the same time it was greeted with relief and hope. For example Kristian Askeland, a young man, recalled: "It was the alluring news of the opportunities and the prosperity in the 'new world' to the west—Canada and the United States—that moved me to cut the ties with my dear people, home and mother country to come to Canada, the land of opportunity. Of course depressing conditions that prevailed at that time in the 'old country' and the lack of opportunity, especially for young people, was to me a real incentive to try and find out what Canada had to offer" (LHB 41:251).

The pain of leaving familiar cultures and social worlds—to "cut the ties with dear people"—was serious, but the anticipation of a better life somewhere else was a strong counterbalance. And, of course, cutting ties was also necessary for those who stayed home. Concern from the parental point of view is well expressed in the following letters written by Hans Mathias Hansen (1832–1909) and his wife, Berthe Marie Osmundsdatter (1845–1917), from Norway to their son Ludvig Horntvedt (1868–1946), who emigrated to the United States in 1888 and farmed in Kalispell, Montana, from 1890.

> Horntvedt Febr 28, 1888
>
> Dear Ludvig,
>
> At your departure I was uneasy and it was not possible for me to express the feelings of my heart. . . . I don't know any other way than praying to God for help, being uneasy. So I do because I'm depressed when you are leaving. Constantly I will be anxious for you. However, nobody can help it. . . . Don't forget us. . . . We will be longing for every letter. We love thee highly. Thank you very much for being good and diligent in the home. . . . Farewell—Farewell.
>
> your tender mother

> Horntvedt Febr 28, 1888
>
> To my beloved son Ludvig Christian Hansen Horntvedt at your departure for America. At your departure I wish for you and your fellow emigrants good luck and rich blessings during the voyage and over there. . . . my beloved son, I admonish you: be careful, discrete, cautious and not overanxious. The dangers are many. . . . There are many failures. . . .
>
> your tender father
>
> Hansen-Horntvedt Letters, p. 169

In the Hansen-Horntvedt letters we recognize parental sorrow and concern for their son, but, although they fear for him, they do not say that they want or expect him to stay home. In other cases, perhaps those in which the circumstances were less onerous, we find parental opposition. Upon her marriage to Dennis Davis, Maggie Gorman Davis left Indiana to homestead in Montana in 1912 against her parents' wishes. She replied to one of her mother's letters, which obviously expressed concern, in May 1912: "Now, mama, honest which way would you rather it would be that we were settled down on a little rented farm or be out here on a farm so big that we can have fields half a mile long and four hundred acres in pasture. Of course I would like to see you folks but aside from that I am well and happy" (Finnell 1980:35).

And for some homesteaders who came as groups of kin and neighbors able to maintain accustomed social relationships, there seemed to be few regrets. Mary Jane Hamilton of Mount Forest, Ontario, came to southwest Saskatchewan with six daughters and five sons, four sons-in-law and three grandchildren: "We were all young and together. We didn't get lonesome, for we had each other; we didn't look back. So we never had a moment's regret for what we had left behind" (LHB 65:181).

Women: "Reluctant Migrants"

The histories and anecdotal descriptions of western settlement until recently focused on the male migrants. The neglect of women's role has been redressed with the emergence of feminist revisions to a male-centered history.[2] While the role of women was perhaps perceived as less dramatic or adventurous than that of men, it was vital to the process, since women were largely in charge of preparing the family and the household for the journey and getting them settled in the new home. In the older literature, westering women were often portrayed as either sunbonneted helpmates or reluctant pioneers, though our source material tells us that there was a considerable range of experience between these two extremes. Historians who reject the Turnerian view of the frontier as a liberating experience for women emphasize women's lack of control over the decision to emigrate, the reluctance with which they followed their men, the unwillingness of women to adapt to the new demands placed on them by frontier conditions, and the hardship of bearing and raising children on the frontier.[3] Sandra Myres (1982), attempting to refute the "reluctant pioneer" stereotype, claims that out of the 259 emigrant diaries she read, 18 percent of the women strongly opposed the move west while 32 percent strongly favored it. Moreover, although the women who filed independent claims (where it was legal) were a minority among the homesteaders (averaging between 5 percent and 15 percent of the total in most areas), single women homesteaders were not uncommon and were often successful in proving up. In the Montana Hi-Line counties, Hill, Blaine, and Chouteau, women comprised at least 13 percent of all homesteaders, as listed in Polk's Directory 1915–16 (for comparable data see Harris 1983, Lindgren 1989, and Patterson-Black 1978).

In Canada, where homesteading women had to prove they were heads of households or the economic provider for a household, female homesteaders were widows with children who had accompanied sisters and brothers to the West. Widows were commonly viewed as women with few resources, dependent upon the good will of their kin. In the West, however, there was a need for women's labor, and where homestead land was available for women their potential social position had changed. Bessie Brower Reesor wrote:

> My mother who at that time was Mrs. Louisa Brower had been left a widow during the winter of 1908. The following spring and summer great news spread far and near, announcing the vast areas of land that had been thrown open for homesteading. . . . Friends and relatives were greatly excited and enthused over the prospect of obtaining ½ section of land for practically nothing. This resulted in mother, along with her 3 brothers . . . and three brothers-in-law, as well as friends from different parts of North Dakota going to Moose Jaw in July to file on homesteads. (LHB 48:26)

The opportunity for unmarried women who were not heads of household to obtain a homestead (limited to the U.S. side of the border) made it possible for a woman to bring to her marriage a self-obtained "dowry" in the form of land or money from the sale of the land (Lindgren 1989).

Far from dreading emigration, some women, like Nannie Alderson, whose reminiscence also records the misery the frontier offered women, seemed eager to move. After marriage, sharing her husband's enthusiasm for heading west, she left for Montana in 1883. The main motivation was to "strike it rich" (Alderson and Smith 1969:14, 25).

Letters from women encouraging others to emigrate abound with reasons ranging from marital opportunities to economic opportunities. For example, Verna Benson wrote long letters from a homestead near Munson, Alberta, to her family in Duluth, Minnesota, telling her sister-in-law, Anna, about the economic opportunities. She wrote to her father-in-law in 1910:

> If Anna cared to do it she could make pretty good money with a bakery out here in some of these new towns. There is so many bachelors out here I should think the baked goods would sell pretty good and there is lots of carpenter work in all these new towns.

She wrote directly to Anna in 1911:

> I will . . . tell you what a good chance there would be for you to make a little money out here if you wanted to do it. The blacksmith's wife . . . keep[s] boarders and baked bread to sell last year. And she says . . . she cleared about $300. Then one of our neighbors went into town last fall and ran a restaurant and they claim to of cleared about $500.

It is tempting to generalize from documents such as the Benson letters that there was little, if any, reluctance among women to emigrate. However, letters encouraging emigration should not be used to challenge other writers who regret the move. Nor does a quantitative count of women who saw the frontier as opportunity deny that some women were reluctant migrants.

Bertha Wilkes's autobiography provides a graphic account of the reasons for emigrations and the ambivalence accompanying the decision:

> The year 1908 and 1909 brought great changes in our home. We were living four miles from Marlington W. Va. . . . The panic came and times were hard. The mill shut down . . . Dad had to go elsewhere and hunt for work. I sold everything I could and stored the rest, took

> my two little boys and went North to my home, hoping for better times to come, but can not say I was sorry to leave the South with its heat, fleas, snakes and poor water.

Bertha Wilkes returned to her parents' home while her husband looked for work. She continues:

> At this time of hard times and worry came word from far away Canada from Uncle Roy, telling us to come as fast as wings could bring us as land was being opened up for settlers and great opportunities lay ahead. So after many long talks with our parents we decided on the far West and our future. Of course many discouraging things were said.

In April 1909 Bertha's husband left for Canada while she, pregnant with her third child, remained behind. After the birth of a daughter, she made preparations to leave:

> As I became stronger I commenced my preparations for my journey to Canada. Again I sold many things, packed several boxes to be shipped at settlers rates, and in September I left the old home. . . . All my friends and school chums and more than all my dear Mother and Dad Wilkes to start a home with my husband and children in an unknown land, with no idea of what lay ahead.

Bertha Wilkes's memories encapsulate the balancing act connected with the decision to emigrate—hard times and the hope of great opportunities tip the decision to leave "the old home . . . with no idea of what lay ahead." Her memoir can be read either as reluctance to leave or as willingness to face the unknown. Most of the debate regarding women as reluctant migrants suggests a male imperative toward the new (the adventurer) and a pattern of patriarchal decision-making where women played little, if any, role. Our data suggest otherwise. We do find that an individual's position in his or her life cycle is significant; thus the demographics of the frontier emphasize its male character and gender but commonly downplay the youthfulness. Separation from kin and family and a search for adventure or for economic opportunity continues to be both expected and encouraged as a phase in the young man's life cycle. In marked contrast, with few exceptions, similar autonomous behavior of young women is discouraged. Women adventurers become admired only if they live long enough to gain social esteem for a unique and particularly interesting life. What becomes clear in reading this and the other documents written by both men and women is the complexity of the factors: perceived alternatives always mitigated by the individual's life situation, encouragement or discouragement by others, and, of course, the particular personal characteristics of the individual emigrant.

Chapter 5

Starting Off: Interactive Adaptation on the Homestead Frontier

The key words—hardship, what social psychologists call relative deprivation, mutual aid, coping, and staying power—define the process of individual settler adaptation on the homestead frontier. While each emigrant had his own particular problems, adaptation was an essentially social process: Hardship could be handled by individual coping but almost always required help from kin and neighbors. If such efforts were successful, a settler was considered by the government to have "staying power." But this did not necessarily mean that the settler would actually stay; the reasons for leaving were many, and frequently settlers would depart to try their luck elsewhere. Staying power, like deprivation, is not a matter of simple or single standards.

The adaptive experience, as described by our writers, was not just a matter of coping skills and interaction with others; it was also affected by available resources, and such availability was often a matter of luck. The homestead regulations were not planned to guarantee every settler the same amounts of land, water, or proximity to transportation but merely the right to claim a small tract of land. Beyond that, settlers were required to find their own resources: cash, machinery, additional land, water, suitable terrain, or transport facilities. Staying power was therefore not simply a matter of attitude but included the capture of necessities and facilities.

And, of course, coping skills varied by individual. Some were remarkably skilled in making quick decisions, taking risks, trading off one possibility against another, persuading neighbors to help out or lend the needed tools. These behavior patterns were as much a matter of personal disposition as intelligence or fortitude. And obviously people who had tried homesteading or settlement more than once were in a better position than those engaging in the process for the first time; experience counted, as many of the writers note. Timing was critical: Successful settlers often showed, in the reminiscences, a keen sense of what to do at just the right time; for example, in certain circumstances it was more important to put in a crop before constructing a permanent shelter, or to put available cash into a good plough horse rather than buy shoes for the family.

We believe that the accounts of the adaptive process in our source materials are reasonably accurate. However, we also believe that the attitudes attributed to the settlers in accounts written years after the experience have some doubtful features. Some of the recollections seem to imply that hardships were actually ennobling experiences—proof of pioneer character—rather than sources of trouble and suffering.

Aside from such potential inaccuracies in the data, we do have materials that add to, and correct, older published accounts of homesteading that neglect the social interaction this type of settlement required. We shall call the process "interactive adaptation" and note that it is based on "overlapping deprivation." The latter term denotes the uneven preparation of the settlers: Everyone lacked something, but what one person needed another might possess. And by borrowing back and forth, interacting in order to adapt, the problems could be solved. There were also more formal kinds of socially interactive support, such as the patron-client system of labor, a form of employment involving a kind of indentured servant or laborer relationship of an emigrant with an established settler.

Thus adaptation was not by any means solely a matter of individual performance but also a social process. Without this trading and sharing, without mutual aid, very few could have settled. In actuality, only a minority of all emigrants stayed indefinitely in their first choice of district, and, overall, the permanent settlers represented a small fraction of all settlers. But those who did stay solved their problems with a combination of personal coping capacities, necessities obtained from neighbors, and a measure of sheer luck.

Arrival

The initial impression of the new place for hundreds of homesteaders evoked dismay and disappointment: "Even though I had been told it was prairie land, my first glimpse of the country . . . was something of a shock, the only break being the different hills and valleys" (Helen Shepard; LHB 48:39). One may imagine the feelings of a farm or village family from Norway, England, or Wisconsin arriving at a dusty spot on a weedy, treeless plain, containing a one-room board shack with dirt piled around the bottom edges to keep out the wind. This was a common situation, and for a great many the final destination could hardly have been considered an improvement over the situation back home. Housing was the first consideration for all settlers.

Arrival at the homestead made instantly apparent the second major necessity of frontier existence: the physical labor required to break the soil and plant crops, to build barns and houses, and to live in temporary shelters for a year or more until income began to flow. And there were physical hazards—rain- and snowstorms, heat, cold, dirt, wind, the scarcity of potable water, the difficulties of keeping clean, and the dangers associated with exposure, illness, and inadequate food.

Everyone experienced financial difficulties, although some settlers were better off than others. Most people brought cash, but for many it didn't last long, and there was a constant struggle to find ways of getting more: searching for jobs, borrowing money, selling or bartering possessions. Free land did not mean free machines, horses, tools—these had to be bought or obtained as best one could. Even when a small crop might emerge at the end of a long first summer, there was the problem of getting it to market, if a market existed. The difficulties of transporting and marketing crops in the early years pinpoints the lack of adequate services and facilities. Post offices, banks, stores, roads, schools, and religious institutions were lacking in the beginning for most districts, or were available only at some distance, or were at best temporary, make-do facilities.

Another problem was demographic. The frontier was at first populated randomly—that is, by people not pre-selected to furnish balances in age and sex categories. This meant that labor might be scarce and every family member had to be pressed into service, that marriageable mates might be hard to find, or that there might be too many elderly people who could not contribute sufficient labor for the farm or help with the children.

Some of these conditions were listed by the writers as immediate deprivations or privations; others were described as continuing problems, recurrent shortages, repeated crises, or a sequence of related difficulties. The size and demography of the settlement unit could influence the severity of hardships. A young, single man could manage in a homestead shack without much difficulty, but if he had a wife and children the shelter situation could be desperate. A family with many possessions and no adequate house to put them into would need to pay for storage in town, possibly inducing a financial crisis; a homesteader with livestock and no means to find or prepare forage might be required to sell the animals and use the money for food. In such cases, interactive adaptation would come into play: Some hardships could be alleviated only through swapping necessities with neighbors.

Such adjustments took place very quickly. The drive to reproduce the necessary conditions of settled life is rendered as a determined one in the reminiscences, and within a few months such herculean efforts paid off; houses, barns, fields, schools, labor, animals, and informal machinery cooperatives appeared quickly. The discomforts and dangers were either managed or accepted as difficult but necessary conditions of the frontier. "If you could get through the first winter, it was easy afterwards." "If you had to, you walked ten miles to get help."

The standards of living of the homesteaders were modest; most had been members of rural communities in homelands where life was frugal. So, while poverty was endemic on the homestead frontier, most writers say that the emigrants were accustomed to it and were therefore prepared to work hard. The material resources required for sheer survival in the first year or two of settlement fall into two main categories: those associated with what we might call the starting phase (temporary adjustments for survival), and those associated with the commitment phase (the relatively final or permanent adaptations for living in one place).

What emigrants were able to take with them to the homestead was the most important factor in the early days of settlement. The quantity of baggage varied, depending on the length of the journey, the mode of transportation, and the amount of cash on hand or possessions that could be sold for cash. The more affluent emigrants, especially some of the Americans from the Midwest, had astonishing collections of household goods, clothing, and keepsakes stuffed into big wooden trunks or bales. The load was especially heavy if the emigrants started from a North American locale in a settler car or came out in a wagon.

Emigrants coming directly from Europe without an intermediate stop had to make do with less, but even for these people there was variation in the quantity of luggage. Some European emigrants brought handmade furniture or accumulated such niceties one by one as other family members came to the settlement. Few were under the illusion that anything could be easily acquired on the frontier; correspondence with earlier emigrants advised the newcomers of the conditions. Everyone knew that when they arrived something essential would be lacking, but they hoped it could somehow be found, thus laying the foundation for networks of mutual aid. Judging by their frequent mention in the documents, there were three essential things to carry in one's baggage: tools, especially basic carpentry items; adequate clothing for cold weather, particularly stout shoes or boots, heavy underwear, and a good windbreaker mackinaw; and, finally, cash, especially enough to buy food for the individual or the family unit for the first days and weeks.

So far as the list of priority tasks are concerned, these appear to have varied by the settlers' degree of preparation and also by the available facilities in the district. The great majority of settlers had three principal tasks to accomplish as soon as possible: build shelter of some kind, find a source of water, and break soil and put in a garden and a commercial crop. Beyond these three vital accomplishments lay a number of other needs depending on settlers' resources and capabilities. For example, if one had livestock it was necessary to find a source of pasture or hay, especially if the native forage was inadequate or appropriated by a nearby ranch or other homesteads or if the country was in the grip of drought. If cash was scarce or lacking, the importance of putting in a crop so as to realize some income was even greater than planting a garden, because if there were other settlers around one could always beg and borrow enough food for a month or two, or even a whole winter. (Bachelors were especially prone to cadging their dinners from other settlers in the first few months, judging from numerous accounts.) For a settler with journeyman skills in a trade, gardening and farming were not so important. Many such men seem to have spent their entire first year after homesteading working for others and accumulating a cash nest egg with which they could buy farm equipment, tools, and clothing in the second year. Adolescent daughters and sons "worked out," contributing their earnings to the household. Women's skills—butter-making, cooking and baking, experience in egg and chicken production, teaching, dressmaking—could also find markets in the settlements.

A patron-client relationship existed in districts where homestead farms were close to established ranches or farms. While the ranchers often resented the entry of the "nesters," there was not very much they could do about it, and many of them felt genuine concern for these ill-prepared pioneers. Frequently one or more of the newly arrived settlers would exchange his labor for supplies with the "big man." Over a period of time, this led to a clientage in which the "little guy" could be called upon for any kind of service or support. Women were also involved in such relationships with the ranch or farm wives, cooking or baking, doing their laundry, or helping with the young children. Such clientage relationships were usually somewhat strained, since an implication of social hierarchy—the "prince and the pauper," as one writer put it—was inescapable. And the embarrassment was felt by both sides, since the relationship tended to preclude the treasured egalitarianism of western frontier culture.

The source documents give the neighborly mutual aid involved in interactive adaptation the special cachet of altruism, as proof of the moral nobility of the settler generation, but in reality there was no alternative: Either you helped the homesteaders next door, or you let them starve. And assistance was needed not only by the ill-prepared but by anyone when unanticipated needs arose. A man might have a good team of horses and a good plow, but if his fields were full of glacial boulders, as a great many were in the northern plains, he might have to borrow a stone boat and neighbors to load it and haul it away. While a horse and wagon did not help you get water if there was no working well, they could be used to haul barrels of water from a neighbor who did have one. A baking oven was not usually something settlers from abroad could bring in their baggage, and the woman who had acquired one (sometimes from little failed cafes in the villages) found it necessary to lend it to her housewife neighbors in rotation.

So the unevenness of preparation and of personal capacities, as well as the fact that no one was *completely* ready to "make it," meant that a value system arose that emphasized a special version of moral pluralism: Everyone is equal, but with unequal skills and preparation for coping; everyone has a right to bring what he or she wants, and if settlers lack the essentials it is not really their fault but the result of the general uncertainty and lack of information; hence, everyone deserves help regardless of personal values and cultural background.

The fact that this emerging value system centered on material objects, techniques, and knowledge is also significant for later cultural development. The strong emphasis on instrumental concerns (that is, material needs and accomplishments) in North American and perhaps especially U.S. culture probably has one of its origins here. The writings are clear on the point that the important things in the first years of settlement were hardly intellectual or spiritual; more important was the wherewithal to survive, make a living, and feed your family. Recreation and spiritual elements were not completely disregarded, but these were things that apparently developed later in the settlement process, after enough settlers had made their commitment and established the basis for a community. And finally, the strong emphasis on the interactive adaptation of equals certainly carried on into the persisting egalitarianism of American life.

Necessities of Life

Patterns of house construction are often described in the local history books. The common procedure involved the making of a crude temporary structure, followed at various intervals by the building of a more permanent dwelling. The texts also illustrate associations of shelter with other factors: water, gardens, lighting, heating, barns, kitchens, and so on. Some people put barns ahead of dwellings and lived in lean-to shanties for a year; others built a substantial cabin before the sheds and barns. If they had very young children, the dwelling house was a more pressing need, especially if neighbors could help out with food and cultivation. If they had valuable livestock or farming implements, they might construct a barn first, leaving the house until next year. This was known as "next year country," particularly on the Canadian side.

The varieties of shelters were, in order of permanence: tent, shack (made of scrap lumber, branches, or brush), combinations of tent and shack, dugout, sod house, a simple one-room lumber house (a flimsy frame building usually built of purchased or donated used lumber), log cabin (very durable, almost always later incorporated into permanent structures), and, finally, the multiroomed frame house built of lumber or, in the rare cases when it was available, stone. This sequence of degree of permanence is also more or less developmental, as may be obvious; the more permanent the structure, the more labor and money must be expended, and these were short in supply for the great majority at the beginning of settlement.

The presence of horses, possibly acquired along the way or immediately upon arrival, was important; they represented the principal available traction power. A cow was equally important as a source of food for the children. Such valuable resources needed sustenance and protection, which meant that the cutting of hay, finding pasture, and providing an animal shelter of some kind—a lean-to shed or a bushy creek bottom—was as urgent as building a house for the family.

Furnishings were, in the majority of cases, extremely simple. There were exceptions, but the typical homesteader had little: some clothing, a small box of valuables, a few tools, a box of kitchen implements, a sewing kit, a few dishes and cutlery, a small wood stove, blankets, three or four books (especially a Bible and perhaps a handbook or two about emigration or pioneering), furniture (a chair or two, a crib, a knockdown bed). Almost every family had a few special items of sentimental value or utilitarian significance: ancestor portraits, a set of china dishes, a sewing machine, an especially good stove, a surveyor's instrument, and, if a horse had been acquired along the way, a harness, plow, or hay rake. These utilitarian items often served the interactive adaptive network of a settlement community, an instrumental process with significant social functions.

Homesteaders were not explorers, trappers, or mountain men trained to live off the land; they were emigrants, people who were in the process of moving their permanent domicile from one place to another and taking as much as they could carry with them. Almost every writer describes one or two very difficult episodes in which something fundamental to survival was missing: heat, light, water, or food. Even some of the North American emigrants who came relatively well outfitted had problems with such vital necessities. To some extent the problem of shortages and the continual struggle to acquire the items necessary for daily life went on indefinitely. The writers of family histories and reminiscences often mark the acquisition of key items—a washing machine, a refrigerator, the change from a coal heater to oil—as milestones in their life history.

Food apparently was a problem for almost everybody in the early days and weeks. Settlers were encouraged to bring essential foodstuffs with them: a sack of flour, sugar, salt, dried fruits, jerked meat. But few could bring a large supply, so nearly everyone found it necessary to buy staples and other foods on the journey. Nearly all settlers purchased food, tools, and so forth at the general store located in the town where the railroad dropped them. These stores were remarkable institutions, full of nearly everything needed for rural existence in the late nineteenth and early twentieth century.

Many families stayed in town for a few days while arrangements for acquisition of the homestead and purchases of supplies could be completed. The stay might be in a "settler accommodation house," a tiny building maintained by the town for settlers without money or accommodations, for one or two nights. More commonly, the incoming settlers stayed at boarding houses or hotels, where they were required to pay nominal fees. In some places, if they had friends in town or word of their arrival had been sent, they stayed with townsmen in spare rooms, outbuildings, or even in a tent pitched in the yard. Their cash was used to pay for board and, of course, for supplies, and when all this was done a typical settler was broke. So out they went to the homestead, and when they arrived they were on their own, or dependent on early-comers, as in this account by Dan Thompson, son of a homesteading family in southwest Saskatchewan:

> The Duncan Thompson family came in 1911 and took up a homestead, which H. E. Hanson helped them locate. Mother and we children were left on the homestead for two years while Dad went out working. We did not have very much to eat. In fact I believe we would have starved to death had it not been for our neighbors, Evan Christianson and Einar Smith who gave us rutabagas and a trap so that we could catch rabbits at night. Mother took the fat off the rabbits to fry our potatoes in and rabbit was our only meat since we did not have a gun to shoot anything with. I used to get so hungry I would eat grass. (LHB 45:36)

For a few days the homesteaders could eat the purchased food and do the necessary chores to create a home, and perhaps the initial land breaking and seeding if the weather permitted. But almost all of the settlers would find it necessary to borrow food at the end of the first week or so, eat the dried or canned foods that many families brought with them, or go out for wild game. Thus the writers describe a period of severe privation at the beginning of homestead settlement that resulted, for many, in discouragement and departure. The specific outcome seems to have depended on the nature of the community. If enough settlers had arrived prior to the newcomers, they could usually expect help until other arrangements could be made, a new supply of cash sent by the folks back home or a job in a nearby town or on a ranch, anything to supply money that could be used to buy more food until the garden came in. During this period of privation, protein was the most acute lack. Dried vegetable foods, flour, and other staple-derived carbohydrate nourishment could be fairly easily found, but meat and eggs were very difficult to come by. Lucky settlers were those who had struggled with a crate of chickens all the way from home, or a pig or two.

In nineteenth-century rural society, cleanliness may have been next to godliness, but it was also work assigned to the housewife (the writings are unanimous on this point). Homesteading women naturally attempted to maintain their standards on the frontier, a task made extremely difficult by dirt floors, sod roofs that leaked dirt and spiders, loose boards and windows that poured dust into the house every time the wind blew (and in some places it blew almost all the time), children covered in dust and mud from playing on the prairie, the sweat-soaked clothing of the men, and the lack of sufficient water or soap for washing in leaky wooden or galvanized tin or copper tubs. The number of items washed was listed in diaries along with lists of visitors and town trips. The following account by Josie Olson Ouelette, the daughter of Norwegian homesteaders in west central Saskatchewan, details the necessary steps:

> Washing clothes was a long and tedious procedure. The children would be sent to the slough with two pails each to bring up the water. It would then be strained of wrigglers and left so that the dirt would settle to the bottom. The water was then heated on top of the stove in copper or galvanized boiler or washtubs. The white clothes were boiled so into the boiler would go Royal Crown Soap, chipped off with a paring knife, and add a little Lewis Lye. There was no such thing as soap flakes. Most farm women made their own laundry soap. This was made from fat and tallow, remainders of Dad's butchering, rendered down and lye added. This was then poured into a wooden box to solidify and be cut up into cakes of soap. If the water was hard Arm & Hammer washing soda was used in the wash water. Clothes were all scrubbed on a washboard, properly boiled, rinsed in clear and then in bluing water. (Ouelette, p. 12)

The Anatomy of Hardship

Virtually all autobiographies and reminiscences recall coping with everyday hardship, but the process of handling really tragic events is rarely described—at least in detail. That is, hardships were routine—everyone experienced them—but tragedy consisted of events with personal loss, profound grief, or deep disturbances of social relationships. Certainly tragedy engenders coping, adaptation, and learning, just as the experience of hardship does, but there is a difference: one never really overcomes tragedy, but only tries to compensate.

While it is difficult to make assessments of the actual frequency of particular difficulties from random collections of documents, it is possible to discern a pattern of linked occurrences. Climate—or really weather—is perhaps the most frequently mentioned starting point of a series of difficulties. Strong winds, blizzards, cold, or excessive precipitation in one form or another could set off a chain. The second most common triggering occurrence is an accident resulting from unfamiliarity with tools and equipment or from primitive conditions and makeshift arrangements. The third might be called general living conditions, especially for settlers without sufficient cash or supplies to make a quick start. Such events exposed them to other hardships in a crescendo of difficulty. We offer several passages that give the tone of the descriptions in the reminiscences and family histories, especially from documents written by people who experienced the events or who used old letters or similar contemporary materials as sources. We are considering hardship in the context of adaptation: problem-solving and coping with frontier conditions, with special emphasis on the first year or so of settlement.

> Blizzards are an awesome product of nature and every family can relate some unique experiences. One nice, winter afternoon our mom needed to bake bread but found her "everlasting" yeast starter refused to work so she walked to her neighbor, Mrs. Kjos, who lived a couple of miles away to borrow some. She was tired enough that she stayed for a cup of coffee and by that time, the wind had started up and snow was beginning to drift close to the ground. The neighbors insisted that their young son, about nineteen, walk back with her. The storm grew rapidly worse but they made it home guided by a light in the window. Then the young man struggled through it again back to his home so his family wouldn't be worried. When mom got home she found the youngest child choked up with croup but she survived. There was no lack of incidents to stimulate their flow of adrenalin.
>
> Signora Eide Volstead, daughter of homesteaders in Montana (LHB 95:278–79)

> The winters were long and we never had much reading material, especially for the early grades, our library was one bookcase about 5 shelves high. We had to work in the garden after school. Pull weeds, hoe or pick potato bugs. My most mortifying job was to be picking up dried cow chips in the summer (to save our coal and wood for the winter). Where we lived there was not a tree in sight. In

today's western stories, the cowboys made camp fires with buffalo chips, however it never made me feel it was the thing to do when I had to gather the cow chips.

Those were the years of the droughts and grasshoppers and all of the money had to be used for food and clothing. Dad would have to go somewhere and work on a threshing crew, sometimes he had to go as far as North Dakota and that would take care of the staples for the winter. Mother always had vegetables in the cellar. Often the spuds were small. She always planted by moon signs and always had a good garden even when others did not. We had no water to irrigate.

Selma Jacobson, daughter of American homesteaders in northwest Montana (LHB 98:105)

In his pioneering days he met with three unfortunate accidents. In the summer of 1914, while raking hay with a team of horses, he fell off the rake on rough ground. The horses ran away and he was dragged by the rake for some distance and was very badly hurt. On Christmas Eve in 1924, one of his horses kicked him and broke his leg. It was a really cold, wintry day and, as he was living alone, he had to get help some way. He took a chair and dragged himself along with it, through the deep snow and cold, to Tysselands. Mr. Tysseland took him to the hospital, where he spent many painful days. In 1926, he broke his hip on the same side, falling from a load of hay. This too caused a lot of suffering. From that time on, I have been told, shaking palsy set in, making him an invalid for the rest of his life.

Written by Kristian Askeland about Louis Moldeseter, a Norwegian homesteader in southwest Saskatchewan (LHB 41:644)

A source of data on hardships other than reminiscences is the local news sheet. Most of the towns and even some of the crossroads settlements acquired newspapers within a few weeks or months after establishment. These papers were usually published weekly, many of them into the 1920s and '30s. By the 1930s the papers began disappearing or merging into larger weeklies published in the largest service-center community and covering a much larger territory. The earlier papers were quite personal in tone, making an effort to report events affecting anyone in the district, which, given the small populations involved, was most of the "news" anyway.

Hardships were reported without embroidery or effusive sympathy.

"Ole Swanson had the misfortune to lose a finger in his mower." "Mrs. L. Jones has been suffering from the grippe the past week." "William Coxey lost one of his horses last week, leaving him with only one to do the work." "Terrible hail storms did damage to crops in the Aavord District last week; people there will have a hard time of it." "Little Laverne Schnabel injured her knee quite badly when the family team ran away with the wagon. The family is very concerned." Terse as these items may be, they do indicate that hardships were indeed hardships; that there was a community awareness of the fact that events of this kind could have serious consequences. However, the items are reported simply as happenings, and they are rarely used to testify to the moral or physical courage of the settlers. Such attitudes come much later, in nostalgic retrospection.

Perception is also influenced by expectations. A few settlers expected instant prosperity, but most knew things would be difficult and conditions harsh. Young people might care less about keeping their clothes clean and mended since they had not reached a point in their socialization to learn that one must care for one's garments. But these differences in expectations, as well as the differences in preparation for frontier life, were quickly leveled in the typical homesteaded district, and in a short time hardship achieved standardized definitions. The documents show that the women discussed the lack of water, health hazards, and food problems, discovering they all shared them though in different degrees, and these differences immediately created an interactive body of coping strategies. Likewise, the men learned from each other how to find help on the farm, to repair a pull-type harrow, to deal with townspeople. The emergence of a standardized rhetoric of hardship served to lessen the burden to some extent, since there was comfort in numbers. N. K. Neilson, a Danish homesteader in southwest Saskatchewan, wrote: "There was one good thing—we were all in the same boat. When it came to distress and sorrow friendship and the neighborly spirit was a wonderful thing in those early years. . . . It all helped to make me forget the daily task" (LHB 45:46).

Material in the reminiscences and letters generally offer more details about attitudes toward hardship than the shorter, more descriptive accounts in the local history books. We believe that this is mainly a result of the public editorial climate of the latter; writing for them was influenced by a shared model featuring condensation and an avoidance (but not complete omission) of conflict and grief. The reminiscences or letters, on the other hand, represent attempts to reconstruct the writer's or his relatives' experiences.

We examined two collections of letters, written by Roy and Verna

Benson from Munson, Alberta, and by Maggie Gorman Davis, from Carter, Montana, covering the same period (1910–26). The letters from both families display, in general terms, the same kinds of difficulties and successes, but the outcomes differ. The Gorman Davis letters show increasing concern over conditions, and eventually they leave Montana and abandon the attempt to establish a homestead farm, returning to Indiana. The Benson letters, on the other hand, display accommodation and acceptance of conditions, and they remain in Alberta primarily thanks to Benson's success as a well-digger. Roy Benson writes in January 1911:

> I suppose you are wondering what kind of country we have struck well there are a lot of people right here that are doing some wondering. This past year has made a lot of them sit up and take notice. Some have left the country, some couldn't. . . . I had a 10 a[cres] broke a year ago (cost me $50) last July. Last spring I let a fellow put in on shares and put $20 into a fence—this fall I told him he could have it all but the fence.

Verna Benson writes in May 1911:

> I surely don't care anything about putting in another winter like last winter. I went to one of the neighbors New Years day and I wasn't away from home again until the last of April. There was two months last winter I never saw a woman and in fact the only persons I did see during that time was Roy and our bachelor neighbor. Then the men all wonder why the women don't like it here and the women all wonder what there is about the country that the men like so well.

Roy Benson, May 1912:

> You wanted to know about the chance to start a hardware store here. The chances are good and the chance to broke is d-m good too but it is something I don't know much about. Every man that has started here has made good so far. . . . I am not able to buy a cow and not able to stay home to milk if I could get one but there is no use of kicking I am getting along getting three meals and a pretty fair sleep every night and got plenty of work ahead. When I started out here we had $500 in the bank. I have been here three years now have my homestead duties done all but the residence will prove up next year. That calls for a house worth $300 thirty acres broke and two crops. I have

45 acres broke and fifteen more paid for and three crops. The buildings are worth over $600 have a waggon, disc, plow and harrow.

November 1919:

> Say if I don't grow a crop this year I am going to be in one h——l of a fix next fall. You see the 100a [acres] I have ready stands me in $1000 The seed $500 and I am going to get another 100a ready that will mean $1000 more and that has all got to come before I even know that the seed is going to sprout. Oh Well! I'll have lots of company whichever way it goes.

The Gorman Davis letters begin with optimism. In one letter she writes about available land:

> February 28, 1911:
>
> It [abandoned homestead land nearby] will cost $50 to contest and $22 to enter besides carfare here. You could enter and go back there till fall. . . . I promised myself that I would never say any thing to persuade any of you to come out here but this is such a good chance that I can't resist the temptation. If Edd was only old enough it would be such a chance for him. If there is anyone you know of who wants to come tell them about it (that is if they're married) for they will be our closest neighbors. (Finnell 1980:25)

A letter from Maggie to the *Burnettsville News* dated 21 December 1911 has a headline: NO REGRETS FOR LEAVING HOOSIER STATE FOR WEST (Finnell 1980:25). However, future letters document an increasing interest in leaving.

22 February 1914:

> You don't need to think there is any danger of Dennis getting discouraged out here for wild horses couldn't drag him away. . . . He says for the first time in his life he has an opportunity to make good. Mr. Wiley was offered a loan of $4,500 on his farm and I see no reason why we could not get that much so you see we could get that anytime and pull out, but we'll never get another farm give to us, so we had better stay with it till land advances to $50 to $60 and then we can sell and retire or travel or something. (Finnell 1980:36)

8 December 1919:

> Dennis says if he sells out he wants me to start for Ind. with him. I tell him I never resigned yet (from a teaching position); he'll have to go without me. (p. 55)

In a letter to her sister Mae, Maggie responds to her sister's statement about some land for sale in Indiana. She tells her sister to "keep an eye on it" (p. 56).

12 December 1921:

> Yes I realize we could make a living there [Indiana] at least. But Dennis is all built up on "next year". . . . Yes I wish too we could sell out but if you could realize that there is not much chance but while there's life there's hope. (p. 58)

23 April 1923:

> Our prospects in every way were never poorer. We have had a dry winter. Winter wheat is going or gone. . . . Everybody that was left is planning on going now. It seems it isn't for us to stay. Even the bankers have nothing encouraging to say any more. . . . I don't know what will become of us. If we could sell the land I would be for coming back there [Indiana] but as it is I don't see any hopes of ever coming. Dennis wants to go South where they get rain and rent land and I suppose we'll have to do that for we can move there without so much expense. (p. 59)

26 September 1923:

> So how are we to come home? I think we should be encouraged to stay instead of to leave for it sure takes courage to stay. But mama I know you and papa wouldn't give up and leave everything. We have debts here and we couldn't pay them if we went and I can't bear the idea of taking "the cure" as they say here like the rest most all are doing. . . . [The letter ends with a discussion of the type of farm they would want to rent.] (p. 62)

24 March 1924:

> I hope we have a crop too but I have no faith in it. If we don't have a crop we can't come and if we do have Dennis will want to stay and

try it again so prospects are slim. And I hate the thot of giving up broke, too. (p. 69)

8 June 1924:

It isn't any use to plan. We hate it here. We never know when we will have a total failure again and be caught with a lot of stock. We were getting pretty nervous when this rain came. . . . Some that have gone have returned. They are talking of having school again this winter. (p. 70)

On the whole, the two sets of letters do not suggest that hardships for the Davis family were empirically worse than those experienced by the Bensons. The difference lies in the attitudes. Increasingly the Gorman Davis letters show a negative response to difficulties, and there is a suggestion that perhaps their expectations were higher than the Bensons' in the beginning. Eva Gorman Finnell, a niece of Maggie Gorman Davis who prepared the letters for record, wrote that while she was growing up she was "held spellbound" by her aunt's stories of the Montana homestead, but when the aunt was asked to write them down she refused, saying that the experiences were so hard she "wanted to forget them." The niece adds, "A certain hardness and bitterness had crept into her life during the years in the west, caused by the difficult life and disappointments she had faced."

The Gorman Davis letters show the gradual change from optimism and a willingness to cope to a desire to give up the hard life. They also suggest that a key factor in the process was the lack of encouragement to enter into homesteading by the Gorman family back home in Indiana. Many of the letters suggest a desire to defend the decision and to make light of the hardships, but also to express regret at the inability, due to financial and other reasons, to come home for a visit. In the year of the decision to leave (1924) letters indicate that a crop may be possible despite the persistent drought, and this vacillation occurs in other places in the correspondence. The niece suggests that the letters downplay hardship because of her aunt's "Irish pride," as she calls it.

To attribute the difference in the Davis and Benson outcomes to differential perception of hardship is to oversimplify a complex decision process, although certainly the hardship issue functions as a symbol of the ordeal. We note the continuing attraction of the Indiana homeland for the Davis family, and the lack of approval of emigration by the Indiana family members—both of which probably exerted a strong pull homeward. Roy

Benson energetically sought out job opportunities in order to earn additional cash, whereas Dennis Davis did not do so, although his wife took a teaching job. Dennis also suffered from arthritis, a physical hardship made worse by the hard winters and extremes of temperature and humidity. All of these elements, and others not revealed by the letters, were no doubt involved, but the fact remains that the context of experience for the Davis family tended to emphasize the difficulties of homesteading on the northern plains, while in the Benson case these were matters requiring acceptance, or an adaptive response.

Staying Power: Some General Considerations

The capacity to endure hardship is, of course, relative to situations and to the passage of time. The initial experience of homesteading required considerable endurance. But some settlers were able to accept difficulties indefinitely, or at least long enough to prove up the homestead, acquire additional land, raise children, and establish a home and farm. Others endured the difficulties for a few months or years and then gave up. Hardships reflect experience, but they do not necessarily relate directly to the capacity to plan, struggle, save, work, and remain in one place and make the best of it. Obviously other factors were involved.

The writings make it clear that the experience of hardship is related to expectations: People with high expectations might be able to accept hardships as well as those with low ones, but they would be more likely to give up the task of homesteading because it did not match ideals of security or wealth. Many homesteaders viewed the experience as a gamble, adventure, or as a high-risk investment, and if it did not seem to be paying off in the early months or years, they would be inclined to leave. A great many tried two or more locations before deciding to see it through or give it up. Given equal abilities, fortitude, and expectations, the quality of available resources, like land, cash, or labor, might lead some to stay and others to leave.

Physical resources were obviously crucial for many settlers in the more difficult climatic and edaphic situations, but these factors were qualified by all the other influences. In this book we tried a different approach: to examine the source materials in order to see if certain qualities were associated with staying power or the decision to leave. Long-term success at building a farm and raising a family was considered to be the most important criterion of staying power.

We selected a district in southern Saskatchewan where we had not worked previously, and matched it with a somewhat less comprehensive sample of cases from a district in northern Montana not far from the Saskatchewan district. We used the local history books for both places. Both districts were ethnically mixed, with no preponderance of one group over another and with no important differences in settler ethnic background in early and late comers. We ruled out personal accounts of motives and reasons for staying or leaving; we used only second- or third-person accounts, almost always writings of children or grandchildren.

We transcribed relevant passages and then coded or classified them into seven trait categories, as follows (in order of frequency):

1. Ability to take chances; make hard decisions; accept risks.
2. Possession of diverse skills, either as an individual or as a family (e.g., carpentry, horse-breaking, good at arithmetic).
3. Ability to work hard or steadily; to "keep at it," finish tasks begun.
4. A high quotient of patience; ability to accept reverses and try again; willingness to wait for outcomes in order to test out the means used.
5. Modest expectations; ability to recognize the limits of human endeavor and the constraints of the physical and socioeconomic environment.
6. A liking for solitude; ability to work alone and enjoy it, but not excluding friendliness when neighbors present.
7. Ability to laugh at mistakes; a wry, humorous attitude toward the tribulations of settlement on a frontier.

Conspicuous by their absence in this list are the traits allegedly associated with achievement in the contemporary urban world: strong ambition, high ideals or expectations, lots of energy, high intelligence, and so forth. Traits shared with the settler picture include the aptitude for hard work, ability to take chances, and sense of humor. This suggests that success is to some extent relative to situations and that different situations call forth different personal qualities. Or, in line with our emphasis on adaptation, success and achievement are simply aspects of adaptive behavior. They come to pass in different contexts with different behavior patterns, although there is probably an overlapping zone of behavioral traits common to all situations.

So we turn to the leavers, those individuals or families who gave up on the homesteading effort after trying it for about a year. In our source materials we noticed that most people who left after a few weeks or months were not serious about homesteading to begin with, or were simply trying out a particular locality and expected to move elsewhere if necessary. Settlers who stayed a full year or longer and then left were likely to give up homesteading entirely. A few cases did eventually return to the fray after, for example, a relative stayed in a particular place, built a good house, got crops under way. There is no easy way to sort out people on the basis of black-and-white motives. Many things influenced attitudes toward the homesteading experience, and this is why the leavers are important. If some of the trait categories tend to suggest opposites of those associated with the stayers, we may have a pattern. The categories, in order of frequency, are as follows:

1. High expectations of success, of early evidence of financial gain, and perhaps correlatively less patience.
2. Strong drive to succeed; perfectionistic attitudes.
3. Inability to handle solitude and personal insecurity; desire to associate with others; liking for community life.
4. A general set of factors indicating complete unpreparedness; lack of necessary physical resources, physical weaknesses, overly hard work, lack of money.

The leavers also shared many of the traits noted with the stayers: diverse skills, ability to work hard and consistently, ability to take chances. The differences lie in the level of expectations, the "patience" factor, and the ability to live in sparsely populated areas with few neighbors and limited community organization. These last three traits, then, probably constitute the crucial markers of reasonably competent people who elected to stay and build a farm and a home, people who were absolutely serious about the homesteading opportunity.

Some differences in attitudes toward solitude appear in the Canadian and U.S. materials. The Mounted Police played an important role in Canada; we found many passages in which the regular visits of the local policeman, out on his circuit of the homesteads, helped to relieve the sense of isolation, giving the settlers the feeling that someone was watching over them. This factor was, of course, absent in the American cases. We have no evidence that the presence of the Mounties might have induced some people to stay longer; at least none of the writers mentioned it. Two of the American settlers did comment that they wished that someone like the "Mounties across the line" could ride circuit on the U.S. side, but there is no evidence that this was a particularly important consideration. On both sides homesteading neighbors could relieve the loneliness for those who felt it.

Coming to Terms with the West

Considering the large numbers who tried homesteading, those who stayed for a lifetime—or at least long enough to amass land, be reasonably successful at farming, and create a home and family—were very few, and ranchers were often the most numerous among them. Out of ten homesteaded districts in Montana, Alberta, and Saskatchewan in our sample, only one retained about half of the original peak population of settlement as long as a decade after arrival (this allows for the replacements of the original or initial settlers in the first decade or so). The others lost between 60 percent and 90 percent of the peak within five years after settlement. The one district had a preponderance of ranchers or cattle-farming enterprises and sufficient water resources. The acid test of the stayer was pursuit of an agricultural occupation until retirement, providing the resources were adequate. Since most homesteaded districts were overpopulated, the stayers really represent those who bought or acquired the vacated homesteads.

Coming to terms with the West did not mean passive acceptance of the economic situation by the majority of farmer settlers. While they might learn to cope with uncertainty and fluctuation, they also did what they could, technologically and politically, to improve predictability. Even with the uncertainty, the West was a great place to be, with natural beauty and remoteness from crowds and hustle. Those who stayed came genuinely to love it.

But one aspect of coming to terms was a fundamental and irreversible change in lifeways. The rapidity of this change is attributed to the specialized environment to which these people, regardless of their origins, had to adapt. The change took place in one generation. The children of the settlers, and especially those born in the West, were the "new people" of whom some reminiscence writers speak: "We were Westerners now." "Even our parents put [the old ways] behind them because they knew things had to be different." "My folks had a chance to start over—this doesn't happen very often in history, and they were willing to change, though it was hard for them." "We became more open out here."

On the other hand, some of the homeland ways not only worked on the frontier, but could be consciously fostered, even at considerable cost and effort. The combinations and compromises varied by individual and family. The material realm was the most obvious. Some settlers worked hard to reproduce the house type and the gardens of the homeland village in an effort to recreate the familiar symbols of culture as they knew it. In an earlier study we called this attempt "symbolic adaptation." The familiar symbols provided an emotional buttress, compensating for the necessary changes in behavior and social relations. And in later generations many of the old customs could be revived (even if the language was lost) as a symbolic representation of times gone by, of nostalgia and return, as part of the heritage movement. But at the same time pride in being "Canadian" or "American" and in having made the transition successfully was equally evident. The sadness and dismay at the necessary changes passed with the first settling generation.

Thus we can perceive a kind of dual adaptive posture among the stayers: pride in the capacity to change but also in the retained or revived symbols of life in a humid environment or in the gentility of rural life in Europe or eastern North America. Some of the latter features found their way into the agricultural establishment via the farm extension literature. Pamphlets and technical manuals treated tree planting, special shrubs and varieties of ornamental plants; designs for the "prairie farmhouse," incorporating traditional North American styles and decor but adapted to the harsh winter and abrasive winds of the Great Plains, were featured in the second-generation pamphlets of the 1920s, '30s, and '40s. Some elements had genuine practical significance. Tree belts were not only useful in breaking the wind for the farmhouse and gardens, but would shelter crops and promote moisture retention in the fields. Drought-adapted fruit plants had symbolic value but also improved the diet. Most of the experimental stations in the region still have significant acreage devoted to raising new varieties of ornamental as well as commercial crops.

As time passed, the landscape changed. The grass and scrub lands became dotted with clumps and rows of trees, enclosing farmhouses, calving sheds, home gardens, beehives. Pride in this distinctive landscape emerged: By the third generation, these features were no longer instances of symbolic adaptation but simply "our landscape," our distinctive plains world. Thus the duality of the adaptive process was transformed into a single homogeneous and indigenous cultural posture.

Chapter 6

Settling In: Family and Household in the Homesteading Experience

This chapter looks at the role of the family and kinship in emigration and settlement on the homestead frontier. The chapter is framed by ongoing scholarly debates over the significance of western settlement, and homesteading in particular, for theories of family and kinship structure and the roles of men and women. The principal themes concern the failure of the promises made for prosperous settlement, the fragmentation of family ties, and the increasingly individualistic character of North American culture.

A more immediate goal of the chapter is to assess the impact of frontier life on household relationships, asking in particular whether frontier life engendered greater independence and autonomy for women or more cooperative or egalitarian relationships between husbands and wives.[1] The chapter is based, for the most part, on women's autobiographical materials and personal letters. When women write about their past experiences they tend to emphasize matters connected to family, life cycle, and the principal phases of gender relationships (courtship, marriage, parenthood). The historical sense is personal, defined by the events and personages of kin groups. Men, on the other hand, generally organize their remembered experiences around work, community, and public affairs. One consequence of this pattern is the sparsity of material about family and household relationships written by men.

The Role of Family in Emigration and Settlement

In her introductory comments to three accounts of families undergoing settlement, Lillian Schlissel (1989:xvi) sees "disassemblement" and "fragmentation for family" in these family histories. Most certainly the experience of settlement required a good deal of self-reliance, the breaking of certain bonds of dependence, and the assumption of greater self-determination. But, at the same time, most emigrants traveled to the homestead frontier with family members and friendship groups, or as advance parties for other members of the kin group who stayed behind. The popular image of the self-sufficient, lone male settler referred to only one kind of emigrant. For most settlers, it was the kin group—the nuclear family and other kin—that provided the economic resources and moral support for emigration. Geographically extended kin units functioned as they continue to do today, as solidaristic units to sustain members who claim the "rights" of kin.

Emigration to the North American western frontier can be viewed as an extension westward of the widespread migrations throughout Europe associated with increasing population, capitalist development, urbanization, and changes in work opportunities. These social and economic changes created a new social context for individual choice, thereby changing concepts about family rights and obligations. Affiliative ties remained, but the ideological underpinnings of what constitutes kin, shared by emigrants to the North American West, permitted considerable variability and flexibility (and still do).

Euro-American kinship is based on the concept of bilateral descent, with the individual tracing ancestry to both the mother's and the father's sides; only in a few special cases or places does it specify a paternal lineage over a maternal one (or vice versa). The absence of specific or enforced rules for association, inheritance, and occupation permits choice for individuals, and it is possible to ignore, revive, or keep dormant kinship connections according to the demands of a particular situation. A second aspect of this system is based on the principle of the neolocality, a principle in which marriage marks the separation of the couple into a separate household, creating the nuclear family.[2] While settlement households did include others in addition to the conjugal couple and their children, inclusion had an optional characteristic (Freeman 1961). There was freedom to include in the household as many relatives, and from whatever side of the family, as the settlers might choose (or put up with). Connected to this freedom from other kin is individual responsibility in which the newly formed household is responsible for their own support and for the support of their children. Marriage, the entrance into adulthood, was dependent upon finding the resources to establish a household, to live independently, and to raise children.

Just as economic changes in Europe laid the base for the formation and increased recognition of the conjugal family as a social group with increased individual autonomy, so, too, did the opportunities of the New World. On one hand, it would seem that the opportunity for individual land ownership without the encumbrances of other family members would lead to the disassemblement and fragmentation of family ties suggested by Lillian Schlissel. From an alternative view, however, the inherent flexibility and optional character of the Euro–North American family system had an adaptive function, since the ideology of kinship could be expanded indefinitely in either maternal or paternal lineages. The connections with the homeland were often not broken so much as stretched and refined. Regular communication led to chain migration, the recruiting of family and friends for the new settlement by sending back instructions, tickets, and information on what to expect and how to make the journey.

Family histories in local history books, written by the children of homesteaders, generally have little to say about relatives and friends who were left behind. Lineal descent from the initial homesteading household and the subsequent ties in the new home community are emphasized, and the settling family is given the status of the kin group.

> Mr. and Mrs. Andrew Schile came to Harvey, North Dakota from Russia in the early spring of 1908, with two small children. . . . They lived there for about two years, and one more child . . . was born. In the year 1910 they came to the Bow Island district [Alberta] and then homesteaded about seven miles north and west of Foremost.

> Six more children were born. . . . These children all received their education in the rural school at Remainder, in the district north of Foremost. Through the years, members of the family married and started homes of their own. (LHB 20:418)

A list of the children's locations, work, marriages, and parents' deaths follows, ending with the statement: "There are 28 grandchildren and 54 great-grandchildren in the family." Family remains important, but, at the same time, the independent actions and careers of children are given recognition. Recently families have begun to pay attention to their "old country" ethnic heritage in line with the themes of the heritage movement.

While complete autonomy for the single emigrant or a small kin group (a pair of brothers, a young married couple) was rare, despite the availability of land and the considerable number of locations available for homesteading, nevertheless individuals were able to follow personal wishes to an extent not possible in the homelands. At the same time, however, starting out required social contacts and work partners and a whole set of new responsibilities toward others; thus communities emerged. Both the bonds of family responsibility and her own aspirations for autonomy are evidenced in Anna Guttormsen Hought's autobiography. Encouraged to emigrate by her brother, she promised her family she would only be gone five years. And in five years, in 1912, she went home intending to stay only three months. However, her mother's ill health prevented that, and she stayed in Norway until 1916, when her brother entreated her to come to join him on the Hi Line in Montana, to take out a homestead and be company for his pregnant wife (Hought 1986). Anna recalls that it was only when her mother recognized that her brother's wife needed her that she received parental encouragement to leave home. Her wish to emigrate coincided with her brother's need, and so by moving she could fulfill both her own desires and her responsibility to the family. Although from Anna's point of view the decision to migrate may have been clear-cut, from a sociological standpoint it is quite complex. On the one hand, individualism was fostered by the needs of the individual, biological maturation, and generational change in the family. On the other hand, her case also demonstrates how an emigrating person accommodates individual needs with family responsibility.

An emigrant family had to face up to the necessity of balancing the need of the family group to stay together and help out against individual opportunity or the necessity to earn money. Mae McQuigg, who homesteaded in northern Montana in 1916 with her mother, recalls how she and her husband, James, made the decision for Mae herself to take a homestead:

> [We] decided that my husband would stay on the railroad job and I would take my Mother . . . and two small sons to live on the land. . . .
>
> There was one shack 10 ft. by 12 ft., and it was built on the line with a bed on each end so that mother slept on her claim and I and the children slept on ours. . . .
>
> It was not too lonely, and we could always expect my husband out on Saturday with the mail and groceries and ready to listen to all of the news about the homestead. I must admit I did have two fears one was a prairie fire and the other was for my children and my mother. (LHB 98:131)

So Mr. McQuigg stayed in his money-earning job with the GNR in Chester, Montana, on the Hi Line, and Mae and her mother stayed on their homesteads thirty-three miles north, near the international boundary. This solution was typical. We have records of at least a hundred cases with similar dimensions: families carefully dividing up their members in two or more domiciles or locations in order to maintain sufficient income so as to keep the whole group functioning according to traditional family patterns.

We are dealing here with the classic sociological distinction between household and family. The household is a residential unit that changes with the developmental cycle of the individual, economic matters, and mobility of residents. A family or kin group involves an ideology or set of values about relationships. Homestead regulations required setting up an independent household, but this did not mean the breaking of kin ties. When a family remains in one place, earning its living and functioning as a single unit, household and family become one and share members. This group, however, is always in flux, changing as the individual members mature. When the members break away, exploring new opportunities, marrying, or earning a separate income, the distinction between household and family emerges as a problem requiring decision and compromise. Such decisions typically involve the weighing of emotional and cooperative-work ties against the need for maximizing opportunities for the individuals and also for the group. In other words, in nuclear families like those of our settlers, "household" and "family" become analytical rather than empirical concepts.

Thus, there was a kind of paradox in the dynamics of the frontier family. Granting individual members the autonomy to make their own way diminishes the solidarity of the household, but it can also protect family ties; in other words, the household—the working group of individuals in a single residence—is sacrificed in order to preserve the kinship group. Despite the extreme pressures and divisive tendencies of homesteading life, the basic social relationships of the Euro–North American family system in large measure were preserved; the system simply adjusted to the greater mobility of individual family members.

Couples and families who arrived on the frontier carried patterns of relationships forged in the homeland but had to adjust their relations and household forms to fit prevailing conditions, and these were very different from those of the homeland. Under the adaptive pressures and shifting cultural contexts encountered in migration and frontier settlement, family and gender roles often became problematic. Relationships, particularly those between men and women and between parents and children, which may have been clearly defined in former contexts and were often represented and legitimated by religious dogma, did not always stand up to the social and adaptive realities of this new setting.

The most general trend we found in our source materials regarding these topics is the transitional nature of the anecdotes. Role expectations or behaviors show combinations of Old Country or at least nineteenth-century social relations, featuring male dominance and wide separation between male and female roles, with the more relaxed egalitarian forms that emerged on the homestead frontier. Necessity, not ideology, directed these changes. In our materials, we find numerous (and humorous) accounts of change in traditional interaction between men and women. Anecdotes recalling problematic sleeping arrangements and visiting patterns abound. For example, because of a husband's early return, sleeping arrangements became a problem for a female visitor: "The question of sleeping arrangements was solved by the resourceful Cora (Colwell). 'Shove over against the wall Maybelle (the friend who was visiting in the husband's expected absence), and I'll sleep in the middle, and we'll all be snug till morning.' When all was quiet and the light out, Cora inquired, 'Are you comfortable Maybelle?' 'Oh yes thank you. . . . All but my conscience' " (LHB 65:257).

There seems little doubt that in the early days of settlement, authoritarian fathers, repressive husbands, and submissive women gave way to their opposites, or at least to a more cooperative and egalitarian pattern (Kohl 1992). But the reminiscences also include evidence of tension between men who intended to adhere to the old customs and women who were making the shift toward more autonomous and assertive roles. In a sense, each family had to construct its own combination of the old and the new and adjust these to the emotional needs of the participants.

Courtship

Courtship exemplifies the pattern of transition in that young people of marriageable age, eager to consummate the relationship in order to get going on settlement tasks, found it necessary to violate parental expectations of slow, graceful courtship. Elopements, or something like them, were common.

Life before marriage was a time of relative social freedom for young women on the frontier (whenever they were free from family duties). They were "popular" with neighboring bachelors and widowers, and there was no dearth of social life: dances, picnics, church and school functions, women's gatherings, and clubs. Barbara Alice Slater visited her brother on his homestead near Stoppington, Alberta, and noted, in a letter dated "Xmas 1910": "Our nearest neighbours are ¾ of a mile away but it seems no distance. Folks are all most neighbourly, & you go *miles* to a party! Every Monday & Thursday there are skating parties on the Creek, from 6 p.m. until any time you like. The bachelors keep fires going on the ice & lanterns in the bushes at the side! It is very jolly, & then there are sleighing parties & surprise parties."

In her 1986 reminiscences, Pauline Diede writes about the social life of young people in the context of acculturation of the German-speaking settlers in her district in northwestern North Dakota:

> The neighborhood young people were invited for [a husking bee party] . . . and we would all sit on the floor . . . boys on one side and girls on the other. . . . Whoever found a red cob, . . . he/she had a choice of kissing his/her favorite. Here is where an occasional romance sprouted. The neighbor boy married his neighbor girl. The case of either one having had one and only one match experience . . . probably not much more than a friendship encounter . . . yet they were married whether the course was for better or worse, they stuck! . . . The barn dances, that drew young people from far and near together, naturally attracted . . . as when a dancing couple held hands assisting each other down the barn ladder, then went on a moon-lit stroll. The word was said as they embraced and kissed. . . . And the smiling moon shone down with a shine of approval for a re-

sourceful and ethnic-mixed marriage . . . a culture enhancement for America! (pp. 123–24)

Diede also writes about changes in courtship from the old-world practice where parents traditionally chose the mate. She emphasizes that courtship was a brief process and was usually initiated at a community social function or at church. In her book of interviews with early settlers in Mercer County, North Dakota, Diede quotes Bill Bockfish, who worked as a ranch hand before filing for his own homestead in 1911: "I was a bachelor for a few years. . . . It was tough all around, especially for a greenhorn like me, facing the hazards alone. To ease a 'loner's' problems, there would be Saturday night dances. . . . I met my girl there. There wasn't much time for courtship . . . as most marriages were hurried affairs. Ours was" (LHB 109: 11–12). However, in many cases, after one or two meetings, courtship had to be carried forward by letters. Although Anna Guttormsen Hought lived within two miles of Ed Hought's homestead and was a good friend of his sister (who also was homesteading), she saw him no more than a half dozen times before she accepted his proposal of marriage (Hought 1986:88–89).

A foreshortened courtship emphasizes the individualistic dimension of the marriage tie, placing all responsibility for the matter in the hands of the would-be partners. The decision to marry, in many cases, was made with little consultation among the various parties, and the ideology of individual choice was reinforced by the informal social patterns of the frontier. But even in situations where extended family members were available for consultation and advice, the economic value of a marriage partner, the loneliness of bachelor life, and the relative lack of single women increased the social pressure to marry. Thus marriage was an individual choice, not determined by family values but by situational needs.

Most women expected to marry and have children, but sexual ignorance was common (Ladd-Taylor 1986; Silverman 1984). Mary Weeks reconstructed her Aunt Cora's thoughts during her aunt's wedding service: "Cornelia [Cora's mother] not only never told her daughters what life, love, sex or reproduction were all about, she chastised them if they so much as talked about it, saying, 'Animals, not people do such things.' . . . the later it got, the worse Cora felt, for she knew that she was going to have to go home with Rouke, and she was afraid of the intimacies of marriage. But it was too late now for she was his wife" (p. 130).

The topics of courtship and marriage assume greater importance in the reminiscences written by women than in those written by men. For example, in reminiscences of similar length (both approximately 2,500 words), R. C. Morrison and his wife wrote about his arrival in Maple Creek, Saskatchewan. First, Mr. Morrison: "That day I met the lady who, seven years later, became my wife. Slow you say! No just all the time broke" (LHB 45:20).

But his wife includes many details about the circumstances leading to their meeting, circumstances that, like many of the marriages on the frontier, had everything to do with proximity. Her husband's family had come from North Dakota to homestead with their relatives, who were neighbors and friends of her family. On the other hand, as Eliane Silverman (1985: 53) points out, marriage—and we can add courtship—was for some not the momentous event depicted in contemporary romantic representations.

We find, however, that most reminiscences, those included in local history books as well as those independently produced, show that the writers attached considerable importance to courtship and marriage. In the independent reminiscences we find details of intimate relationships revealing marriage as not only an important episode but often a very difficult one as well. Local history books do not include these sorts of memories; a marriage in these books is often depicted as successful both personally (especially if a family enterprise is involved) and collectively (for example, we see in Mrs. Morrison's recollection of her courtship that her relationship with her husband only cemented a prior friendship with neighbors). Such presentations reflect editorial conventions governing the writing of local history that mandate that a single personal event demonstrate, albeit quite indirectly, the bonds of community.

Husbands and Wives

For both men and women, marriage meant the assumption of adult roles. Households had a relatively clear division of labor: Women were responsible for household management; men were responsible for the farm; children were subject to parental demands. Since the time before marriage was a period of relative social freedom for women, daughters, though responsible for regular household chores, were not responsible for household management. Upon marriage women may have gained independence from parental supervision, but a wife was subject to her husband's authority and was as well responsible for the household. In Mary Weeks's description of her Aunt Cora's early days of marriage, she writes about how her aunt felt about her freedom from her parents: "Rouke and Cora were invited to a party . . . and Cora was excited, for now as a married lady, she could go to a party if she cared to without her parents' permission. She felt quite grown up" (p. 134).

A subsequent anecdote illustrates the increased household responsibilities placed upon new wives. Cora, concerned about the devastation caused by gophers, spent a morning catching them. When her husband returned for his noon dinner his response was anger at her desertion of household chores (p. 141). For men, the change from son to husband meant the responsibility of building and maintaining a farm, or a business or trade, if the couple moved to town.

Wives were dependent upon personal responses of their husbands for their position in these families, as was the case everywhere in Euro–North American society at the time. The ability of the husband to control the household and the opportunities for the wife to make her own decisions depended on cultural ideology, the juridical status of women with respect to property, and, of course, personalities. In the personal dimension of household life there were (and remain) important differences among the members in ideas about appropriate behavior for women, patriarchal power and control. Despite a collectively shared gender experience of household responsibilities, women have not uniformly experienced the same reality. Generalizations about and judgment of power and autonomy within the domestic group need to be explored in the context of the particular household relationships and associated cultural expectations of that kin and ethnic group. For example, Helen Potrebenko (1977:17) talked with her father about his relationship with her mother. She asked how her mother managed when he was away from the homestead during the winter. His reply:

> She did whatever it is women do when looking after small children. She was a good mother. There was lots and lots of work to do, all that wood and water to be brought in.
>
> But what did she think about it all? . . . Was she bitter then?
>
> I don't know.
>
> Did you talk to each other?
>
> Oh sure, we talked. But . . .
>
> Was she bitter?
>
> Maybe she was, but she was never afraid. I have never known another person like her. She was never afraid. Even, I had a gun at her head once and she spit in my eye. How are you going to look after the children if you kill me? she asks. She was never afraid.

In reviewing her father's comments Potrebenko writes: "He was only her husband so he wouldn't know. Like all peasant women my mother never accepted the inferior role handed her. But I was her daughter and I know she was afraid. Afraid of freezing, afraid of starving. No, that's not right for death itself has never had any particular threat for her. What she was afraid of was cold, hunger, illness."

In her 1983 memoir of her Russo-German family, Pauline Diede tried to explain the differences between the role of the wife on the North Dakota frontier and in the Old Country (i.e., German farming communities in southern Russia). She claims that many young wives felt a "homesickness" for the Old Country, where there was more of a community among women, and that this was especially the case for a woman who was "married to a man she hardly knew" (p. 18). Diede makes the point that without the support of other women, wives on isolated homesteads had nowhere to go for help. There were no effective voices in the community that could restrain an abusive husband. In her mother's case, an attempt was made to control her father's sexual demands after the birth of a second child: "Today Frau Jaeger was even more high-strung, for she knew why Ludwig [Diede's father] had come and she did not want this already bereft young woman to become pregnant again. She ordered Christina to keep the baby sucking to prevent impregnation and told Ludwig Christina was still in the menses from childbirth and he should abstain [*Du sollst 'fast' haben*]" (p. 48).

The marital relationships portrayed by Diede and Potrebenko concern families characterized by religious and patriarchal authoritarianism and existing in a state of relative poverty. The picture of marriage presented by homesteader Barbara Alice Slater is quite different. She wrote in 1912 about her intention to visit a friend: "After Xmas I want to go & stay a few days . . . & let my men batch! Marvin [stepson, about 9 years old] can keep the house clean & his Daddy is an excellent cook. If ever I am delayed, out anywhere, Marvin will have the meal ready as far as he can get it—once they had had it, & the dishes were washed, stove brushed, & floor cleaned. I hate to come back to a dirty house."

Even in families where male authority was not pronounced, negotiation between husbands and wives for access to limited resources was necessary. In a rare case where women's manipulation of male-controlled resources is remembered, Edna Tyson Parson writes about her mother's campaign to purchase a piano: "One day a salesman came to the farm, he had just the piano she wanted, very good price, in excellent condition. Sight unseen, she decided she would take it. Anthony was working on Olson's quarter . . . , the salesman drove Rosie in his car to the outfit. Anthony stops the horses to see what is the matter. Rosie tells him about the wonderful bargain for a piano. He says, 'But I don't have my cheque book.' Rosie says 'I brought it!' There was no further excuse" (LHB 57:120).

Rosie Tyson may have gotten her piano, but Anthony Tyson still controlled the check book. Male control of economic resources was taken for granted, although in cases where women controlled decisions concerning land, consultation between husband and wife was common. Anna Hought (1986:134), for example, recalls the decision to return to Minnesota after her husband had looked at land during a cattle sale trip: "When he came home . . . he said, 'Well I bought a farm in Minnesota.' 'Oh no! Without me seeing it?' 'Yes' But Ed was smiling. 'But that's not fair!' I protested. Then it came out. Ed was teasing me. He hadn't bought it. 'But you and I are going back to look at it.' "

The concept of "fair" expressed in Hought's memoir is rooted in individual values, and, regardless of the homeland ideology, egalitarian imperatives in settlement society fostered mutual respect, as reflected in Pauline Diede's 1986 summary of the difficult marriage relationships she observed among authoritarian German immigrants: "A wife, to be the subject to her husband often proved a miserable experience, married to a man she hardly knew. . . . On the whole life was tough on the man too. He held responsibility to feed the family. . . . And everything had to be done by the sweat of a man's brow. . . . At best when man and woman jointly worked . . . together" (p. 26).

The Birth of Children

The topic of children is handled with indirection and ambiguity by most of the writers. Accounts in the family histories in the local history books are simply informative—"so-and-so had her first child when. . . ." Only the reminiscences give more details, particularly those pertaining to the difficulties of having babies in the rough conditions of the homestead frontier. Most women considered children inevitable, something to be accepted calmly and stoically. In nineteenth-century rural culture children were the natural consequence of marriage, the raison d'être of family life, and a necessary part of the labor force. Ambivalence and anxiety associated with the birth of children were usually expressed with reference to inadequate medical facilities or the burden child-rearing placed on the entire household.

In families for whom contraception was forbidden, the ceaseless childbearing placed great demands upon limited resources of time and labor for everyone in the household. Mary Weeks described her Aunt Cora's anger with her own mother's continued pregnancies: "When Cora came home from school, she was told that she had a new baby sister. She was furious, refusing to even look at the baby. Taking care of Mary was enough without having to help with another, but there was work to do and she being the oldest had to help her grandfather with the housework until her mother could be up on her feet again" (pp. 42–43).

Controlling conception remains part of the "hidden history" of frontier women, and there is virtually no mention of it in our source documents. Summarizing from her 130 interviews with women who settled on the Alberta homestead frontier between 1900 and 1930, Eliane Silverman (1984:60) discusses the interviewees' hesitations to talk about contraception. Information about birth control, while certainly exchanged among women, was limited and inaccurate, and the distribution of birth control information and devices was illegal (Jameson 1987:151–54, Smith-Rosenberg and Rosenberg 1973, Gordon 1976). Nevertheless, a variety of measures existed in the public domain and were used by women to limit births. Silverman (1984:60) lists the use of the diaphragm (obtained with difficulty) and prolonged nursing, also mentioned in Pauline Diede's memoir. Condoms, withdrawal, and abstinence were rarely mentioned in interviews and never written about in the family histories and reminiscences.

The raising of children meant that women's lives entered a new period about which many women write in terms of constraints on their freedom and increased isolation. In her autobiography, Nannie Alderson, a ranch wife, recalls how children limited her activities so that she couldn't leave the house for weeks at a time during winters (Alderson and Smith 1969:27). Ranch women who lived with extended family members, or the farm women whose residences were closer to towns and to neighbors, were less constrained in their activities. The degree to which women suffered isolation varied depending on their social preferences or needs, their access to transportation, the composition of the household, and the degree to which parents were willing to leave children unsupervised. But all seem to have felt the limitations, and many were able to articulate them in reminiscences and letters.

Husbands and Wives: Working Together

Despite laws that denied married women control over the family's finances and a cultural ideology that insisted that women were dependent on men, marriage was considered by the women writers as an economic partnership. In the interviews we conducted with third-generation housewives as part of our earlier research, homestead settlement and enterprise development were retrospectively described as joint ventures, using "we" when family and farm decisions were discussed (Kohl 1977, 1988). In addition, many wives routinely did the farm work when husbands were off on a job to bring in cash. As Mary Weeks wrote about the early years of her aunt's marriage to Rouke DeBoer: "Her worth as a farmers wife was quite evident, for that fall when Rouke found a job in the coal mine, Cora worked up in the fields for the fall planting. While Rouke was away, she hitched up their five horses in the morning, plowing, discing and harrowing until noon. At lunch time she went back to the house, ate a sandwich, then walked the three miles to Henry Schick's house, where she hitched up his five horses, working in his fields until supper time" (p. 150).

All women were not as well prepared or competent as Cora Zeestraten DeBoer, who had been her father's favorite helper and thus was trained to be skilled and self-sufficient. The degree to which women had to learn new skills was, of course, related to their previous situation; women raised on farms had a great advantage over those from cities in that they were "pre-adapted" to the conditions and to the expectations of their contribution. The letters of Verna Benson indicate that there was little change in her economic activities with emigration. She was a farm girl with prior experience in egg and butter production. She frequently wrote about the necessity to bring in cash: "1911—I am going to try and make a little money off of our eggs next summer. My chickens are doing fine now." "Nov. 1919—the cow is giving a nice lot of milk I sell 7 qts a day, then have about three qts to use ourselves. I get 10c a qt. then the man I sell to delivers it around town for 10c."

In contrast, marriage and homesteading was for Barbara Alice Slater a deliberate means to change her life. She wrote in a letter that she had "deliberately chosen hard work and plenty of it, with disadvantages and inconveniences." A former school teacher, a city girl, she served as a hired hand working as a team with her husband.

> Oct. 10, 1911
>
> I did some ploughing before my accident—with 3 & four horses, & last week I did some seeding with the drilling machine.
>
> 28:1:12
>
> My birthday was spent on the trail hauling coal. George had one wagon & team & I drove another. We go 22 miles for it, & pay 8/4

> for all we can put on our wagon. Five tons cost us 16/8 & it is excellent coal. It is too much trouble and takes too long to go to the "Cutbanks" & mine it for ourselves free of charge. We have had to decide to stay for the winter because of the work to be done—there is so much to do to get ready for the spring. . . . We have some hay to haul, too; George has one hayrack & I drive another.

Members of most families had to "work out," taking jobs outside the home in order to supplement the income of the farming enterprise, and wives often took outside employment in addition to their domestic responsibilities. Teaching, for example, provided a livelihood prior to and after marriage. "We finally found land and farmed for several years. Times were hard but when things got too bad mother could always teach school. She had taught off and on for thirty years. I worked out quite a bit" (G. W. [Bill] Rankin, LHB 95:537).

The teaching salary earned by Maggie Gorman Davis made possible a visit to the old home and also helped support the farm:

12 May 1912:

> I was so disappointed . . . [Dennis, her husband] was unable to come visit on the weekend. . . . I like to go out there [the homestead] but it is so hard to get back in time for school Monday. I have at least six weeks yet. That will make 9½ or 12 month altogether or $780 I have got since I have been in Montana but I think I have earned it all and more too. It looks like I ought to save enough to bring us home [for a visit to parents in Indiana] but I won't have enough left to buy a cow. . . . I am so tired of school. (Finnell 1980:34)

3 May 1920:

> If we are here in June I think I'll try for a certificate (teaching) as I may have to keep the farm going again next winter. (p. 56)

Women also worked as nurses and midwives, sewed, cooked for threshing crews, took in boarders, and supplied neighbors with garden produce. When these activities are recorded in local history books, however, the cash income brought in from these activities is usually omitted. On the other hand, men's work outside the homestead almost always includes the actual amount earned, as proof of its value and necessity.

There is plenty of evidence in reminiscences and life histories that men and women did share similar views on homesteading as a way to ensure a future for their families. Most young husbands and wives agreed that men, women, and children would "do what was needed" for the survival of the family and their farm. In her diary, kept during the first year of settlement (1907–8), Sarah Roberts described her reluctant participation in cattle branding: "I stayed with my job until it was done, and I am glad that I never had to do it again. I think that it is not a woman's work except that it is everyone's work to do the things he needs to do" (Roberts 1971:226).

Homesteading required both sexes to learn new skills and put aside, or hold in abeyance, traditional concepts of "feminine" and "masculine" behavior. For example, Roy Benson wrote his father in March 1911: "You are not alone on the trouble question. For one thing I have a son Fred Benson Jr. That's as it should be but I can get no one to stay here and take care of the folks and I wasn't cut out for a nurse cook and baby tender. They say you never know what you can do until you are up against it Well! I am up against it." Verna Benson wrote a few weeks later: "Ah yes Roy makes a splendid nurse and a fine cook. He can make better bread than I can when he finds there is no way out of it. I told him how to make it and when he got it baked it certainly was fine bread."

The local history books often retell anecdotes in which this expansion and even reversal of gender role expectations are at work: "Grandma soon realized the need to shoot wild game for the table. She had never used a gun in her life. On her first attempt someone handed her a .22 rifle, whereupon she took aim and fired at a 4 gallon oil can from a distance of ten feet, missing it cleanly. Undismayed she practiced until she became a crack shot" (Ruth Masters; LHB 39:287).

Revision of gender expectations has become part of the lore of the homestead frontier, and such adaptability became one of the essential characteristics defining the ideal pioneer. Even the settlement propaganda of the time promoted flexibility. Would-be pioneer women were advised in a CPR settlers' information pamphlet: "Don't be prejudiced in your minds in favour of English methods of cooking, baking, washing etc., or be too proud to ask advice when you come. You will find new methods those more suited to the country and your altered circumstances. . . . New settlers can be taken by the hand by earlier arrivals, and information, receipts, etc., are freely tendered to those desirous of learning. There is a great social freedom amongst settlers" (Jackel 1982:38).

What this "social freedom" ultimately meant for both men and women on the homestead frontier is the subject of scholarly debate. Women's participation in "male" areas of work can be viewed as both liberating and exploitative. It was liberating from the rigid confines of gender roles with concomitant expansion of opportunity, but exploitative when it lacked either a reciprocal exchange on the part of the men in the necessary "female" work in household activities or shared economic and social rewards. Controversy persists among historians about the evaluation of women's workloads. We must remember that our knowledge of the experience of this "freedom" comes to us in an inevitably adulterated form, a consequence of time, changing social values, and legal rights. Nevertheless, when we review these written memories the repeated anecdotes do make a prima facie case for women's increased autonomy on the homestead frontier. On the other hand, we must also remember that, as time progressed, the region was more and more exposed to wider currents of thought and ideas that may in fact have revised gender expectations, strengthening the mythic or folkloric nature of the memories of "social freedom." In any event, changes in accepted behaviors between men and women eventually became comfortable, even if not sanctioned by tradition, and the ultimate consequence was a transformation in the expectations passed on to the children.

Chapter 7

Growing Up: Memories of Childhood

Although recollections of childhood appear in over half of our reminiscence documents, they are unfortunately among the least reliable in terms of providing a full and accurate account of the events, experiences, and feelings of children. Since children generally do not write autobiographies, nearly all the accounts we have of childhood on the frontier were written by mature or aging adults years later, usually when the individual had moved away from the settlement district. The majority are rather wistful, nostalgic re-creations of what it felt like to be a boy or girl growing up on the homestead frontier. Hardships and privations are represented, consistent with the themes of the heritage movement, as character-building experiences—which they probably were, though not always along the lines suggested by the writers.[1]

It is not easy to determine whether the recollections refer to real events and experiences in the writer's early years or whether they are re-creations influenced by shared memory and the heritage themes. We also had problems of interpretation based on the relationship between actual childhood experiences and the way the adult writer remembered them. For example, many values and expectations carried over from earlier generations could influence the adult writers' interpretation of their experiences as children, not to mention the reverse situation, that is, how contemporary values could transform the remembered significance of childhood experiences. Adults who were children on the homestead frontier almost invariably consider their childhood experiences as conducive to a maturity and stability rarely encountered in today's children. A majority of the documents contain explicit or implicit criticism of current child-rearing practices and the way contemporary society treats children. These critiques are evidence of the writers' belief that the privation and hardships of the homestead frontier experience created a special and better person.[2] The following is typical:

> As a child, one of the happy memories was the good preserves that my mother used to make after we kids had picked pails of saskatoons. . . . Fruit sold at the stores was unfamiliar to us. . . . Around Christmas we would see a few oranges and candy. Picking the wild berries seemed a pleasure. . . . but when we were called to pick up the bushels of potatoes . . . it was far from interesting. It was back breaking, dusty, hot, heavy work. . . . I can look back and smile to myself on the joys of childhood. . . . Why the poor kids today have nothing to do but play and many of them can't do that without leadership. I wonder what their childhood memories will be. (Mrs. J. Cotrell; LHB 52:30)

Remembrance of childhood is a favorite theme of novelists, and readers of childhood novels tend to accept at face value the depictions and interpretation of children's thoughts and interactions with adults. However, when the aims are scholarly and veracity is at least as important as authenticity, this becomes more difficult. In reading the accounts we found it necessary to distinguish between the memory of an experience and the way the writer used it to summarize his or her beliefs or to instruct or impress the reader. For example, Robert Collins in his reflections about his childhood and relations with his father writes that he "fought like a panther for the right to help the Ole Man (although I never dreamed of calling him that). I pleaded for the back-breaking labor that, forty years later, Canadian farmers begged young men to do for board, room *and* $180 a week—and were refused" (Collins 1980:66).

Readers of childhood reminiscence need to be wary of generalizing from past social and economic contexts to contemporary situations.[3] One must recognize how time alters the content of memory and how memory is constantly revised to fit an individual's current self-knowledge. Memories may be based upon what should or could have happened but did not necessarily occur; their salience changes over time as do the number of negative memories (Linton 1987). Memories may not be exact in detail, but they are true in the "sense of maintaining the integrity and gist of past life events" (Barclay 1987:82).[4] The issue of memory exactitude is ambiguous and complex, but memory is not devoid of meaning.

There are differences between the recollections of childhood written by men and those by women, although the variations are, for the most part, found in the interpretation of experiences rather than in the details of the experiences. The general similarity of recalled events and experiences from document to document—work, play, poverty, and the role of parents and other adults important in the writer's development—gives us confidence that the recollections, for the most part, provide an accurate picture of growing up in homestead communities. In this setting schooling was absent or sporadic, yet it was valued by the parents' generation; they had worked hard for the establishment of schools. There were few material possessions and little money, yet the deprivation was optimistically seen as a necessary part of establishing a successful farm or business. There was a good deal of hard work and children had little chance to have experiences outside the familiar setting of home and district or neighborhood, yet there was much informal learning within a culturally or ethnically heterogeneous social community whose residents shared similar goals and problems. Because of the need for their labor, children participated with adults in work and social events, yet they were usually given very little supervision. Although the cultural values of the time retained the distinction between child and adult responsibilities, homestead children had to take on adult tasks very early. Also, "working out," living outside the parental household in other families and communities, children learned the same skills as did their parents, often more effectively. Parents or adults, however, were not necessarily the ideal or most effective teachers.

Children broke with the conventions their parents had grown up with, and as they did their parents changed as well. Elvie Jones's autobiography in Chapter 13 recalls how her parents came to accept dancing. Other reminiscences describe how parents learned to accept or tolerate behaviors such as drinking, lack of manners, and illiteracy. Children whose parents did not speak English or who followed religious practices different from those of the Anglo-American and generally Protestant majority population were usually inducted into the frontier culture more rapidly or more effectively than their parents. In such situations, the young taught adults, women taught men, Indians taught Europeans, the unschooled taught the schooled. Thus learning was an experience that of necessity ignored or played down differences of all kinds and thereby contributed to egalitarianism, mutual dependency, and shared experience.

The Work of Children on the Farm

In his reminiscence, Robert Collins (1980:60–70) devotes an entire chapter to what he calls the daily "round of chores spinning inside the greater circle of seasons." The list of jobs was endless, and children were introduced into the routine as early as possible. The family farm system of homestead settlement formed a structure in which the relationships of parents and children developed out of their respective contributions to both household and farm chores. Thus, the work of children was a routine part of everyday life, but the expectations held for children varied with the family cycle, enterprise needs, and available economic resources and labor. Children's work was taken for granted by most of the writers, and their contributions, such as baby tending, milking, and weeding, were usually mentioned casually. In families with adolescents, younger children, although still responsible for chores, were more likely to be released from farm labor to attend school, as in the case of the younger Zeestraten children described by Mary Weeks. She also notes, however, that with changes in the family cycle, expectations also changed: "Neal's role changed too after Cora [his sister] married, for although he was only six, he became his father's right hand man. Too little to stay on the cultivator by himself, Cornelius [his father] would tie the boy to the seat, put the reins in his hands and tell the team, 'get up.' Neal felt very grown up and an important partner to his father, for although he was doing a mansized job, he knew it left his father free to do some other back breaking chore that a child could not do" (p. 136).

The labor needs of the homestead placed great responsibility on children and also made age and gender restrictions impractical (West 1989: 75). Where there were sons, daughters worked in household production; where there were no sons, daughters worked in the fields: "Our clan of growing girls were brought up to strict hard work, especially the two eldest . . . who became field workers and received harsh treatment from pa. They were expected to do as much work as a man. . . . Dilda, a young teenager [age 10–11], sat on the rig's seat and took on this dangerous work to drive the horses as well as stepping on the lever, regulating for straight rows" (Diede, 1983 memoir, p. 84). Where there were no daughters, sons worked in the household. Barbara Slater, pregnant with her third child, wrote on 30 May 1914: "I couldn't get a girl for love or money so Marvin is my Mary Jane, & much better than most girls. He washes the dishes, does the men's bedroom, peels potatoes, sweeps & dusts the sitting room every morning & on washing day turns the washing machine, & helps with whatever is going. At a pinch he can get a meal as well as I can & then he has ponies, cows, & chickens to see to outside."

For the majority of writers, especially those writing for the local history books, the labor of children is seen as an integral part of the character of the homestead frontier and a valuable learning experience. A minority of the writers disagree and use the memories as an indictment of parents. Similar disagreements are found among the recollections of schooling. The local history books record parental struggles to establish schools and maintain teachers, but even parents who desired schooling for their children were dependent upon their children's labor and felt that school competed for their services. This conflict gave rise to continual trade-offs between children's schooling and their work at home. As in all situations where child labor is a vital resource in maintaining the family enterprise, virtually all children were regularly kept home from school for planting, harvest, child care, and particularly demanding tasks. The North American school year with its long summer holiday was based upon farm labor needs. However, parental emphases on the importance of school and the need for children's labor varied. Vera Johnson Kuenzel wrote: "School was an important part of the children's life. Most of their fathers hadn't had too much education. My father had to leave after the fourth grade to help on the farm in Iowa. My Mother had been a school teacher and they were determined I should have an education" (LHB 104:82). But another writer from the same Montana Hi Line and international boundary district, called North Havre, remembered how her parents forbade continued schooling: "Marjorie and I had finished the eighth grade and were supposed to go to town to take the final examination. The folks wouldn't let us go, but our sister-in-law, who was the North Star [school] teacher, got the County superintendent to let her give us the tests. We passed and that was the end of our school days (1918)" (Doris Jones; LHB 104:105).

In families where Old Country authoritarian values were preserved along with a strong emphasis on the duty of the child to work for the family, children were more likely to be kept home from school to help. Pauline Diede wrote in 1986 of being kept home from school in western North Dakota to help with washing (p. 69). She also noted that Russo-German settlers discouraged schooling for their sons so they could do chores and preserve their knowledge of the German language and traditions (p. 50). In less patriarchal households, where children (and their mothers) had greater autonomy, and in households with greater economic resources, mothers and children would move into town for the school.

For the most part, memories of living in town with children during the school year are presented as examples of how one had to cope with inadequate rural facilities. It reflects as well shared commitment on the part of families for schooling, and acceptance of independent action by women. Children also lived away from home to work and bring in cash; often the two objectives were combined. So children were accustomed to a variety of arrangements that included both being subjected to strong parental control while working at home and having relative autonomy while attending school or working outside the home. The matrix of family relationships in the context of labor and cash needs was a flexible and adaptive one, and this very flexibility, we suggest, was a crucial element in the socialization of children who grew up on the homestead frontier.

Working Out

The periodic moves for schooling were part of a cyclical pattern of movement among households in which children moved in and out of the homes of their grandparents or other relatives. Older children worked out for cash or were given board in exchange for help with relatives or neighbors. The experience of working out differed according to gender. Girls or young women usually found housekeeping jobs or worked as waitresses or maids in the town hotels and boarding houses, while boys took farm or ranch jobs. Opportunities for such work were abundant, and working out promised both cash and relief from crowded living quarters at home.

For many young people, leaving the household provided an opportunity to learn technical and social skills. Mary Weeks described a typical situation experienced by her mother at the age of 14: "[She] begged her mother to let her work for the people [the Highway Commissioner and family]. 'I would get plenty to eat, so you wouldn't have to feed me, and I might learn a great deal about keeping house.' Cornelia acquiesced. . . . she could do with one less at her table, and it certainly was time for the girl to learn something about housekeeping besides living in a dugout" (p. 97). Working-out children were significant contributors to the household, helping out with cash as well as expanding the family's store of knowledge. Weeks's mother brought home gifts from town and new ideas about social relationships, food, clothes, and household decor. Some of these new ideas were welcome (girls learned, as Weeks put it, "how to talk and act like a lady"); others threatened family ideas of propriety, particularly those connected with women's autonomy and male-female relationships. Weeks's mother, for instance, during her time working out, met and fell in love with a man, but her parents refused to allow her to marry him.

Working-out situations were open to exploitation and victimization. In her diary, Sarah Roberts recalled neighbors who abused two young boys "poorly fed and thinly clad" to whom they gave foster care, not permitting both to attend school at the same time, whipping one "because he wanted to go all the time" (Roberts 1971:144). Some writers, on the other hand, recall work and working out as part of their personal maturation and character development: "I think the time spent [as a 13-year old earning seventy-five cents a day] was good training for me. It helped in getting along with other people and developed qualities that made handling any job better. I found that men weren't judged by rank, size or wealth but how they stacked up as men, how they did their job whatever it was" (Carl and Averil Jacobson, p. 23).

For many young men the memory of work on threshing crews came to be seen as an important masculine rite of passage, a time during which men were isolated from women—the "place where you become a man, or you don't" (Braithwaite 1984:200), a theme echoed by Orland Esval: "I learned the satisfaction of being on a winning team. . . . What I learned of this craft was by sink-or-swim survival, and by observation. It was a pleasure to be part of this team. True it was very arduous and demanding but the rewards were more than wages. . . . There had been a challenge, a mountain to be climbed. With painful effort and teamwork, it had been conquered" (Esval 1979:159–60). Not all writers shared this view, however. James Minifee (1972:75), for example, wrote about threshing gangs as "overworked, underpaid, poorly housed, and exploited by the wealthy farmers whose ranks they hoped to join one day."

Working out was for many young men part of an apprenticeship prior to taking out a homestead or a way to accumulate the beginnings of a herd. The family letters of David Christie illustrate this pattern. Each of the Christie sons left the family household in Bridger Canyon, Montana, to work for local ranchers. Their letters record increasing responsibility as they changed jobs and moved from place to place. They shared work and land purchase opportunities and exchanged information about agricultural practices. In the Christie case there was a concatenation of the need for labor, the availability of homesteads, and personal experiences. The Christie sons came of age before the large influx of farm homesteaders; they grew up on the frontier and apparently had no goals other than ranching. In time, each brother homesteaded his own place and purchased additional land, eventually forging a partnership with his brothers and father. This pattern of working out continues in the contemporary population (for the description of the process in southwestern Saskatchewan, see Kohl and Bennett 1971).

Like the boys, young women found working out was part of growing up, providing opportunities to gain a measure of independence, earn money, and learn skills. For the most part, their outside work was a continuation of their household chores: cooking, washing, and helping with children. Girls also helped out neighbors in times of crisis: illness, accidents, childbirth, or during particularly heavy work periods such as harvesting or branding and other tasks in the vital mutual-aid networks. However, unlike their brothers, young women could not expect work to lead to land ownership; so marriage and the creation of a new family were the objectives. As working out was an apprenticeship for young men, for women it provided a training period outside her family's household in anticipation of the establishment of her own.

The Community as Socializer

Despite the goals and desires of parents, socialization in any society is never unidirectional from adult to child, and children are never empty vessels to be filled.[5] It is an interactive process in which children can shape and redirect parental intentions. Socializers come in all ages and forms of relationship, and peers play important parts. School was recalled by homesteaders as the center of community social life, particularly for children's social life. Visiting and social events were family affairs and for the most part included all ages, so friendships between children were often established in the context of relationships among whole families and networks of mutual aid. But, given the work demands of the enterprise and the distances between homesteads, outside the school children had little opportunity for friendships with people other than family members. Siblings were the primary playmates, which led to many nostalgic comments in the local history books about the closeness of family members. A more complex record is presented in the longer autobiographies that contain descriptions of differences among siblings and among parents, leading toward a recognition that close interaction among family members can both reinforce family ties and also exacerbate conflict.

Even though schooling was often sporadic and of short duration, school was a place where children established their own world outside of adult supervision, making it a powerful agent of socialization. Memories of school often emphasize the social learning experiences over the academic:

> I remember the years I attended . . . school as some of the greatest of my life. . . . My first teacher was a war veteran. . . . I was afraid of him so I did my reading in the coal shed to the older students. . . . None of us learned much about the 3 r's but we learned how to play games, take our lunch to the coulee for picnics and other games, steal sticks, fox and geese, etc. . . . Next year we had a beautiful young teacher. She fell in love with a young man in the neighborhood. We had long lunch hours and recesses when he would ride over . . . to see her. (Vera Johnson Kuenzel; LHB 104:83)

School was also the primary acculturational force for non-English-speaking immigrant children as they learned the language, the history, and celebrated Canadian or U.S. holidays. Growing up was part of learning to be a pioneer, a Canadian or American. Pauline Diede's 1986 memoir describes her experience: "This was a typical American country school . . . in work and play alike, where we spoke English and where the children were taught to conform to American ways. Learning English and being patriotic were vital steps in the Americanization process. At this point immigrant parents were willing to let their children take the step but they did not want them to lose the native tongue, the German background families especially. Rightfully speaking, it did cause problems" (p. 110).

The degree to which there was controversy about preserving the language of the home country seems to have been dependent upon the diversity or homogeneity of the settlement community. For the most part immigrant parents were willing to allow their children to speak English in school, and in turn children taught their parents English and served as interpreters. Helen Potrebenko (1977:299) recalls, "Most of our parents could not speak English and even fewer could read it, so we had to do their form filling and letter writing as well as our own." In some instances teachers punished students who did not speak English. Pauline Diede, who began school without any knowledge of English, recalled her teachers using whips, belts, and sticks to punish the children who spoke German (Diede 1986:88). Diede also recalls the conflict she experienced between home expectations and those of school. The rapid socialization of children of ethnic immigrants is viewed by some writers as a triumph of national educational programs and also, more doubtfully, as discontinuity in Old Country practices and values. But assimilation was also part of parental desires for a better life for their children.

For most children the social world of the frontier was both restrictive and expansive. The constant daily routine of work, the few social options, the lack of urban amenities, and the absence of anonymity all placed restrictions on experimenting or challenging the status quo. At the same time, adults, who in heterogeneous urban or less-impoverished rural settings would not be involved in children's lives, sometimes had considerable influence on young people. "It may seem like trivia, but the appointment of 'Billy' Peck turned out to have a momentous effect on my future life and career. Each morning, on his way to school, he passed by our homestead door driving a horse and buggy, and he would pick me up en route. He not only became my teacher, but we became warm friends as well. As a result of our conversations back and forth from school he got to know me, my interests, my dreams, my plans far better than most teachers ever could" (Eggleston 1982:49).

Children's experiences outside the household and learning from nonhousehold members were remembered with clarity. For Pauline Diede, the neighboring ranch families provided new cultural opportunities. "The two Crowley ladies [neighboring ranch women and school teachers] necessitated the English language and made the German-speaking parents realize the importance of America's standard language" (1986:51). With few institutional resources, other adults served a variety of needs:

> Chris Cummings . . . retired gambler, miner was a kindly, old man and spent many hours teaching the children card games. Edna played cards before going to school. . . . This is how she learned arithmetic. (LHB 95:652)

> What brought chubby, cheery George Marriott from England to his windswept farm, when his lively mind and bent for natural science might have graced some university? Lucky for me, whatever it was. He told me the origins of strange rocks and let me pore over his collection of Indian arrowheads. . . . He produced the first binoculars I'd ever seen and said "Have a look at the moon." (Collins 1980:45–46)

Such relationships met the needs of lonely adults as well as the needs of young people. For instance, if the homesteading nuclear family did not come with other relatives, people on the outside could function as uncles, grandparents, and the like. The reminiscence writers often take special pains to describe these instances and to convey gratitude to the surrogate kin for providing company, caring, and intellectual development in a setting of minimal social experience.

Alternative Views of the Homestead Experience

We have noted that childhood memories are especially subject to nostalgia and self-justification. While family histories written for local history books emphasize positive attributes of family, especially cooperation, when these recollections include hardships they also recall the learning and personal benefit gained from the experience. Not usually present in these accounts are the anger and pain that are visible in letters, private autobiographies, or autobiographically based fiction. Thus we find accounts of children left alone while their mother chased cows or accounts in which women recall tying their children to chairs as a way to keep them out of trouble while the mothers went about their work. These incidents are generally recorded as matter-of-fact solutions to getting on with one's work. Rarely mentioned in the local history books but commonly discussed in the autobiographies is the anxiety induced by parental absence.

> We children got frightened. Could Mother ever find her way home: We waited—it seemed a century—but she did not come. At last we could stand it no longer. I cautioned the children—I always called them "the kids" to stand right in the doorway until I got back. I ran down the road around the bend to see if she was coming. Of course I could see no farther than if I had stayed at the house. . . . I turned back. But I could not quiet my fears. Would Mother never come! (Adelaide Rowley, p. 15)

Conversely, parental anxiety about children being left at home is also recalled: "When Winter came I had to drive the sleigh with the hay, while my husband forked it out. My little children, three of them now, had to be left in the house all alone, and many a time my heart was in my mouth as the saying goes, wondering if they were touching the fires" (Catherine Neil, p. 46).

We find two different responses to the absence of adult supervision. In the first, largely male view, children had freedom of action: "It was not to the narrow confines of a quarter-section homestead that our parents brought us in the spring of 1912, but to a vast kingdom of boundless sweep and almost infinite variety. . . . We children were free to roam as far as our tired legs would take us. . . . Meantime our seniors, the 'grown-ups,' were facing grimmer realities" (Eggleston 1982:36, 38). Wallace Stegner, who spent his early years on a homestead in southwestern Saskatchewan, expresses the same view more graphically. "There are certain advantages to growing up a sensuous little savage, and to tell the truth I am not sure I would trade my childhood of freedom and the outdoors and the senses" (Stegner 1962:25). In Robert Collins's memory childhood was insulated from the cares of the adult world: "Barely into my teens when the worst years [he was born in 1920] were over, I never truly understood the tense murmurs through those paper-thin walls after bedtime, as my parents fretted over the money we never had. We had enough to eat, although it was plain, and enough to wear, although it was plainer. I had no yardsticks for poverty and so no envy. We had our land and we had the house, our fortress against the world. I thought we were the luckiest people on earth" (Collins 1980:28).

While male writers generally recall growing up on the homestead frontier as a time of freedom where children were spared from the cares of adults, most women writers feature poverty and hardships. Cora and Dena Zeestraten remembered the grimness, the authoritarian parents who insisted, "Children are supposed to work, not play" (Weeks, p. 86). Pauline Diede's 1983 memory of the one-room shack, while acknowledging some "good" aspects, plays up the hardships: "Eight people sleeping in one room with a mixture of odors; and yet, in my memory there lingered a last close-family repose in the rectangular sod-made room. Where four out of the six children were born in. The room contained family history. Both bad and good. We were the poor of the poorest. Baby after baby, wailing from malnutrition and the wrong treatment-beliefs" (p. 60).

A more neutral image is evoked by Wilfred Eggleston:

> For two years we all lived in a single room, with curtains to screen off the beds. I think the first cash returns, from the little pile of flax seed harvested in 1913, must have gone in lumber to build a small lean-to back of the cabin. . . . In fact we were poor, and growing poorer, and the calamity of 1914 made us destitute. I suppose it was easier to bear because all of our neighbors . . . were in the same boat. I don't think this hardship left any permanent scars on us children. (Eggleston 1982:48)

Memories of parents also tend to differ with the gender of the writer. Although men remember their fathers as important figures, they usually give their mothers heroic stature. James MacGregor (1968) dedicates his book this way: "To my pioneering father and to my mother who, every morning carried her five-year-old son over the floating corduroy of the quarter mile slough so that he might not have to sit in school all day in wet clothes." Fathers may have been dominant figures, but for these male writers mothers were the sources for affection and solace: "He didn't seem to know how to show affection except by maybe a pat on the back or just a touch. The result was that we would tell mother our troubles and ambitions rather than him. Still we weren't afraid of him. . . . We certainly thought a lot of him and our love for them both was great" (Carl and Averil Jacobson, p. 2).

In reminiscences written by women, admiration or love of parents is usually mixed with criticism of their mothers and ambivalent feelings about the pressures put on the child. Melody Graulich (1984) suggests that the daughter-writers reject their mothers since they see their mothers' lives as too painful—to survive they must be like their fathers. The memoirs written by Pauline Diede and Mary Weeks support this hypothesis.

Recollections or reconstructions of growing up on the homestead frontier are not always given the same meaning. Nevertheless, all writers reflect accommodations between what may have been desirable and what was seen as necessary. The widespread abandonment of homesteads in the post-frontier period and in the drought and depression of the 1930s—and the current historical revisionism stimulated by the heritage movement concerning the whole homesteading episode—requires writers to evaluate and in some cases to defend their (or their ancestors') attempts to establish farms and businesses in this marginal environment. In this process hardships are viewed from the perspective of a whole lifetime. As one homesteader wrote, "The nicer things always stand out." Or, as the man we call Fred Haas ended his autobiography (chapter 13), "I look back over my life it has been one of struggle after struggle but I have enjoyed it all."

Children of all ethnic backgrounds and economic levels shared similar experiences. As experience changed them, they also contributed to changes in their parents. Schools and community social events introduced new patterns of behavior and new ideas; the simultaneous learning and relearning on the part of both parents and children led to rapid social change and increasing homogeneity of the district culture. Farm work and the restrictive boundaries of family and community life provided similar adaptive problems for the homestead population, resulting in a shared identity and common values.

The children who grew up during the frontier settlement period learned the need for self reliance along with mutual aid. As children they knew little other than hard work and deferment of gratification. They saw their parents incorporate the flexibility and pragmatism needed to cope with the frontier, and those skills served them well when things got really difficult in the drought and depression years. Although this point cannot be proved, it seems clear that the upbringing of children on the homestead frontier and in the little towns and villages of the West helped to forge a character and culture which eventually influenced the national cultures of North America.

A Photographic Portfolio

The settlement of the Canadian-American West has been called the Railroad Frontier for obvious reasons, the Model-T Frontier, because automotive transport was available or began shortly after the peak period, around 1910, and the Brownie Frontier, referring, of course, to the fact that a great many settlers owned one of those little square, black boxes and used them to document their experiences. Our selection of the photographs in this portfolio was made from hundreds we looked at in the several major museums and archives and the smaller, local historical museums in the Canadian-American West. While we found examples of the themes we wanted, we often had to compromise on the quality of the prints. Accessibility was the principal problem. While hundreds—thousands—of suitable and good-quality pictures exist, to obtain good reproducible prints for publication is another matter. The local history books display superb photographs, but these come from the private collections of the many people who lent them to the editorial committee, and getting and using them becomes a project of its own. Since our main mission in the study was not really photographic, we lacked the time and funds to make a thorough search and go through the many steps necessary to locate, obtain, copy, print, and return the originals.

For some reason the Canadian collections were more abundant and accessible than those on the U.S. side, so the portfolio contains more pictures from Canadian sources. But the whole settlement process was simultaneous, and the technology, arrangements, and the origins of the settlers themselves were substantially similar in the two countries. Moreover, in several of the photos, the reader will note that people of American origin appear on the Canadian side, and vice versa.

Warning sign at international boundary, about 1915, looking into Coutts, Alberta, from Sweetgrass, Montana. In the early days there was little to mark the crossing, and the customs offices were one-room frame buildings. People moved freely across the line, and still do on the whole, although at the present time the heavy commercial traffic through this particular crossing has been responsible for large permanent customs buildings. (Courtesy of Glenbow Archives, Calgary, Alberta, NA 1293-2)

A ranch family's private museum, 1962. This is one of three rooms filled with memorabilia. The building is an old log "railroad car" type of ranch house built in 1908, when the family settled the area. A newer ranch house adjoins this structure. The museum celebrates the family's history as well as that of the locality and region. (Photo by John W. Bennett)

A roundup of Indians in Havre, Montana, 1894. These people included groups of Cree, Ojibway, and probably some métis who fled from Canada following the Riel Rebellion in 1885, as well as similarly mixed tribal bands from North Dakota. Many of the people in this photo eventually became the nucleus of the Rocky Boy Reservation, established on the site of old Fort Assiniboine, south of Havre in the Bear's Paw Mountain area. Note the telegraph poles in the background marking the railroad line. For an account of the Cree saga, see Dempsey (1984). (Courtesy of Al Lucke Collection, Northern Montana College Archives, AL-892-11)

English settlers arriving at a station in western Canada on the Canadian Pacific, 1904. The two jaunty travelers in the center of the picture appear to be "remittance men," a term used to describe well-off young Englishmen, often second sons, who came to Canada to start businesses and ranches beginning in the 1890s. (Courtesy of Saskatchewan Archives Board, R93-196)

American settlers arriving in Canada, about 1910. These are most probably settlers from North Dakota, many of whom moved to Canada during a period of considerable economic difficulty in the state. Some were Scandinavians who were making their second migration. Note the bicycle, a commonly used form of transportation among farm homesteaders. (Courtesy of Saskatchewan Archives Board, R-B3387)

The homestead shack and the "first furrow," 1910. The picture was taken with a snapshot camera in order to record the signal event of breaking ground on a new homestead in southern Alberta. The shack was a wooden, temporary structure erected to demonstrate the homesteader's serious intention of living on the claim. This building was about sixteen feet by eighteen feet and a family of four persons lived there for two years before a more permanent structure was built. During this period, water came from a neighbor's spring. The dirt piles near the shack were for banking around the foundation in the winter. (Courtesy of Glenbow Archives, Calgary, Alberta, NA 2543-1)

Skinny dipping in the river, about 1904. This photograph was taken by a professional photographer from Medicine Hat, Alberta. It records a common activity for boys and young men and was most likely taken along the South Saskatchewan River near Medicine Hat. Recreation like this reflects time of freedom from adult constraints. (Courtesy of Saskatchewan Archives Board, R93-196)

Woman sewing in front of homestead shack, about 1910. A tarpaper shack with a sod roof was a temporary shelter. Note the outhouse, washboard, wagon, water jug, and poles for laundry and canvas shelters. Weather permitting, it was common to perform household chores outside. (Courtesy of Glenbow Archives, Calgary, Alberta, NA 4625-5)

Children playing in front of the family's first farmhouse, about 1910. This building was the immediate successor of the homestead shack. It had better siding, a shingled roof, and a new screen door. The generous woodpile and the elevation in the background indicate the homestead was near Bear's Paw Mountain, south of Chinook, Montana. This picture was taken by a professional photographer. The children are relaxing without toys, although the title of the original photo is "Play." (Courtesy of Al Lucke Collection, Northern Montana College Archives, AL-912-9)

Interior of a dry goods store, 1890s. The dry goods store was one of the very first of the specialty retail establishments that opened after the general store period of frontier days. These stores, invariably located in the center of the town, were quite dark even at noon. The low light and the formal dress of the clerks projected a restrained urban elegance in contrast to the crowded character of the general store. Note the large stock of yardage material. At that time most clothing was made at home. (Courtesy of Saskatchewan Archives Board, R-B9120-2)

Sunday picnic of town and country people on the prairie, 1890s. Picnics were among the most important forms of social gatherings during the frontier and post-frontier community periods. This is a mixed group of townspeople and country settlers, many of them relatives, out on the prairie of southeastern Alberta, south of Medicine Hat. Country settlers as well as townspeople customarily wore relatively formal attire to these special social occasions. (Photo courtesy of the Medicine Hat Museum and Art Gallery Archives, P.525.247)

Club women going to a district meeting, early 1920s. Women's organizations offered both recreation and the opportunity to share current concerns about household work and community welfare. Although cars were in use during this period, access to them was limited. In reminiscences, women recorded the various ways they managed to get to meetings. Usually they walked, sometimes pushing baby buggies or pulling sleds, and wagons were a common means of transport. (Courtesy of Glenbow Archives, Calgary, Alberta, NA 4283-1)

Railroad station garden, about 1903. The Canadian Pacific Railway was known for its efforts to decorate the station areas in the small towns along the main line as a welcoming sign for settlers, as a symbol of "civilization," and as substantiation for the railroad's propaganda about the verdant countryside. These beds in Medicine Hat, Alberta, are designed like an English country-house formal garden. (Courtesy of Glenbow Archives, Calgary, Alberta, NA 2003-18)

Getting water during a dry period, 1903. The country suffered from intermittent drought throughout the period of settlement, although denial was common, in the form of the aphorism "Water followed the plow." Wells were few, even during rainy spells, and many of the homesteaders had no reliable source of water for several years following settlement. This water wagon supplied people without wells in the town of Maple Creek, Saskatchewan, prior to the establishment of a town water supply, and also served many of the homesteaders outside town. (Courtesy of Saskatchewan Archives Board, R-B10047)

Chapter 8

Coming Together: The Formation of the Homestead Frontier Community

The community is usually presented in classic sociology as a discrete object, a thing with concrete existence and form. This corporeal image is based on the fact that social scientists began their study of communities with established examples in the western world and then extended the work into existing peasant and tribal societies. Few or no studies were made of the kind of social interaction that might produce the shared ideas and behaviors found in communities, but it is precisely this process that occurred on the homestead frontier.[1] Although a model of community existed in the minds of adult settlers, since they were all born and raised in one, actually reproducing that social form on the frontier was something else again.

"It has been justly said, 'There is no other civilization without the association of men.' It can perhaps be said, civilization of these parts of the prairie started to take shape in our minds when we finally located our homesteads—Mr. Smith and I, and hundreds of others, who later became our neighbors" (Evan Christianson, from his reminiscence of homesteading in southwestern Saskatchewan; LHB 45:48).

Robert Redfield, in his 1955 study of the "little community," proposed that communities take different social forms depending on the culture. Some communities are arranged like onions, with rings of occupational groups surrounding a kinship group core; others are organized hierarchically, in a vertical fashion, with all-powerful authorities at the top and poor people at the base. The community that took form on the homestead frontier was, initially, an egalitarian network of dyadic (two-person) relationships, each member of the dyad helping the other. But as time passed the dyads expanded into networks and hierarchies; organization-planning groups emerged and were charged with the task of creating the institutions necessary for economic and social survival.

We have therefore divided the process of community formation into several phases or steps, depending on the amount of staying power of the settlers, their willingness to cooperate on community tasks, and the relationship of the local group to externally based organizations and institutions. These steps will be described in more detail later in the chapter, but, in brief, we make distinctions among the early homestead frontier with its informal interactive adaptation, the subsequent planned emergence of local institutions and organizations such as churches and schools, and the later creation of connections between the local community and the outside world, a phase we refer to as the "postfrontier community."

The formal planning was aided by the existence of a familiar model or template: the concept of community in western—that is, Euro-American—culture.[2] The model contained specifications for formal organizations, modes of decision-making, the regulation of everyday life, and the basic services. Moreover, the model was reinforced by the rules for settlement and creation of political entities provided by the central governments of Canada and the United States. Many localities organized their own facilities—post offices, railroad stops, roads, and schools—with the help of state and provincial funds. Such funding was, in effect, a reward for local initiatives.

If there is a general theme running through descriptions of frontier communities in all phases of development, it is the intimate, friendly, face-to-face nature of social organization, the relationship that sociologists and anthropologists writing in the nineteenth and twentieth centuries called *Gemeinschaft*. The specific term was featured in the writings of the German sociologist Georg Simmel. It refers to a level of intimacy that emerges in small groups in daily interaction. The homesteaded district and the small towns and villages had *gemeinschaftlich* qualities, and these are almost universally recalled by the writers of our source materials as the chief characteristics of a kind of golden age: that early frontier period when everyone was equal in poverty and hardship, and also in the circles of neighborly mutual aid. We can accept the desirable features of the *Gemeinschaft* but at the same time suggest that the writers neglect the negative or conflicting aspects of small-community existence: the boredom, jealousies, resentments. A few of our documents do mention these or provide humorous anecdotes about especially difficult people and social friction, but on the basis of interviews and other firsthand contacts with the former homesteaded communities we feel that much has been omitted. Without doubt the continual outmigration resulted in communities with residents able to live in what one of our writers called a "fishbowl."

Speculations and theories about how communities take form go back to Aristotle's *Politics* and down through Rousseau's *Social Contract*. The creation of organized social life and communities on the western frontier provided an opportunity to observe this ancient social process firsthand. But few sociologists were able to study it in part because the topic of western settlement became the province of historians, and sociologists specialized in the study of urban communities. In addition, the frontier communities were virtually instant creations on the overly familiar Euro–North American model. The community that finally took shape had some special features created by the frontier milieu. First, they were formed with extreme rapidity, made necessary by survival needs and, in the later institutional phases, by the need to have state, provincial, and national governments recognize the existence of the community. Incidentally, this rapidity also meant that frequently the communities overbuilt—created too many organizations or overly complex forms of local government that could not be sustained with the slender resources or the fluctuating populations typical of the western frontier.

A second main feature is demographic fluctuation, felt in both the country districts and the towns in the form of a varying but general trend of population loss as economic difficulties and climatic disasters created uncertainties and unacceptable risks. The classic population curve for the homesteaded districts in the northern Great Plains consists of a steep rise followed by a steep decline; differences in the shape of the curves are found for different modes of production. Ranching districts had a flat, low curve, while farming districts showed a marked rise-and-decline pattern. Towns generally showed a fluctuating pattern, depending on economic conditions. Figure 5 shows 1901–1960 curves for every township in a large rectangular area of southern Saskatchewan and displays these various demographic patterns.

A third feature is the strong "booster" spirit that characterized nearly all of the country districts, towns, and other forms of community and local government. In order to obtain resources and favors it was necessary to advertise and to boast, or "boost." The settler recruitment pamphlets quoted in chapter 1 are good examples. The attitude was also reinforced by the considerable optimism and hope associated with emigration and settlement. The adventure represented a new start, a possibility for achievement unobtainable in the homelands, and success at settlement and community life was part of these very high expectations. Optimism about the conquest of nature, the importance of planning, the confidence in the technology of the late nineteenth century, the progress of industry and public education, and the rise of science were also evident. This was a period of cultural enthusiasm and belief in progress, despite economic uncertainties.

A fourth characteristic of the developing western community was its incipient linkage with national societies through railroads, the telegraph, the automobile, newspapers, and eventually the telephone. By 1910, the Old Northwest frontier, while still a frontier in the sense of its lack of economic development, was already a mosaic of instant country neighborhoods connected to the long-settled parts of Canada and the United States and even European countries by their emigrant population and their eagerness to maintain their ties to the homeland and re-create a "civilized world" in their new home. The railroad towns were mostly settled by businessmen from eastern towns who were in regular contact with their bankers and supporters back home and who regarded the new frontier town as an investment rather than an experiment in social organization.

While the pattern was, on the whole, similar for Canada and the United States, there were a few differences. The settlers in many Canadian rural districts appear, from articles in the local history books, to have had a more vigorous organizational drive. In his study of a southern Alberta community, Paul Voisey (1988) makes the point that most small towns had so many organizations that directed or concerted civic action became difficult to achieve. Similar findings appeared in some of the reports by the Center for Community Studies at the University of Saskatchewan in the 1960s. The Montana communities appear, from the lists and descriptions

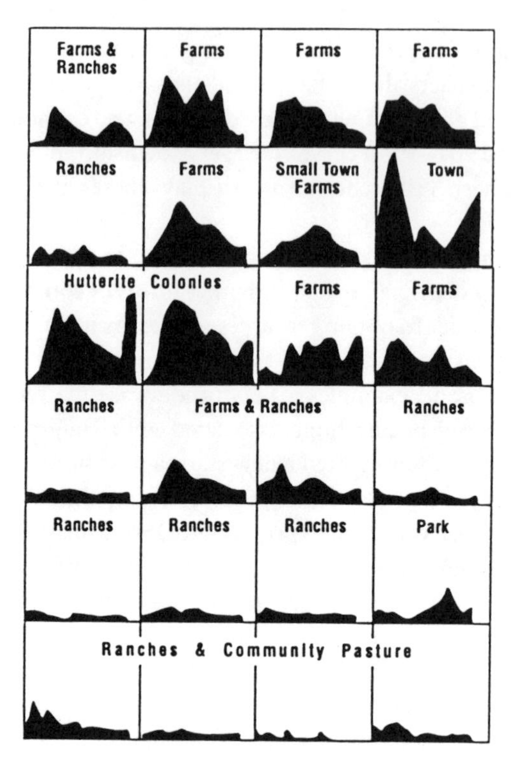

Figure 5. Population and principal activity in a region of southwestern Saskatchewan. The gross population curves for each township illustrate a number of patterns: (1) the rapid buildup of homestead settlement in the farming townships; (2) the rapid decline of the farming population, due to environmental and economic difficulties; (3) the generally larger population of townships where grain farming is the main activity; (4) the smaller and more stable population in the townships where cattle ranching and livestock farming is the principal activity; (5) peaked populations in the townships settled by Hutterite Brethren in the 1950s and '60s; (6) unusual shapes for the curves in the "town" and "park" townships due to intermittent population inflow and outflow. All curves were constructed with the gross population data recorded for each of the censuses between 1901 and 1960, although for some townships one or more census figures were missing. The vertical axis (as shown on the graph to the right) for each township square represents a total of up to 500 persons, except for the "town" square, where the peak is about 3,000. The horizontal axis of each square represents the time period from 1901 to 1960.

available to us, to have had fewer organizations, and a more individualistic spirit seems to have prevailed.

The reader will note in the following quoted passages concerning community spirit and development that we have relied more extensively on Canadian accounts of experience than American. This is not simply a bias in our source materials; it reflects the greater emphasis on heritage-inspired comments in the Canadian writings.

Since the emigrant stock was composed of people with similar origins on both sides, this difference needs to be addressed. We believe that differences in aspects of community formation can be attributed to the influence of British-trained government officials, the Mounted Police, and the restrained patterns of behavior associated with the English middle class. Most Canadian districts had a plurality of Ontarians and people from the British Isles. As we may guess from the novels of Robertson Davies or from John Kenneth Galbraith's (1964) reminiscence of his small-town Ontario origins, the culture of these people emphasized Protestant restraint and conformity combined with strong sectarian and small-group pluralism. The general cultural background of the Canadian postfrontier communities may well have been more conducive to the reproduction of these *gemeinschaftlich* characteristics. In Montana, on the other hand, the less developed frontier and the living heritage of the mountain men and cattlemen combined to produce, in the early settlement, a more rough-edged and individualistic community pattern.[3]

The rapidity with which a particular community was established varied depending on the time of settlement. In Montana, métis and Euro-American squatters colonized the territory prior to the passing of the Homestead Act, and these people found nothing but earth, sky, trappers, and a few Indians. There were numerous métis squatters on the Canadian side, but the majority of Euro-American settlers arrived after homesteading became official and after the North West Mounted Police had arrived on the frontier to control the Indians and patrol the regions opened for homesteading. In Montana early settlers, including the earliest waves of homesteaders, entered a region without government, while settlers on the Canadian side were preceded by the Northwest Territorial Government, which had already, in the 1880s, passed laws and established some facilities for the promotion and regulation of agriculture.

The local history book *Long Shadows*, a history of the rural townships south of Lethbridge, Alberta, describes the services that antedated the opening of the area for homesteading in 1910:

> There was already limited settlement in that general area at the time on a squatter basis. The N. Kingsburys had come into the area in 1908 and had soon recognized the need for services to these people, consequently they built a small combined store and post office which adopted the name of Lucky Strike. With the opening of the territory to homesteading, and the resulting increase in land-seeker activities in that area, the Kingsburys soon added eating and lodging facilities to their initial assembly of buildings. This, then, was the scene when our first homesteaders arrived in the district. (LHB 4:12)

The differences in national preparation for settlement seemed to have had little significance for the typical settler. In both cases necessities were lacking or hard to get, and in both countries the establishment of a house, farm, and social contacts required strenuous labor. Perhaps the main difference was psychological, and on the Canadian side the principal factor in this context was the Mounted Police; their duties included supervising and checking up on the homesteaders and enforcing some of the provisions of the agricultural regulations, especially the Herd Law, which required settlers of all types to control the movements of their livestock: "At midnight the police came and almost put us in the coop for not putting our horses in the barn. We stabled the horses. It did not matter if we slept out, but the horses had to be in" (Ole Wenas; LHB 45:41).

Irritation with the regulations aside, the police did seem to confer a sense of security and protection, and this, along with other emerging differences between U.S. and Canadian national culture, had a long-term effect. As time passed, Canadians developed a sense of the differences between themselves and "the folks on the other side of the line" (even though in many cases they were connected through ties of kinship). "It seems as though people across the line do things more on their own, if you know what I mean. It's a more progress kind of thing," commented a second-generation farmer-rancher in southwest Saskatchewan.

Phases of Community Formation

The writers marked the advance of the community or their own success at forging a more or less permanent home by citing specific improvements: the building of a road into the village, the first post office, the first schoolhouse. Although there was considerable local variation in the phasing and order of community formation depending on locality and time of settlement, it is possible to generalize the major steps based on a compilation of events recorded in the local history books for the country districts and towns.

Phase 1: The Early Homestead Frontier District Community

Most services were supplied by dyadic mutual aid and altruistic help, and social life was based upon individual or family household activities. In places where there were two or more waves of settlement, the earliest settlers (for the most part ranchers) had to assume responsibility for assistance to the later waves and become, thereby, honored pioneer "founders" of the community. As the community emerged, services were increasingly supplied by organized rings or networks of people with similar needs or complementary resources, or, later, by local entrepreneurs who combined services such as a post office or general store with farming. Social life and recreation was based upon informal neighborhood and friendship groups that included virtually everyone on an equal basis. The system would become a matter of local tradition for the second- and third-generation descendants or for latecomers.

Phase 2: Formal Community Establishment

This phase was marked by the formal creation of school and church districts and various social, recreational, economic, and political organizations. The earlier spontaneous, informal assistance patterns continued to provide neighborly support, needed resources, and recreation.

Phase 3: The Postfrontier Community

This phase included the establishment of villages and towns for providing services to the country people. In some cases nucleated centers could precede country homesteaded settlements, but in most their founding tended to follow homesteading. Many towns along the CPR and the GNR lines in a sense preceded settlement, since the railroads established them as station stops and division points. Soon thereafter they were used as drop-off points for the settlers and pick-up points for farm produce, initiating town development. In the country districts, the formation of village centers often focused on a post office (intensive campaigns had to be mounted to persuade the governments on both sides of the border to establish one), and then a general store, agencies for such basic needs as food and fuel, agricultural extension services, catalog offices, and so on. The towns introduced a structural element in the frontier and postfrontier society—differentiation of individuals and groups by ethnicity, occupation, origin, and income. For example, the elite elements were usually of eastern North American or northern European origin, and the railroad yard districts became the abode of laborers, transients, and other people not definitely associated with property ownership circles. But so far as the country people were concerned, the main function of towns and villages was to serve as conduits for needed exogenous resources and services.

The order of these phases in any particular place would depend on the settlement pattern and the time it took for the population to reach a critical mass. If an organized group settlement of people from a European village arrived, complete with priest or pastor, the church might be built immediately after the individual temporary shacks or sod houses and certainly before the school. If the district filled up with unrelated families of mixed ethnicity, the school could precede the church. Stores usually preceded the homesteaders in key railroad stops where railroad employees established and used them. Some districts never proceeded beyond phases 1 and 2; others developed institutions and organizations almost immediately. And in many sparsely populated country districts the intimate social relations and mutual aid of the early settlement frontier continue to exist.

The Cognitive Model of Community

The needs of the settlers refined the most generalized cultural pattern of the settlements, the Euro–North American template of how a society should be organized, how children should be raised, and how needs for affiliation and cooperation should be served. Underlying this protocol is the classical ethical dialectic of individualistic democracies: that while people succeed or fail as individuals they still need help and social services.

The model provided the means for "social reproduction," a term referring, in this case, to the obvious desire on the part of most of the homesteaders to replicate the institutions of their homeland. But there were two problems. First, the frontier had its own imperatives and needs that the homeland institutions of either the country district or the small town would not necessarily serve. Second, most settlement districts had a high proportion of strangers—people coming from everywhere, with different religions, varying ethnic origins, differing and potentially incompatible personal and familial cultures and outlooks. In one sense these differences were not as important as ethnologists who emphasize culture differences might assume, because so many of the emigrants were "pre-adapted": They had experienced separation from their past lives on the journey out, they expected they would be in a difficult situation, and they knew they would have to depend on other people.

Creating an organized society on the frontier involved both social reproduction and considerable innovation. The institutions organized by the district settlers had a degree of continuity with the past, but they also had an element of novelty. The first school might have both Catholic and Protestant youngsters in it, something unheard of in European countries or in many districts of eastern North America. The first church could be the community hall, which allowed people of any denomination to use its facility. The first neighborhood clubs might be organized around particular needs, like the building of roads. And the social contacts themselves were something new: committees for establishing a local governing body could consist of people who spoke three or four different languages and a little English and who had different traditions of political representation but who in the atmosphere of the frontier somehow found it possible to make collective decisions.

The beginnings of the country community required a sense of time, space, and social limits and boundaries, however vague these might be at first. The two English words used by homesteaders and townspeople to describe these latter coordinates were "district" and "neighborhood." The former term was borrowed from administrative concepts, in particular the school district, which existed either before or soon after the initial wave of homesteaders entered an area. "Neighborhood" is the more socially based term; it has been used in all English-speaking countries for several centuries to describe a group of friendly inhabitants who depend on each other in varying ways to share the tasks of ordering social relations.

Initially, space was a variable. The cognitive model lacked a definition, in precise square mileage, of how large or how small a "community" —a neighborhood or district—must be. The earliest homesteaders were spread out over large areas, often across the international boundary, and used towns as the markers of neighborhood boundaries. "Our neighborhood [ca. 1902] went from Maple Creek [Sask.] to Chinook, Montana, and east and north to East End [Sask.] and consisted of the Boltons, Laurel Reid and family, the Freels, Spencer Pears, Oswalt Gibson, the Hermans, Joe and Harold Bull and a Mr. Hardy, Walter Humphrey, Beddington, and the Wylies" (Otto Moir, son of a pre-homestead rancher; LHB 45:72).

When towns or other settlements were absent, geography provided the initial means for identification or location. The Cypress Hills lie close to the international boundary and stretch across the line between Saskatchewan and Alberta. Reaching altitudes of 4,200 feet, they constitute a forested geographical anomaly in the rolling high plains, and location in space was commonly given as south or north of the Hills: "At that time [1913] Maple Creek boasted six lumber yards and the same number of livery barns, and after supper in the evenings, the sidewalks were thronged with homestead people. The standard query was 'Are you from the North country or the South country?' " (George Shepard, homesteader from England; LHB 51:3).

Without established social ties, individuals and their "places" provided identifying markers. Luella Forsaith, a member of a large ranching clan in southern Alberta, researched the origins of the place names there. For example: "Bill Maffity came from Texas with Negro John Ware on one of the early cattle drives to Montana. He worked for the Spencers for a number of years. During this time he took up land in the bottom of the Milk River between the lower Spencer and the Dutchwoman's Crossing. This area has been known as the Maffity gap for as long as I can remember" (LHB 1:4). Remembering sources of names is an important feature in the recovery of local history, and virtually all the books note origins of place names. Compilations like *Names on the Face of Montana* (Cheney 1983) are available, and in most of the local history books the origins of the names of the neighborhoods are given. Naming identifies for readers a reality of person or place. Without a name, a place does not exist. Names provided connecting links in time and space and between people, as Edna Tyson Parson notes in her account of Neidpath, Saskatchewan: "To live in a place with no name was never tolerated by the settlers. Names were speedily chosen by them, fanciful names, unusual names, but more often than not, names that reminded them of home. Thus it was that one of the first settlers . . . suggested the name of Neidpath. . . . The settler had been born within a half mile of the ruins of Neidpath Castle [Scotland]" (LHB 57:55).

As spatial constructs, districts, neighborhoods, or communities never had stable and precise boundaries. Boundaries changed over time with changes in the pattern of movement within the geographical area and in the centers of social life. The recollections of George Lane, an early settler near Consul, Saskatchewan, illustrate the fluctuation of district boundaries. Initially there was no "district," only a landscape and a list of settlers near his homestead in 1909. He writes:

> I have been asked to chronicle some of my experiences when I first came to the "South Country," so called south of the Cypress Hills. . . . There were only a few neighbors there yet and we spent a day getting acquainted. McKinnon's were located where Buck Schmidt's are now. . . . Lou's ranch was one and one half miles up the creek from

McKinnon's. Jake Wells had a shack a mile down the creek. . . . Pete Reesor had the same place that he has now. Ike Stirling and Earl Nash were about ten miles South and the Gilchrists were about five miles up the Creek. (LHB 48:23)

With the entrance of more homesteaders and the establishment of a post office and store, the locale was named Kelvinhurst:

When I got out to the homestead [after returning to North Dakota for six months] I found many changes. E. J. Peachey had started a store near McKinnon's and later ran the Kelvinhurst P.O. at that location. . . . A great many came to their homesteads in the Spring of 1910, to name a few in the Kelvinhurst District. (p. 24)

But later, with the establishment of the branch CPR line-town Vidora, Kelvinhurst became the Vidora District, incorporating the geographical area served by the town:

The C.P.R. steel was laid in the Summer of 1914 [establishing the town of Vidora]. . . . The Kelvinhurst P.O. and the Union Bank was moved to Vidora. . . . We farmed in the Vidora District until 1954. (p. 25)

After the abandonment of the branch line and departure of most of the original homesteaders during the drought and depression of the 1930s, Vidora disappeared as a populated village about 1960. However, the original settlers do not disappear: wherever they may live now, former residents are identified in the history book as from "the south country":

We sold out (1950) and retired to Maple Creek, where a number from the South country are now retired. . . . The old pioneers who settled the district are getting fewer as the years go. . . . I sincerely hope that the effort we made in opening up that country will make it a little easier for those who follow us. (p. 25)

Ranches established prior to farm settlement and villages were another means of spatial location for the incoming Euro-American homesteaders. The circuitous means of identifying his ranch site is illustrated in the way Earl Nash recalls his early days south of the Cypress Hills in Saskatchewan in 1902:

> We finally arrived at our destination on Battle Creek about 5 miles South West of the present site of Consul. . . . There were no trails to follow . . . and the J. S. Gaff ranch in the edge of the hills, 16 miles away was the nearest habitation. . . . There was no rural mail delivery in those days. Our mail was addressed to Coulee P.O. in Assiniboia, N.W.T. via Maple Creek. The N.W.M.P. would bring it from Coulee P.O. to the Barracks where Gaffs would pick it up. . . . It was only a few years however until Battle Creek P.O. was established at the original Isaac Sterling [Stirling?] ranch about 3 miles above the Police Post. (LHB 48:21)

Geographical distance did not necessarily mean social isolation, since there were means of keeping in touch and gaining access to schooling, medical care, and recreational activities. Cooperative ranch work created large masculine establishments, since range or limited fenced cattle management required a large force of live-in ranch hands, reducing the costs of isolated living. Since women were scarce everywhere, both men and women had to do without female companionship until settlement filled out the social categories of sex and age. The family histories and our own earlier fieldwork attest to the frequency of marriages between farmers' daughters and ranchers' sons, which created bonds between the families and the modes of production. While families could be relatively isolated for months at a time, they included aged parents, unmarried siblings, and, in some of the larger ranch outfits, the wives of hired hands who helped the ranch wife. The arrival of a new bride (or sister or mother) was greeted with joy, and social "dropping-in" could last from three days to a week or longer.

Among the early ranching families with children, meeting the need to associate with friends and schoolmates was left to the individual. Schooling or medical care varied depending upon economic and social resources. In the absence of a country school, mothers and children often moved to town, or children boarded in town by themselves. Such decisions depended upon the mother's value to the ranching operation and on the importance placed on school attendance. In other situations, particularly in large families, a live-in teacher was hired. If the mother had some formal education she might act as teacher for her own and the neighbors' children, taking advantage of correspondence courses provided by the province or state.

The old names of districts, schools, post offices, and so on continue to be used to locate places or to define organizations composed of retirees in towns and in such distant places as California, British Columbia, or

Idaho. Despite loss of population, the names of districts, schools, and post offices remain in memory, preserved in the local histories and included on local maps. The local history book committees usually use the initial pattern of settlement to organize their lists and presentations of homesteading families and individuals. Neighborhood friendship networks, residence in school districts, and homesteading in a particular township or small railroad town are used to recall the character of settlement and the social-emotional ties that remain from that shared experience. From a sociological perspective, district, neighborhood, and community are constructs that permit individuals to capsulize their social relationships, creating—or re-creating—a social world.[4] In reminiscences these initial ties assume priority and the writers emphasize the social ties in their reconstructions of the settlement experience.

The Retrospective Concept of Community

The use of such terms as "community," "neighborhood," and "district" in local histories and by contemporary residents continues to suggest a clear ideology of altruism, mutual aid, friendship, and collective support. The recollection of the special associational life and mutual aid characteristic of the early phases of community formation provides an empirical foundation for values now incorporated and reinforced in the local history books:

> Neighbors helped one another build houses and barns and went to Maple Creek together for their loads. The community spirit was wonderful. Everyone had a smile and a cheerful word at all times. . . . The neighbors were all kind and would lend a hand at any time. . . . The pleasant memories still live in the minds of us left behind of a good neighbor never to be forgotten.
>
> Mrs. Andrew Skauge, Norwegian homesteader in southern Saskatchewan (LHB 45:37–39)

A refrain runs through the history books and reminiscences of the "lives we have lost." For example, Evan Christianson, who homesteaded near Robsart, Saskatchewan, in 1909, sums up his nine-page reminiscence: "Would I homestead again, if I were twenty-one years old? No!—Still I don't know. I long for the return of the community spirit of those days" (LHB 45:58). Or as one writer expresses the same nostalgia for the closeness of a community brought together through common hardship: "We had some trying experiences in those early days . . . [that] drew us closer together and that made for better friendship and better living." The remembrance of past experiences is a mechanism by which contemporary social life is viewed, measured, and often found wanting:

> School houses that were used for dances, church services, meetings as well as for education are now all closed up, most of the old folks have passed away and the younger ones have moved away to brighter fields. . . . The ones remaining have bought up all the land. . . . There's so little of the pioneer spirit left, but I'm so happy that I lived to see it. The stamina, the faith and struggles, the happy times and well-deserved pleasure of lending a hand, is something I shall never forget. (Moorhouse, p. 35)

"Lending a hand"—the concern for others—remains in the cultural rhetoric, as is evident in the following passage from an article in the *Maple Creek News* in 1974: "The . . . Kinsmen Club with support from the Ken Club was quick to bring into play the old-time spirit of helping neighbours or those to whom misfortune had struck, when they had an executive meeting and decided to sponsor a dine and dance in aid of Mr. and Mrs. Alvin Lightfoot and family, whose home was destroyed by fire last week. There may be better places to live than this, but people nowhere." The altruism and mutual aid of the homestead neighborhood remain a major symbol of pioneering experience and affiliation. The relative recency of the frontier era reinforces the ideas, but equally important are the national media, which treat the pioneer past with affection and nostalgia. Mutual aid remains economically and socially functional today: It saves money in a high-cost economy, and it continues to furnish social rewards in sparsely populated regions.

Contemporary rural society in the Canadian-American West retains much of its *gemeinschaftlich* quality. The limited social and economic alternatives require dependence upon neighbors and kin. One welcomes and supports neighbors since they may provide important help in situations of need. This is both an adaptive response to present needs and a continuation of frontier behavior. In reminiscences it has been elevated from survival necessity to an idealized goal of community, involving suppression of the original de facto needs for social control and access to resources. However, while mutual aid and other affiliative phenomena on the homestead frontier were certainly survival necessities, they were also carried out, for the most part, in a spirit of friendship and cordiality—the aspects of the process that the writers of the reminiscences choose to celebrate.

Chapter 9

Institutions and Services: The Postfrontier Community

Settlers came to the homestead frontier with an implicit model of how communities should be organized, and that model featured the idea that schools were to be provided by the community, although home instruction was not prohibited and was frequently practiced. Few of the country localities filling up with homesteaders and settlers had school districts, except some parts of Canada where districts had been created prior to settlement. Whether in Canada or the United States, the early settlers had to get together to build a schoolhouse, hire a teacher (or petition the authorities to send one, as in later times in Canada).

> It had not been possible to get the school started earlier. . . . Of those residents upon whom fell the burden of organizing the school, there were nineteen fami-

lies with children of school age. Some homesteaders were childless or had families already grown up. They had nothing to gain by having a school. Neither did the twenty-four bachelors, although thirteen of them were destined to marry in the future. Many of the people who lived in the school district were but recent arrivals and they naturally dreaded any more taxes.

> In due course the school district was set up and empowered to sell debentures; and finally the money was raised. The selection of a site came next. The best compromise was to locate the school on Paul Cantin's quarter. Paul, as I have said, was a bachelor; but he donated two acres for the school grounds. The building was largely a community effort—and a creditable one. It became a frame school and, except for the Kipps' home, it was the only frame building in the district. Fortunately Jim Allen, who lived just across the road, was a carpenter, and he guided its construction. Everyone chipped in to raise the walls and the roof. The only hired help was for the finishing carpentering and the plastering. (MacGregor 1968:106)

Schools were not always located in the home district, and schooling was often erratic, as is illustrated in this recollection by May Griesbach Clark, a teacher and homesteader in Montana:

> My first schooling I received at home: my father taught us to say both the German and the English alphabets and to count up to one hundred. He made a sort of game of it and I think he enjoyed it too. We had some children's books printed on linen; they had pictures, words, and stories. They were actually worn out by us children. When I was eight, I went to the country school for a term of four or five months. Our school terms were always short and teachers were hard to get. Until I was thirteen, we never had a nine-month term. That year our teachers added American literature and algebra to the work my class had. Then the next year we had all high school work. Then the state issued eighth grade examinations to the country schools and my class reviewed their grade school work and took the exams. We received our diplomas by mail. I think that was the year the Fort Benton High School was established. (LHB 95:242)

The collective nature of the school campaigns is evident; settlers with similar needs got together to work out a solution. Regardless of what facilities or resources might be obtainable from nearby or distant authorities, the people had to get together to seek support locally. (In Montana the authorities were the county governments, if and when they were organized; in Canada, the Northwest Territories, later provincial education departments, or rural municipality school districts.) Above all, the community had to prove they needed a school, that the expenditure, either local or by some higher government agency, was justified by the size of the potential student population. While schools and schooling were certainly approved and sponsored by the people of the districts, there are persistent accounts of underfinancing, neglect, ignorance of educational needs, and abuse of the teachers. While the basic ambivalence toward education does not show up in the later local history books, it does emerge in many of the reminiscences. Archives also contain numerous documents illustrating the conditions of the country schools, especially during the Great Depression, beginning in the late 1920s. A good example is a letter in the Saskatchewan Provincial Archives (file 3284) from two teachers in southwestern Saskatchewan, who, in despair over the failure of the government to provide the regular grant, eventually led a teachers' strike and were discharged. The letter preceded the strike and dramatizes the conditions that led to it:

> Re fall grant to Abbey S.D. No 3284, which is some months overdue. We have suffered in silence so far, and take this step as a last resort for immediate action. Please know the need is great. We are both married men with families. Obligations continue to mount, and still no money with which to meet them.
>
> We do our part faithfully. Surely the gov't. can do theirs. Kindly advise us as to some course of action, and oblige.
>
> Very respectfully,
> [signed by the principal and vice president of the school district]

While the school building was probably the most important general-purpose structure in the district or the small town, there were also the village halls, the lodge buildings, the shacks used by incoming homesteaders, the local "hotel" or boarding house, and the vacant second floor or attic of a store building. The uses put to these various structures were always similar: political assemblies, dances, parties, musicales, speeches, religious meetings, lodge meetings, and the like. The significance of the school building in comparison with these town edifices was simply that the school was a genuine communal structure, usually well built, and, in the earlier years, it was located in the country. So the "one-room schoolhouse" went into folklore and history as a vital symbol of self-help, collective effort, and respect for civilized life.

Churches

After schools were built, there usually came churches. In the early days homes and school buildings served all denominations—or at least those considered Protestant. This ecumenical character lasted into the 1970s in isolated country districts throughout the Canadian-American West. For example, in the remote districts of Merryflat and Battle Creek, between the Cypress Hills and the international boundary in Saskatchewan, services were held by a student minister from Consul, a town 30 miles from these districts, and were given on alternate Sundays at the two country schools in the area. The liturgy was that of the United Church of Canada. Virtually everyone in the districts attended, including members of Protestant denominations not included in the United Church. "Nobody minds, we look on it as our district church," said one resident in a 1971 interview. The local inhabitants viewed the arrangement as a nostalgic link to their pioneer generation ancestors and as a symbol of the special frontier character of their community.

From the reminiscences and local history books alone it is hard to assess the priorities concerning the construction of churches, because the need for a local church was perceived differently by the various sects. Simply using school buildings for services was easiest when the community had a number of congenial, usually mainline Protestant sects. When evangelical or Catholic congregations were present, however, except in very early days, it was not easy to do this, and such groups of worshippers met in homes, store buildings, or garages until separate churches could be constructed. All of the first churches in the country districts were served initially by itinerant pastors, since the homestead communities lacked the money or the facilities to support a full-time minister.[1]

Lloyd Diemert describes the beginnings of St. Ann's Church in Rudyard, Montana:

> Matt, Pat, Margaret and Anna Carr [brothers and sisters] all homesteaded east of the bridge on Black Coulee 17 miles south of Rudyard. Anna donated a spot for a church from her homestead land. She and Pat were on the north of the road and Matt and Margaret's homesteads were on the south side. They had church services in Matt and his wife, Catherine's home for quite a few years before they moved

> the old church building from Kremlin, Montana onto Anna's homestead. Anna and Margaret had gone back to Minnesota by this time. The church was 16′ × 24′ and they moved it with an iron wheeled Big Brother International tractor. Twelve more feet were built on right away. It was called St. Ann's. (LHB 83:895)

The location of churches in villages or towns was quite deliberate, since it provided an opportunity for country families to leave the little farmsteads at least once a week and make their way to town, shop, and exchange visits with folks other than the neighbors. Typically there were at least four churches: one Catholic, one or two representing various Protestant denominations, and at least one for non-English speakers, such as the Norwegian Lutheran Church. Many of these congregations have since withered, and a common sight in both Canada and the United States is a church that has been converted into a granary, a temporary house, a social hall, a town library, or a museum. The Canadians consolidated several Protestant sects into the United Church of Canada in 1925, partly as a response to the multiplicity of sects in sparsely populated western communities.

The role played by religious belief on the homestead frontier is something of a sociological mystery in that not much is known about it outside the sects themselves and their patient efforts to write the history of specific churches. As to the social functions of religion, sociologists and historians of the West tend to emphasize three points: 1) settlers of religious persuasion attempted to reproduce their churches and their faith on the frontier, often with great difficulty; 2) religion was useful in giving settlers, beleaguered by a forbidding climate and an uncertain economy, a sense of purpose and security; and 3) sects and churches were vital for ethnic groups and corporate settlements, where reproduction of homeland patterns was a matter of deliberate planning and forethought. The Washington Prairie district in northeast Iowa is exemplary of all three points. Norwegian settlers clustered there in the nineteenth century and constructed two churches, one Lutheran and the other Baptist. (The Lutheran one is still in regular use and both are restored as historical monuments.) While most of the Iowa Norwegian congregations eventually moved west into the Dakotas and Canada, their first churches were important as a focus for the ethnic identity of the community. However, they could not compete with ambition, restlessness, or the growing shortage of land in the second homeland in Iowa.

Our source materials contained a relatively small number of histories of churches or religious groups. Several of the later, comprehensive books do not even mention them, yet the districts and the nearby towns contain many churches. There are two reasons for the scarcity of formal histories of rural churches. The first has to do with the extent to which religion, or at least worship, was viewed in Euro-American rural culture as something apart from ordinary life and existence, and therefore not considered to be part of the history of the community. The history of a church typically was treated as a private topic, and this is consistent with the North American separation of church and state. When the account of a particular church is found in one of the local history books, it is usually presented as a special contribution, although there may be some recognition of the fact that the church building in the town was one of the structures contributing to the town's physical mass or, in a few cases, its up-to-dateness.

The second reason for the scarcity of sources has to do with the proliferation of sects. For example, sixty-one different religious affiliations, ranging in size from an exotic Asian group represented by a few immigrants to 96,564 Presbyterians, were listed in Saskatchewan's 1911 Department of Agriculture Annual Report (p. 259). "Religion" in the local history literature is a sociological rather than cultural category. None of the books or reminiscences contains a named category, "religious life" or "religion." The varied and often antagonistic Christian sects resisted a combined classification: Catholics must not be lumped together with Protestants, Christian Brethren with Lutherans, and so on. The sects might have a long history of mutual recrimination, and while the battles would never be fought openly on the frontier, a residuum of suspicion, or at least exclusiveness, remained.

Several Mennonite communities, especially in Canada, have in recent years published local history books, with such titles as "The Eigenheim Mennonite Church." The books of course include histories of the churches, but they are organized on the standard local history book pattern, attempting to include every person who settled in the area. The church in the title refers to the fact that the settlement is considered to be coterminous with the congregation, a feature of most sectarian settlements and communities.

Medical Care

Josie Olson Ouelette, the daughter of a Norwegian homesteader in southwest Saskatchewan, titles one section of her reminiscence "Thank God for Doctors."

About 1910 Mrs. J. W. Haas was instrumental in getting a Dr. Finnerty as a resident doctor and also a Miss Campbell as a Registered Nurse. The doctor in those days had a hard life as the nearest hospital was in Saskatoon and only the near dead were taken there. In winter the doctor would travel to the country, no matter how far. They were usually driven by the livery man or were taken by the people who needed him. There were poor roads with lots of mud or snow and the babies were born at home. Many did not survive.

Diseases were difficult to control. Diphtheria, small pox, whooping cough, measles, mumps and scarlet fever to name only a few. All farm wives had doctors books explaining the symptoms in detail and even pictures of the various rashes. Many a child was saved by a mother's intuition; a wonderful gift of God. When an epidemic broke out, the ones who contracted the disease were put in quarantine for a certain length of time and no one from that house were allowed out of their yard. Some good neighbor would bring supplies for them until they were released but not before the whole house was fumigated. This was done with sulfur put to burn, giving off a blue flame and it smelled terrible. I wonder do people appreciate the good life now with so many less worries? (pp. 17–18)

The problems of distance from medical care and transportation, home births and infant mortality, the identification of local resources and local remedies mentioned in Josie's reminiscence were common. Virtually every family history or reminiscence has similar stories about childbirth, illness, and farm accidents. Ouelette's account makes clear the fact that although many homestead settlements were established simultaneously with village growth and accompanying medical service of a doctor and nurse, distance from town meant that for the most part settlers were dependent upon their own resources. These resources varied from home remedies to the presence of a trained doctor or nurse on the next homestead.

The state of maternity care was precarious at best. In 1916 the U.S. Children's Bureau conducted a series of rural surveys in response to letters to the bureau from women, state boards of health, and volunteer organizations. In Montana 463 women in Dawson County were surveyed. The survey found 104 women left the area for confinement. Of the 359 who did not leave, 129 were attended by a physician. Husbands delivered their infants in 46 cases. For the remaining 184 women, the attendants were relatives or neighbors, few with skills, none a licensed midwife. Three delivered alone (Paradise 1919:10).

Women tried their best to anticipate the date of birth and made what arrangements they could to find a doctor or get into town, where they could find at least semi-professional help. Anna Hought successfully managed to make necessary arrangements for the birth of her first child in 1920: "How does one plan for the birth of a baby in a home thirty-five miles from the nearest town? In our case, we decided to take no chances, and plans were made for me to go to Mrs. Ebaugh's Maternity Home in Malta to have my baby. I would go in early and stay at a hotel until the time of delivery was imminent" (Hought 1986:102). Anna Hought was among a minority of women able to arrange for professional care. Most babies were born at home with the aid of neighbor women. Adequate medical care became, with suffrage, an early demand of women's national organizations.

In each district certain people were singled out as having competence to help in medical crises. In some instances it was only necessary to be of the appropriate gender. Women with nursing skills were highly valued and played crucial roles during the homestead period and beyond. Women's organizations were often instrumental in providing care. The lack of medical care remained a problem for rural areas long after other social services had been established (in some areas it still is a problem). The following letter was written 22 July 1922 by A. K. Buckham, grazing supervisor and member of the Tilley East Board, to R. G. Reid, minister of municipal affairs in Saskatchewan:

> Now the great blunder of settlement of these areas, after years of progress, reached its climax possibly on the average about 1914 to 1917. People lost their balance wheel and ran wild. So we find common among these folk, eyes that require glasses and can't get them, teeth causing illness, not fixed, operations necessary to health, not done, and children gifted out of common by nature, perhaps cannot go further to school and become independent and function as citizens in spheres nature may have fitted them for—and in short a very full measure of the biting misery of poverty—and that the natural result of a mistake in our system of land settlement in those areas. . . .
>
> These people, by and large, are of a superior type of citizen very industrious and very inured to hardship. An equal number of new immigrants would not replace their economic value to our Province. Their hardships have purged them of nonsense largely. (Saskatchewan Provincial Archives, Regina Branch)

Transportation, Communication, and Retail Trade

Settler expectations for schools, churches, and medical care were based on the way these needs had been met in their homelands: with formally trained professionals, certified by external institutions, replacing people who served informally or in a volunteer or part-time capacity. Similarly, the provision of the expected services of a settled life—roads, telephones, a mail system, access to manufactured products, and recreation—began with informal volunteer activities eventually to be replaced or supplemented by more formal institutional responses.

Roads

Emigrants arriving at any of the railway stops or towns found a rosette of dirt roads radiating out in all directions, or at least in the direction of surveyed areas opened for homesteading. These early "roads" were really tracks made by the hooves of horses and the wheels of wagons; many of them followed old Indian routes, trapper paths, or deer and bison trails. They were rarely straight, meandering across the prairies and hills or along creek bottoms. They can be seen on modern road maps of counties or smaller districts as a fine net of curving road lines with a rectilinear grid of modern country roads superimposed over them (see figure 6).

The grid system became the topic of intense campaigning on the part of the settlers some years after the population had shaken out and left behind a committed group of families interested in improving their economic position and reducing the costs of transportation. Moving heavy wagons or early low-powered farm trucks over curving trails built of dust, mud, or coarse gravel that had been given little grading to compensate for low spots or slopes was an increasingly onerous and frustrating affair. People living along the right of way were expected to do volunteer work along that stretch of road, and most did since it was in their own interest; but the custom became increasingly hard to sustain as traffic increased and individual settlers moved away. As townships and counties began to acquire horse-drawn scrapers and other equipment, assistance in maintenance could be provided, but this did not really fill the bill either, so the country people began intense campaigns for the construction of modern roadways. An account of such a campaign, plus a history of the road that eventually emerged, is provided by Joe Pleskac in the local history book for the North Havre (or "St. Joe") district. The road in question extends

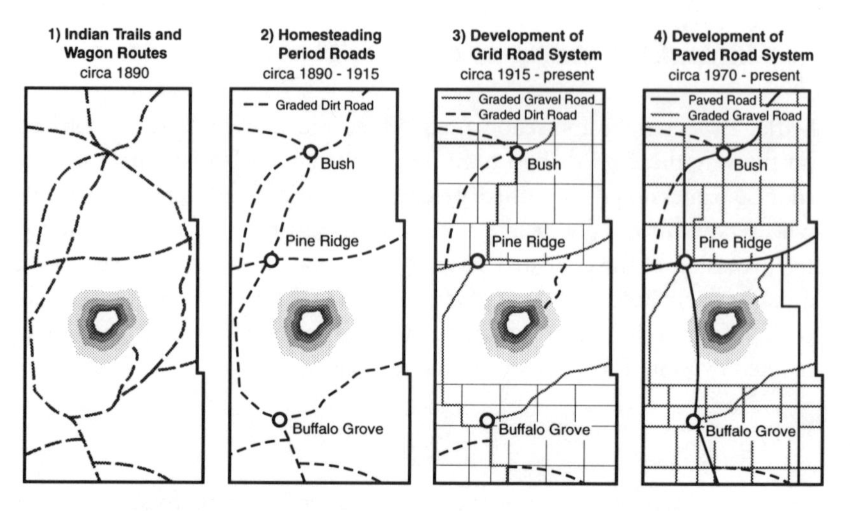

Figure 6. Evolutionary sequence of transportation facilities. We have drawn a stylized landscape type illustrating the differences in elevation so typical of the northern Great Plains, and especially the Canadian-American West heartland area. The evolving road pattern assumes a more and more rectilinear form as the land survey, tenure systems, and road-building capabilities develop.

from the Hi-Line town of Havre north to the international boundary and is used by both Americans and Canadians for shopping and visiting. However, the concern of the writer was mainly the convenience of the farmers who settled the area between the Hi Line and the border.

> The railroad with its many switch tracks, was a road block for access to the country to the north of the Milk River. An underpass was built under the Great Northern railroad tracks and a bridge built over the river. Thus travel was made easier to the part of the country north of the Milk River. Because there were no fences or section lines in the area, the early wagon trails fanned out over the country in many different directions. As time went on, two major trails began to be used by people traveling north from Havre and on into Canada. The west road that became prominent was known as the "Wild Horse Trail," now State Route 232. The north was served by the "Willow Creek Trail." This trail was to become what is now the "St. Joe Road," state feeder 233.
>
> . . . As the years went by and the road was being used more and more, some upgrading was done on the bad parts of the trail.

> In the early thirties, the U.S. Government W.P.A. work relief program was started. When money became available, crews of men with horses, "slip scrapers" and horse drawn road graders, went to work on the road. . . .
>
> About 1937 the county started a full scale road building program on the St. Joe Road. The road bed was elevated all the way to the Canadian port of entry at Willow Creek. The road was then graveled with crushed gravel as far north as what is known as the West Fork turn off to the east. This was done with state of Montana Highway Funding. From this point, approximately the last nine miles, the graveling was done by the area farmers and ranchers. The county equipment did the loading and spreading of the gravel and the farmers and ranchers, using their trucks, did the hauling. This was pit run gravel furnished by some of the local residents. . . .
>
> As larger trucks and more Canadian traffic began using the road, the road bed was deteriorating badly. About 1960 the North Havre Community set up a meeting with the Hill County commissioners to see if something could be done to repair or improve the road. This meeting did not produce any results as far as repair or improvement of the road was concerned.
>
> As the years went by the road became almost impassable. Then the women of the St. Joe Community Friendship Club took things into their own hands. On a cold January day in 1970, they armed themselves with picks, shovels, rakes and even a little tractor and went to work on the road. Several ladies came down from Canada to lend their support. (LHB 104:6)

(Eventually this road was taken over by the county and given further treatment. It is now a wide, well-maintained route to the border.)

Telephones

Telephones were initially a luxurious convenience; they were rare everywhere in rural North America in the late nineteenth and early twentieth centuries. In parts of the Great Plains full telephone service did not materialize until the 1930s, and some areas in the Canadian-American West were without telephones and even electricity until the late 1950s. And there were phones and there were phones. The simplest and earliest in many districts was the "barb wire telephone," merely a wire strung along the top of the fences and powered by storage batteries and magnetos. Any two users could start such a system, and it was a simple matter to expand it. However, the longer the line, the weaker the power and the more frequent the failures.

As people settled in and the social network expanded, communication needs also increased. The vagaries and uncertainties associated with weather, the labor supply, agricultural prices and costs, medical emergencies, and the like all bespoke the need for rapid and reliable communication. Emergencies were not the only reason people wanted phones—social communications, gossip, passing the time, and eavesdropping were all part of the system.

> Murray Johnson was a very community-minded person. He along with several other men, (I think Tom Strode and Frank Laird) were the ones who organized the Sweet Grass Hills Telephone Co. I believe this was about 1915. This was a telephone line which ran to Chester where it was connected with the Chester Exchange which was run by George Ainley. Everyone on the line had a ring. The Johnson's ring was two longs and two shorts. You rang the old wall phone by turning the handle. Of course, anyone could take down the receiver and listen in on someone else's conversation, as these "rings" rang into everybody's place. This telephone company was in existence until the 1950s when Northern Telephone Coop. came into the area. My father was president of that company all those years and it seemed as if he was responsible for keeping the telephone lines up and working. Many a day he and Pearl Alvord would take off to fix the lines. Sometimes it would be by horseback or with a team of horses and sled. This telephone line brought aid and enjoyment to the people in the Hills, by getting doctors out from Shelby or Chester, bringing help from neighbors, calling for groceries and repairs to be put on the stage at Chester and just good old visiting when one was completely snowed in, in the winter. Of course "rubbering" (listening in) was a pastime.
>
> Descendants of Murray and Myrtle Johnson, homestead farmers in the Montana Hi Line (LHB 95:374)

Post Offices and Stores

Just as settlers had to petition or campaign for schools and telephones, they also had to petition for post offices. "E. J. Peachy was busy in those days circulating a petition amongst the settlers asking the government to grant postal services and to grant appointment of himself as post master. A name had to be submitted for the proposed post office. Mrs. Tom Russell signed the petition on the understanding that the post office be named Russell. Mrs. Mike Thornton would sign if the office was called Thornton. Peachy promised that he would do his best and cleverly dodged the issue with a compromise and the post office was named Russthorn" (C. E. Lightfoot; LHB 45:74).

The country district store and post office were not mere services, but also a focus for community social life and communication. They also provided a small cash income for the operators. Edna Tyson Parson describes the Neidpath Post Office in southern Saskatchewan:

> On August 1, 1909, the Neidpath Post Office opened in the home of John Mitchell who had replaced his original sod shack with a somewhat large home built of lumber hauled from Herbert. Mrs. Mitchell served as post mistress and she continued in that office until they left the district in 1924. Mr. Mitchell carried the mail twenty miles from Herbert by horse and buggy. For these labors the Mitchells received a salary of thirty-five dollars a year.
>
> Loneliness was never again felt in the Mitchell household. Lack of privacy was more likely the concern when approximately 120 people passed in constant flux through that prairie post office. When daughter Sylvia came howling into the house because brother Johnny let go his end of the see-saw and dumped her in the barn, the neighborhood knew. Mrs. Mitchell took everything in her stride and managed a diversity of interests with efficiency. She introduced into the post office a travelling library case. A cold drive for the mail in the winter meant, for the settlers, a cheerful chat, a warm-up by the stove, a book exchanged and another dreary week of winter hastened on by the thrills of the printed page. (LHB 57:58)

Many women served as postmistresses, combining the job with household chores, child-rearing, and farm duties. Dispensing mail and store-bought necessities, they also dispensed information, advice, and gossip.

In a similar fashion, the role of mail carrier was more than the transportation of mail; he carried oral messages, gossip, and useful information along his route. The following was recalled by Shirley Lothain in her reminiscence of a district in southeastern Alberta.

The mail route was approximately fifty miles one way and for years most of it was wagon trail with no bridges where it ran by the Lost River.

Winters were especially rough. Rocks and footwarmers were taken in the sleigh but their warmth was soon gone and many times Bill walked beside his sleigh to keep awake and warm. The bitter cold and storms never stopped him as he was a very determined fellow. He never missed a trip in the eighteen years of his contract. This meant one trip a week. In the winter he went by horse and sleigh as far as Comrey the first day and to Onefour and Wild Horse the second day. Coming back he stayed at Comrey overnight again and the next morning back to Manyberries which meant four days on the road. (Sometimes stormy weather necessitated a full week spent on the road, but he was always back by Monday night, ready to start over Tuesday morning.) Many times during blizzards he was uncertain where he was and his faithful team got him through safely.

. . . Bill's first car on the mail route was a 1914 Chev. He always had a team on hand as he seemed to have it pulled more than the car ran itself. His next vehicles were Model T's with extras for parts. A 1928 Chev entered the picture and after that a 1929 Chev. A small Model A truck was then purchased and was used until he quit hauling mail.

Bill took a few passengers on his route. We recall one, a school teacher by the name of Mrs. Scobie. She left Wild Horse with him in a sleigh in bitter cold weather. Mrs. Scobie got so cold she wanted to sleep and Bill had to slap her around to keep her awake.

No matter where he stopped he and his horses were well fed and had a place to sleep. In times of blizzards or bad roads each post office tried to keep track of him. (LHB 1:97)

Recreation

Recreation had to be provided by the settlers themselves. It is hardly necessary to point out that at the beginning there was no radio, television, or movies; and storytellers, lecturers, singers, magicians, or small theatrical groups began to appear in the little towns, and occasionally in the country schools and churches. Revival meetings also became more frequent as churches and congregations became available to furnish space. Radios, usually battery-powered, came in everywhere during the 1920s and television in the 1950s, though southwestern Saskatchewan and a few remote districts in Montana did not have reliable electric power until the 1950s or television until the early 1960s.

In the early years of settlement in a particular district the two most common forms of organized recreational activities were picnics and dances. The picnic was probably the very first, since it did not require a special building and could be staged with any number of people—an extended kin group, a few neighbors, out in the open, in a little grove of trees near the creek, or in somebody's farmyard. Preceding the onset of organized gatherings and confined to the individual homesteads were card parties and musical sessions, the latter often held in the front room of the one house in the district that had a piano, laboriously dragged all the way from the East. The developmental sequence of forms of recreation progressed from homestead shacks to community school houses. Catherine Neil recalls:

> These new settlers soon felt the need of comradeship, and get-acquainted parties were held at each other's homes, and later on as the schools were built, concerts, box socials, and dances were held. It was quite common to hear a noise like a lot of coyotes howling, and on investigation to find out that it was several sleigh loads of folks from all over the district coming to spend the evening. They brought eatables and all you had to provide was the tea and coffee. They did the work. Beds were taken apart and piled on top of each other to make room for all who came. Elegance had no part in these gatherings. A good time was all we looked for. (p. 48)

These homebound forms of entertainment continued even after the community had developed social clubs, musical groups, and other organizations. The nature of this activity, whether in the home or in larger groups in public places, was its obvious and dual function: it was both enjoyable—an occasion to let off steam, find relief from the daily tasks and the anxiety and boredom of homestead life—and it was practical insofar as it created and cemented social contacts and friendships. There were social pressures for community participation. In a setting with few organized social occasions it was hard to avoid pressures for "good fellowship." Neil recalls:

> One night when I was doctoring my husband for a bad cold, two sleigh loads of neighbors drove up to our home and took the place

by storm. Jim was forced to get out of bed and look pleasant. Next concert this was the skit on him:

> What's the matter with Jim Neil?
> He's a sleepy head.
> When we go to visit him
> There he lies a-bed.
> Tho we arrive with bustle and din
> And tho Jim hates to get up, like sin,
> He gets up and puts on a grin.
> Jim's all right. (p. 49)

The anthropologist is tempted to recall Navajo song therapy, when a circle of relatives and neighbors gather around the bed of a sick person and are led in a curing ceremony by the shaman (Leighton and Leighton 1944). Getting well is a benefit to all in a society so dependent on mutual aid.

Dancing, one of the more common forms of recreational activity, was prohibited by certain church groups and was often a divisive issue, creating conflicts within families and between neighbors. However, almost everywhere it gradually became generally accepted and dances were heavily patronized. Clara Coverdale gives some evidence for importance in her recollection "Country Dances" in a local history book for southeastern Alberta:

> Everyone went to dances which were often held in the school houses in the rural areas or in the assembly halls in the two towns.
>
> Baby-sitting was no problem as the whole family went to the dance. Coats were stacked high on the benches and as the dance progressed, babies and smaller children were stacked on top of the coats to sleep. Country dances were a mixture of the various ethnic groups that were represented with square dancing the most popular.
>
> The only transportation for many of the young ladies was by horseback, so she would put on a pair of overalls and take her dress in a bundle on the back of her horse. Reaching her destination, she would shake the wrinkles out of her dress and change along with the other girls. We would go for miles to attend a dance. (LHB 48:514–15)

Attended by virtually everyone in a district, dances and picnics cut across differences between generations, ethnic groups, ranchers, farmers, townsmen, and country people, reinforcing affiliative ties as well as relieving everyday burdens of work. In retrospect the affiliative ties provided the foundation for re-created meanings of community life in the reminiscences and local histories.

Chapter 10

Women's Organizations: From Country District to Nation

The women would come in from the country . . . with their husbands. He might do his business and then go to the bar. Well, the women with the children had no place to go: no place to change their babies, warm their bottles, nurse them, and so on. . . . The Women's Institute decided that they were going to do something about this. They first rented and then bought a little old building and fixed it up. They put in a stove and utensils so there would be places for the ladies to make a cup of tea or to warm something for the children to eat. There would be somewhere for the children to go to the toilet.

From an interview with a member of the Carmangay Women's Institute of Alberta (Silverman 1984:183)

Organizing by women for a restroom in town fulfilled a simple yet important need on the homestead frontier. Reflected in this reminiscence are the roots of change in ideas and ideals concerning gender roles common to the late nineteenth and early twentieth century in North America.

The generalized ideology was that of the late Victorian period: Women were defined as "feminine," nurturing, more sensitive than men, the "weaker sex," in contrast to men, who were seen as the strong, practical, "doers," the breadwinners of society. These values may have controlled much of the behavior of the sexes in urban settings, but they were not typical of working class or rural people. This was particularly the case on the homestead frontier, where the exigencies of survival required a practical equality of responsibility and labor among sex and age groups and, as in the Carmangay quote, organization for their own welfare. Yet as literary values or symbols, the stereotypical ideas were conventionally enunciated to country people by ministers, local pundits, newspapers and magazines.

Recognition of the disparity between ideal and actual gender roles emerged in the first two decades of the twentieth century, as farm economists and home economists attached to the agricultural schools developed a scholarly and practical "science" of domestic management. This acknowledged the importance of the woman's role in the household as one that could save money for the farm and home establishment, thereby providing a pragmatic rationale for recognizing women's roles as something other than purely nurturing ones.

The rapid formation of women's organizations characterized the frontier period after 1910. They started as small groups in farmhouse kitchens, and within a decade or so had become formal local clubs, many affiliated with state, province, or national women's associations and political advocacy groups. In one sense this movement was simply the rural version of a continentwide consciousness-raising on the part of women. The period of the late nineteenth and early twentieth centuries was one of social ferment and populist idealism in North America and Northern Europe (particularly England and Sweden), and activities promoting women's rights blossomed. This movement for social change was known to many of the homesteading women, especially those who came from eastern and midwestern communities with a longer history of numerous women's organizations.[1] Still, the frontier roots of women's associations were strong and stimulated organizing—with or without wider models.

As frontier became postfrontier, women formed their own clubs and sodalities, mainly with social service functions, as the men formed their roping clubs, work-assistance networks, masculine fraternal groups, and sports teams, with recreational and economic functions. The gender division persisted regardless of the recognition of the social and economic significance of women's activities, introducing a degree of "equality" of the sexes but preserving a number of inequalities, including prejudice against women's role in politics, full property rights, and others.

By 1910, the major national groups devoted to redefining rural women's roles in the Canadian-American West were the Extension Home Demonstration clubs in the United States, the Women's Institute and United Farm Women in Alberta, and the Homemakers Clubs and Women Grain Growers in Saskatchewan.[2] These organizations received formal and informal support from governmental and political sources as well as from newly established academic departments of agriculture and domestic sciences. Such groups, affiliated with agrarian reform movements, domestic science, and social and child welfare movements, were advocates of new ideas about gender roles, child-rearing, household production and consumption, and better social services for rural communities.

Women's clubs usually began with informal gatherings for socializing and the sharing of necessities and information, and developed into formal organizations affiliated with national bodies. This sequence took place everywhere, but at differing rates and with various patterns. In country districts informal gatherings in kitchens preceded organized clubs, but in some cases the move toward outside affiliation was immediate if the women were familiar with the means or when a local representative of organized agriculture, like a farm extension agent, was available to provide the information. In general women from eastern and midwestern parts of North America and parts of northern Europe were more familiar with women's club participation than women from central and eastern Europe. Therefore, in the early stages most of the clubs were dominated by English-speaking women.

In many districts the sequence had three phases. The first we have already noted: the informal get-togethers for mutual assistance and company. Phase two would consist of the formation of clubs or groups for particular purposes: sewing circles, committees designed to serve local needs like cleaning the school or providing clothing and food for indigent settlers, or to furnish necessary facilities like the country town restroom, or to arrange for a church service. Phase three consisted of the link-up of such local groups with the national organizations, which introduced a new set of goals emphasizing political and welfare issues in an agrarian setting.

Descriptions in Reminiscences and Local History Books

For the most part, there is sufficient dated descriptive material to establish the sequence of phases, particularly the first two, the early informal gatherings for mutual assistance and the later formalized clubs and committees. However, descriptions of the circumstances or processes by which local women's clubs affiliated with national organizations were lacking in our documents. In any event, such affiliation took place rapidly, since many of the women came from homeland rural communities in which such connections already existed. National agricultural and rural extension representatives appear in settlement communities a decade or so following the homesteaders.

The local history books contain few formal histories of particular clubs and other women's groups. It is not uncommon for these books merely to record the existence of a club and list the founders. ("History," as implicitly defined in the books, emphasizes the experience of individuals and families, and secondarily the story of "private" groups. However, institutions like general stores, railroad offices, and town development programs are given considerable historical treatment since these are viewed as official agencies of community solidarity and evidence of "progress" and continuity.)

We may begin with the early phase of exchanges among women. Most of the accounts are simply anecdotes about coping with the demands of homestead life. Reminiscences contain anecdotes about information obtained from other women, ranging from the use of cow chips for fuel to the safety of drinking water. "One evening at dusk, a lady walked in. Mom was so surprised to see a woman. . . . She had been here a year. . . . She said they had a well, and not to drink that slough water. However her advice was too late. She also told Mom to get a sack and pick up that prairie coals called "chips" for the fire. It had to be dry, it was cow or horse manure. And Mom's appetite was affected by the thought of using it, she soon became thankful for having something to burn" (Moorhouse, p. 6).

The second phase begins with the formation of local clubs, and the personal reminiscence documents contain numerous accounts. Adelaide Rowley recalled her mother eagerly attending a women's sewing club that met monthly in different houses, requiring some women to ride fifteen to twenty miles. At the monthly meeting, women shared the chores decided upon by the hostess: patching, darning, tying quilts, sewing buttons. In exchange the hostess provided dinner. Rowley recalls: "Mother said they always had a nice time and that the only rule the club had was that there should be no gossip" (p. 22).

Descriptions of these women's clubs, when included in local history books, usually omit or gloss over the recreational or affiliative aspects, featuring either the pioneer character of the participants or the significant social objectives. For example:

> Mrs. Wittick found it hard to get out and visit with the neighbours as she had no way of traveling and she had three or four small children. Mr. Wittick had a small "sled" or "stoneboat" made for her to hitch her pony on and haul water for the household. One Ladies' Aid day Mrs. Wittick hitched up her pony, placed her children on the sled (in summer time) and she and her children went to Ladies' Aid . . . about four miles distant. It was just another way of getting around in those first years on the homestead. (LHB 45:9)

Local history books also include frequent expressions of the services to the community made by women's organizations.

> It came the time when many of the Consul children had to have their tonsils and adenoids taken out, so we the people, the Homemakers Club got together and planned to hold a clinic in Consul. We had an ideal empty building. We could clean it up with sweeping and lots of soap and water. We tacked sheets on the walls and ceiling, getting paper from the grain elevator, we tacked down on the floor. . . . Stretchers were improvised as also an operating table by one of the boys that always came to our aide in making things. . . . We had made arrangements with 2 Shaunavon doctors to operate. . . . [When they arrived] they took one look and said, "Well we never expected a real operating room. You people are to be congratulated." We were pleased and quite satisfied with our work. (Mrs. Dave Anderson; LHB 48:44–45)

Mrs. Anderson, an early settler and trained nurse, attributes the success of the clinic to the role of women as innovative workers, reminding readers that the groups, and implicitly all women, were not frivolous or concerned only with socializing. When social activities are described their instrumental functions are emphasized (though not always described in detail), as in the history of the Glengary Homemakers Club of Shaunavon, Saskatchewan:

> The club played a vital part in the life of the district especially so during the Dirty '30s when it was the only organization in our district to initiate the social events that made an otherwise drab existence more bearable. . . . They gathered clothing articles for a more needy family, bought emergency coal for an elderly widow, gave baby baskets to new mothers, . . . bought books, a flag and window blinds for the school and a set of silverware for new brides. At one time they donated toward the expense of a neighbor having to go to Regina for cancer treatment. (LHB 35:465)

One account of Homemakers Club activities in a local history book enshrines their altruistic objectives in rhyme:

> On the nineteenth day of August,
> Way back in twenty-one,
> The Homemakers of Robsart,
> Their Club had just begun.
> Eighteen kind ladies came at first
> And put their names down here;
> And then we had three more who joined,
> Before the end of the year.
> The object of this noble Club
> Is to help where'er we can;
> To help the poor and needy,
> In this and every land.
>
> . . .
>
> Our first big venture was to try
> To remedy our ills;
> To get a doctor who would come
> To give medicine and pills.
> The hospital was needing aid,
> So we thought that we could help,
> By giving of our hard-earned dough,
> Without one groan or yelp. (Mrs. J. Smiley; LHB 45:99)

The third phase, involving affiliations with larger groups, required formal records of meetings, and in these minute-books, in contrast to descriptions of purely local clubs, we find detailed records of social activities, as in these entries from the Lea Park Women's Institute:

July 1909: An interesting though informal meeting was held . . . the numbers being comparatively few. Friendly chat took the place of opening exercises.

Oct 1909: A meeting was called at Mrs. ——— but the prevalence of prairie fire prevented nearly all the members from getting out. The afternoon was passed in conversation.

February 1910: After supper a short WI meeting was held in an adjourning room—while the men discussed Railroads Tarrif and so forth. Our meeting was cut short as no one seemed to hear what was said or done. All knowing that Mr. Goodall had very kindly given us the liberty of dancing a few hours to the excellent music he had so thoughtfully provided . . . dancing was indulged in till the wee sma' hours of the morning—everyone having a very enjoyable afternoon and evening.

However, these social activities were not trivial, because there is little doubt that the clubs alleviated the loneliness and boredom of homestead life. Eva Carter begins her history of the United Farm Women in Alberta with no apologies for women's social needs: "The farm women's organization grew primarily out of a pronounced need for some form of social intercourse. The monotony and isolation of farm life with its consequent restricted opportunities for recreation and development of social services, was the despair of many a thinking farm woman" (Carter 1944:14).

National Country Women's Organizations

We turn now to a different type of document, protocols defining the goals of the national organizations that were distributed to the local clubs. During the last two decades of the nineteenth century the expansion of business created opportunities for jobs that required an extension of education and skill training for women. The period also witnessed the institutionalization of agriculture as a legitimate function of government at national, state, and provincial levels. The creation of agricultural colleges included departments of rural sociology and home economics, staffed increasingly by professionally trained women. The emerging ideology emphasized the important role of women on the farm and featured recognition of the farm woman's function as manager of the household and the importance of that role in ensuring economic well-being in both household and enterprise.

Rural women's organizations accepted and enthusiastically promulgated these "modern" role definitions, and combined them with earlier ideals of woman as the nurturing sex whose function was to create a better world—in the country, a comfortable and secure home for her farmer husband, her children, and the community in which they lived. Fostering this outlook became part of the mission of most of the late nineteenth- and early twentieth-century women's organizations in both the United States and Canada. Such terms as "maternal feminism," "responsible motherhood," and "civic or municipal housekeepers" were used to generalize the link between traditional ideas of women's domestic responsibility and their extension to civic activities. This connection served as an ideological base for government and male support of women's organizations as well as for acceptance by the media of women's activities outside the home (Martin 1987, Myres 1982, Riley 1988, Underwood 1984–85).

In Canada, provincial organizations such as the Alberta Women's Institute and the Saskatchewan Homemakers were patterned after the initial Women's Institutes established in Ontario in 1897. The object was to promote "that knowledge of household science which shall lead to the improvement in household architecture with special attention to home sanitation, to a better understanding of economic and hygienic value of foods and fuels, and to a more scientific care of children with a view to raising the general standard of our people" (quoted in Nicholson 1974:89).

The goal was "a system of women's clubs or institutes, under government patronage having as their object the simplifying of all problems pertaining to the home, and consequent achievement of better home conditions and the increase of the general fund of comfort, health, and efficiency. The study of Home Economics . . . will come in for a large share of attention. . . . In brief, a conscious effort will be made to promote the highest ideals of home and the best standards of community life" (quoted in Bosetti 1983:56). Thus home and community were seen to be intimately connected in the new "science" of domestic economy: If each home runs smoothly, then the collection of homes—the community—will also function well.

Both the United Farm Women of Alberta (UFW) and the Saskatchewan Women Grain Growers (SWGG) were sponsored and supported by their respective male farm organizations and encouraged to take political positions associated with populist farm movements. From the beginning both the UFW and SWGG advocated suffrage, prohibition, better health care, and public welfare (as did the men's organizations with which they were affiliated). Both groups shared similar domestic and community life goals with the less political Women's Institute and the Saskatchewan

Homemakers. In 1915, the United Farm Women in Alberta aimed "to assist our members to educate themselves to be the best possible citizens of the community, the nation, and the world; to interest them in . . . reform in social conditions, particularly those affecting the childhood and youth of our land; to popularize the study of social and economic questions; and to develop local taste for . . . the finer things of life" (Wilson 1977:29).

The same year the platform statement of the Saskatchewan Women Grain Growers listed educational and domestic issues as their goals:

> 1. Make farm life more attractive. . . . keeping young people on the farm.
>
> 2. Beautify the home, home surroundings, and the school.
>
> 3. Ascertain the views of the Provincial members of the Legislature on questions directly affecting farm women.
>
> 4. Increase the efficiency of the homekeeper and raise the ideal of home life and work.
>
> 5. Work for better school boards, with women among the trustees.
>
> 6. Foster and develop local taste for music literature and the finer things of life generally. (Flint Papers)

In the United States, Congress allocated funds for the organization of farm women clubs in 1914 through the emergency bill entitled "To Stimulate Production and Facilitate the Distribution of Products"—an action anticipating wartime. Extension Home Demonstration clubs were initiated and given direction by trained teachers or home economists. Specific instructions by the federal government directed attention to women's important role in food production and in maintaining family health. However in contrast with the Canadian organizations there was little, if any, formal or programmatic effort toward community development.

Canadian and U.S. groups shared a similar commitment to improving the personal well-being and activities of rural women, providing access to information and resources in those areas considered the responsibility of women: household work, child care, education, and medical care. Nevertheless we find cultural and ideological differences. In Canada the hallmark of women's groups, reflecting their middle-class British heritage, was cultural improvement and social commitment, whereas the U.S. programs had a more pragmatic and individualistic stance.

The U.S. Department of Agriculture agenda for farm women emerged from surveys that investigated their household and farm work. One USDA survey of 10,000 farm homes in the northern and western United States identified the following concerns:

1. Shorter working days.

2. Lessening the amount of "heavy manual labor" performed by farm women.

3. Higher standards of comfort and beauty for farm homes.

4. Safeguarding of the health of family members.

5. Developing "money-yielding home industries" to allow for necessary home improvements. (Schwieder 1986:202)

Although respondents mentioned personal social isolation and lack of adequate education for children as special problems, the primary interest, as recorded in the survey, was in changing women's working conditions. Little attention was given to social responsibilities for community welfare or to cultural activities.

In Montana, as elsewhere in the United States, Department of Agriculture Home Extension goals targeted individual change within the domestic sphere; instruction was primarily provided by professional personnel. Activities of the Welfare of the Sages Home Demonstration Club (Montana), first organized in 1923, followed the guides set forth by the Montana State Agricultural Extension office. In a history written in 1947 summarizing their accomplishment in the traditional homemaking skills of cooking, sewing, kitchen planning, nutrition, mattress making, upholstering, and rug making, the kitchen planning project was remembered in detail:

> During this time [1923–28] we had received instructions in kitchen planning for our homes. Miss Miriam Hawkins was the specialist and planned with the various members ways of improving their kitchens, making work easier and having more conveniences to work with. . . . [There was] a kitchen tour . . . to see the improvements each one had made and afterwards a kitchen scoring of each club member's kitchen was made. . . . This project was a very great help to our homes in this community—built in cupboards, water systems, refrigeration and many other things were installed. (LHB 83:712)

With the increasing costs of farm labor, women's help was needed. Specifying improvements in women's workplaces—home and kitchen—was promoted as a way of lessening the domestic burden. The Fergus County (Montana) Farm Home Committee in 1927 proposed to a county economic conference that "home improvements should go hand in hand with improvement in farming practices. . . . Every home should install water, heating, lighting, and drainage systems, and invest in kitchen conveniences, such as a high stool, pressure cooker, and dish drainer" (Mercier 1988:54–55).

As in the U.S. Extension Home Demonstration clubs, food preparation, production, and child-rearing dominated Canadian agendas. Typical meetings of the Women's Institutes included "papers" devoted to a particular topic, considered to be the main program, and "rollcall," during which club members exchanged hints or solutions about a prescheduled topic such as "What to Eat to Keep Warm" or "Hints on Care of Eggs and Hens while Setting." Meeting topics for papers were, for the most part, devoted to children's development and education, women's roles, food preparation, and home management, but at least one program during the year was devoted to women's responsibilities in the political or social sphere. Some examples from the Women's Institute meetings of 1914 include "What it Means to Be a Citizen," "What is the Meaning of Real Giving," "The Necessity of Social Life in the Country Homes," "Current Events and our Special Interest in Them," and "Privileges of Life in Canada—Alberta especially" (from Huxley Park Branch, Didsbury, and Verdant Valley Women's Institutes lists of meeting topics for 1914; Provincial Archives of Alberta, Edmonton, accession no. 786.1255).

Not all women were pleased with the attention paid to domestic activities. An exchange of letters in the *Grain Growers' Guide* of 16 September 1915 illustrates two different views:

> What do you think about this [Women's Institute] program? Is it not merely a program for very young schoolgirls? Does this program give us a larger field than the usual "women's yard"? Always suggestions about housework, knitting, and the main women's distinction: "preparing of dainty side-dishes and salads." Kitchen, kitchen, and again kitchen!
>
> Mary Nicolaeff

Francis Marion Beynon, one of the early organizers of the Saskatchewan Homemakers Clubs, replied to Mary Nicolaeff:

> All great changes require much time instead of being peeved about the domestic character of the program . . . I think you might find cause for thanksgiving in the fact that in the very first year of their existence they are studying parliamentary procedure, the history of their great women, and social settlement work in great cities. Be

patient with these women's clubs my friend, and you will see them grow into something better than you and I could foretell. (exchange quoted in Rasmussen et al. 1976:132)

In general, national-level social and political issues were avoided by U.S. Extension Home Demonstration clubs. Such matters were the province of other types of women's groups, including the Women's Christian Temperance Union, the States Federation of Women's Clubs, and the Montana Equal Suffrage Association, as well as family farm organizations such as the Grange and Farmers' Union, which were part of populist political movements in Montana.

In Canadian organizations, committees were established to examine specific areas of concern—education, health, welfare—and to circulate directives to the local clubs encouraging research, discussion, and action. For example, the Alberta Women's Institute Committee on Legislation issued this list of suggestions for 1928–29:

1. Provincial Legislation.
   (a) the study of the Statutes dealing with one of the following subjects:
   1. Mothers Allowance.
   2. Rights of Widow's and Orphans's in deceased husbands estate.
   3. Domestic Relations Act.

   (b) Make a study of the problem of maternal mortality in order that our organization may be prepared to suggest constructive legislation along this line to our legislature.
2. Dominion Legislation.
   I think each branch should devote one meeting to the study of one of the following topics:
   (a) The Nationality of Women.
   (b) Our food Laws.
   (c) The legalization of gambling on race tracks and at fairs.
   (d) The immigration in laws and regulations. (signed by Mrs. J. P. Ferguson; Alberta Women's Institute, accession no. 86.125)

Between 1919 and 1927 the Alberta Women's Institute passed resolutions to promote provincial scholarships for pupils of rural and consolidated schools; the appointment of women school inspectors from the ranks of women school teachers; governmental support for school play periods with supervision; governmental support for establishing district nurses in remote districts; testing for venereal disease; provision of medical care for tubercular patients; and support for prohibition and its subsequent enforcement.

But in both U.S. and Canadian organizations, the specific needs of the local community were at the heart of clubs' social welfare activities: schooling, charity for the indigent, medical facilities, social events, the erection of community buildings, and the improvement of streets and recreational facilities. Local groups preferred to use any funds they raised for their own sons and daughters, as is clear in the decision of the Ever Ready Women's Institute of Coaldale, Alberta, rejecting a proposal to support provincial scholarships: "[We] decided to vote down the scholarship fund . . . and use the money . . . to aid our own school" (Ever Ready Women's Institute, Minute Book, 5 Oct. 1922). In at least one case, the members of a local organization, the Lowell Homemakers of Saskatchewan, resigned their affiliation with their national organization, the United Grain Growers, over such an issue. "Seeing a great need there [the building of a local hospital] they decided to put their efforts toward this big project" (LHB 41:91).

The emphasis placed on local social and cultural needs by the Women Grain Growers organization was the way they distinguished their activities from those of the male Saskatchewan Grain Growers Association (Marchildon 1985:97). There were no similar women's groups in the United States.

The lack of women's access to homesteads and regulations governing their enlargement was a specific political issue for Canadians. Among the earliest resolutions (November 1910) of the Lea Park Women's Institute in Alberta was a demand for homesteads for women and payment of $13 to send a United Farmer's Association delegate to bring the resolution before the minister of the interior in Ottawa. Other property issues affecting women were also a source of concern. Elizabeth Mitchell, after a tour of women's organizations in 1915, wrote of the Canadian groups:

> The special trouble which has turned the prairie women's minds to politics is connected with the land. The woman so obviously shares with her husband in making the "improved farm" out of the 160 acres . . . that it is felt to be an injustice that this product of their joint labour becomes the sole property of the man, and that he can, if

> he chooses, sell it and break up the home without his wife's consent. Cases where this has been done have raised a great deal of feeling, among men as well as women, and a Bill was actually introduced lately into the Sask. legislature making the wife's signature as well as the husband's necessary. (Mitchell 1981:55–56)

The Saskatchewan Homestead Act, and its Alberta counterpart, the Alberta Married Women's Home Protection Act, were passed in 1915.

The extent to which the local clubs shared the view of national leaders or followed through on the annual resolutions varied, but the conventions, letters, and informational directives did introduce national and provincial policies to the local groups. For example, the Ever Ready Women's Institute minutes recorded their response to a resolution from the 1927 Women's Institute Convention regarding "granting Hutterite colonies special privileges on school matters and the Institute strongly protesting this action. It was asked what opinion our local had on this subject. After a great deal of discussion it was decided to table the matter for next meeting meanwhile to look up and learn more of this subject" (Minute Book, 21 April 1927). Eventually, the group decided to support the resolution.[3]

Opportunities for women to demonstrate their organizational skills were provided in all women's groups, on both sides of the border. Extension Home Demonstration clubs in the United States mounted a collective effort when they saw direct connections between their personal welfare and governmental decisions.

> A Miss Weitske Bydely conducted the school [a short course in mattress making]. . . . During this two day's time all the members . . . decided we would like to have her for Home Demonstration Agent for Hill County. We got our heads together and made plans to have every club member who could in all the nine clubs in the county meet with the County Commissioners very soon and try to get Miss Bydely as our H.D. A. About forty people gathered in the court room . . . and went in a body to visit the commissioner. Guess they thought that when a group of women like that called on them they meant business! Before going in we had decided on who was to be spokesman and present our wishes. A. E. Swift was elected and did she ever talk to those Commissioners! At any rate we got results and in a very short time Miss Bydely was in our midst. Before this time we . . . had been trying to get an agent for our county, but were always told

there were not enough funds. ("History of the Welfare of the Sages Home Demonstration Club"; LHB 83:713)

Such club participation gave women power outside their roles as farm homemaker. Women felt that collective action could be used to solve local problems. Through affiliations with national organizations, they were connected to national and state institutions. These ties afforded access to resources for personal and community needs.

The Transformation of Expectations

Through their activities country women's organizations effectively disseminated a value system recognizing the importance of women's contributions to family and household. Although Canadian organizations were more inclined than their American counterparts to base their programs on a belief in women's unique morality and character, all clubs nevertheless organized their activities in response to the actual experiences of rural women. On both sides of the international boundary, rural women's organizations saw the woman as the linchpin of the home—but a home in which women had dual responsibilities, to both domestic and enterprise spheres. Simply put, women worked on the farm, gave birth to and reared children to provide labor, and provided the household milieu necessary to supply and nourish their services. While some farm men and women may have shared conventional ideologies restricting women to a separate world of domesticity, the exigencies of homestead agricultural settlement and the interrelationship between household and family farm production did not support this separation.

Similarly, child-rearing responsibilities called for participation in community efforts for children's health and schooling, giving women experience in community organization. The extension of family concerns to the public sphere seems self-evident: parents with a sick child and no easily available medical help needed assistance, and women's groups mobilized the resources and human energy to supply that help. Paradoxically, attempts to establish and re-create old patterns of social life, based on traditional assumptions about women's dependent and unique roles as nurturer of children, guardian of morality, and civilizer, led to new alternatives for women to expand their sphere of influence within and beyond the household.

Club programs and short courses and the informal exchange of experiences provided practical solutions to specific concerns of women. Instructional and social activities disseminated similar ideas based on domestic science propositions about food and nutrition, child-rearing practices, family relationships, and consumption. The attention to home improvements was as much connected with the goal to ease the burden of farm living as it was connected to economic and technological changes in the United States and Canada, such as the availability of electricity in rural areas or the development of mail order houses including Sears and Roebuck in the United States and Eaton's in Canada. Rural women and men were not isolated from a national economic system that encouraged an increase in consumption and thus raised individual expectations regarding standard of living. The programs advocated changes in women's workplace, raised expectations, and promoted assimilation to middle-class norms, thereby perhaps diminishing ethnic and class differences.

Although based on women's traditional domestic roles, these programs led to ancillary benefits for women. (1) They made explicit the contribution of women to farm production and reinforced farm women's image of themselves as working partners in a family enterprise. (2) The external valuation of women's household production supported expenditures for household consumption and increased the recognition of women's rights to economic resources. (3) Although socializing was not a formal aspect of either U.S. or Canadian groups, the women's clubs gave their members a chance to meet and discuss common concerns. (4) Through their engagement in local community welfare activities, women developed organizational skills and community recognition, increasing their sense of their own worth.

Chapter 11

Rudyard: A Railroad-Homestead Town as Seen by Contemporaries

We now turn from country communities and their social organization to town centers planned and built by engineers and businessmen eager to make money from services provided to incoming settlers. We do not imply that the first type of community is socially benign and the second purely materialistic. Creating nucleated centers of population and services in a landscape as undeveloped as the northern plains was a necessity, and it took a great deal of skill and energy, whatever the motives. At the same time, we acknowledge the fact that many of these created and promoted towns were ill-conceived and their residents and functions exploited by real estate and other business interests that created them.

Although the towns along the CPR and the GNR were similar in function and history, the Canadian ambience was responsible for some differences. One was the availability of British capital on the Canadian side. Most of the early British investors were interested in opportunities that involved raw materials—potash, kaolin, brick clay—or agricultural products such as beef. They financed facilities in the railroad towns that could collect and process these materials. A few British investors tried their hand at very large scale corporate farms, which were often tied to cluster settlement and rail town ventures, like the Sir Lister Kay enterprises in Saskatchewan. Most of these early town-based enterprises faded as the difficulties of farming became evident and the cost of transporting processed raw materials became prohibitive.

Most of the descriptive material in this chapter is taken from a remarkable document collection serving as a local history book (LHB 83) for a single railroad-homestead town: Rudyard, Montana, on the Hi Line of the Great Northern Railroad, in the heart of the Canadian-American West. The compilation, entitled *Rudyard Images,* was made by Ruby Langel, a former resident of the town. It is a 912-page lithographed manuscript containing hundreds of items, from local newspapers and other sources, pertaining to every facet of town life, business, and politics, arranged in chronological order. It is raw material for a true local history, a history of a town, but our treatment of it is more as a historical ethnography, focusing on the town's heyday, around 1910 to 1920. Rudyard is a good choice for the purposes of the chapter because it is a little bit of everything. It is a railroad town, a homestead town, a *small* town—yet bigger than a country village. It was a town born as the result of conscious decisions but one that also underwent its own evolution: rise, decline, revival, and finally stabilization at a modest level of existence—a trajectory characteristic of many small towns in the Canadian-American West.[1] Rudyard's peak population, in the 1910 census, was 598 persons; it dipped to about 200 in the 1940s, then rose slowly to 596 in the late 1970s.

Towns as Planned Settlements

The first towns in the region appeared in Montana and were associated with the mining frontier of the 1860s. Some of these towns made it all the way to city status, especially if functions unrelated to transient miners could be found to sustain them. (Helena, for instance, became the state capitol and the financial center.) On the Canadian side, most of the mining frontier was in British Columbia, outside our designated territory; instead, the ranching frontier became the chief setting for towns. Calgary, Alberta, for example, was founded as a livestock processing and shipping center.

The early Montana towns had two major functions: to serve the mining labor force and to manage money. This soon led to land and cattle operations—land for the increasing number of settlers attracted by the economic development associated with mining and cattle. But land, cattle, and financial dealings developed their own momentum, generating other urban activities including the construction of office buildings, retail shops, craft and trade centers, and small manufacturing enterprises. By the 1870s, small cities along the U.S. Rocky Mountain front offered a full range of services, an urbane atmosphere, and permanent brick and stone office buildings. But they were surrounded by a largely unpopulated countryside and were, in the beginning, without rail transportation. This anomalous situation was itself one of the great incentives to open the area to agricultural and village settlement.

As the frontier opened, the types of towns multiplied. There were homestead villages, railroad towns, post office centers, crossroad centers, ranching towns, old cow towns, and others. These labels usually referred both to the deliberate purpose of the town and to the functions it fulfilled after its establishment. "Establishment" is the key term here. Most towns, of all sizes and locations, were deliberately planned and promoted. Such towns had "founders," many of whom were in fact *owners,* if they used their own capital or capital supplied by an investor group to establish the first businesses and build the first structures. Occasionally a country district might simply fill up with settlers, and a village would emerge without any preconceived plan beyond service to the local agricultural settlers. But these organic processes of growth were not typical for the larger towns, especially the railroad towns.

The key factor in town settlement was this self-conscious, deliberate act of creation by railroad executives: "We will put the town here." Some towns were the sites of camps for workers, others were wintering villages for crews that had gone as far as they could, others were division points or multiple-tracked centers for refueling, cleaning, and storing cars and other equipment. The division points were true instant towns. In a matter of weeks such a location could acquire tracks, streets, a station, car barns, water towers, and bunk cars; traveling entrepreneurs would set up saloons, restaurants, pool halls, and perhaps a bawdy house or two. The rapidity of development, of course, was helped by the presence of plenty of capital to get the job done. The railroad company simply built its own facilities, and these facilities would then become the locus for independent entrepreneurial effort.

Sometimes the instigation went the other way—a group of businessmen would decide that a particular location along the line, or the surveyed place for the line, would make a good spot for a town because of some natural feature like a river crossing or the intersection of wagon trails. Havre, Montana, "the Metropolis of the Hi Line," was established at a main crossing of the Milk River where trails created by bison, Indians, trappers, cattlemen, whiskey traders, and wagon trains already existed. Then the corporation—for in many such instances that is precisely what existed—would seek to persuade the railroad to establish a station and make the town into a port of entry for incoming settlers. In the early years, the town would literally be the private property of the founding corporation. However, since they desired a return on their investment, the founders immediately began selling land and business sites, thus permitting ownership to diffuse.

The self-consciousness of town and village formation led directly to the booster spirit, which was much more than a materialistic attitude. It was the symbolic aspect of an active, energetic attempt to create a community, to persuade people to invest in it, and for settlers to come and benefit from this little garden spot. Boosterism was a symbolic manifestation of the North American entrepreneurial spirit. Equally significant was the investment angle. People who had put their money into a town project were anxious to sustain its value or make a comfortable percentage. Most towns were in their very inception commercial undertakings, but to say that towns were commercial does not detract from their essential function in helping to create a new society. It was this dual nature that helps to account for the ferocious enthusiasm and determination of their founders and builders.

Another facet of the booster spirit was the notion of progress. Virtually any change could be taken as evidence of progress if the town advocates so chose. Consider this passage from a local newspaper in Rudyard: "H. S. Robinson is building an addition to his store house, with P. D. Reed as head carpenter. Thus we are reminded again of how business in Rudyard is increasing, and our merchants are prepared to care for the trade. To the public we would say, give our merchants a trial. They have groceries down to bed rock, you will be pleased with your purchases" (*Rudyard Dispatch*, October 1910). This defines one essential criterion of a progressive citizen: one who invests in a new addition to his store building. The investment becomes a symbol of faith in the future of the town, a declaration that it exists, that it will progress toward some permanent state of being, that it is not just a speculative gamble but a solid reality. Progress is in this sense not only a quantitative measure but an ideal, a symbolic act of faith.

Towns grew, declined, stayed the same, or fluctuated with the economy. The energy of their citizens was not always the most important factor in deciding which of these patterns would predominate; equally important was the relationship of the town to exogenous economic and political resources. While the attitudes and objectives of the townspeople were "local" in the sense that they were focused on the effort to build a community, they were by necessity externally oriented as well, since the economic wherewithal to keep the town functioning depended on investments and facilities provided by the railroads, land or grain elevator companies, banks, meat packers, and the suppliers of goods to be sold locally. Credit extended by all of these agencies was essential in keeping the town businesses alive and well. Still, the obvious dependence of the town on these external forces is rarely acknowledged in the local histories and newspapers. In the true spirit of do-it-yourself and frontier entrepreneurship, the town's fortunes are attributed to its citizens.

The Model of Self-Sufficiency

The most important general theme of town building in the period from 1890 to 1920 was self-sufficiency. A town was seen as an autonomous entity, a world unto itself, however paradoxical or defective this ideal might have been. It should contain all the facilities needed to permit a continuous social existence, and the townspeople and the folks in the nearby country districts should be able to find anything they need in town without having to resort to long trips to other communities or to mail orders. Sears and Roebuck and other mail order companies had a vigorous business as early as the 1880s and it increased throughout the homesteading era; they constituted major competition to town business. So the goal of self-sufficiency or completeness of services was not simply ideological; it had vital economic implications.

The goal of self-sufficiency had other implications. The town was conceived as an oasis in the midst of a wilderness. It constituted a safe haven for a population exposed to the elements and lacking efficient transportation or sufficient cash or goods. It was the definitive answer to the frontier: in fact the frontier ceased to exist where its deficiencies were made up. Thus the town represented civilization, the settled East brought out West. This civilization was of course capitalist. There was money to be made in providing services to people in need.

The dual nature of the system was understood by everyone, and while complaints over sharp practices of town merchants often surfaced, they rarely reached the magnitude of a boycott. Prices were generally fair; they had to be because the country people, the main customers, had so little cash. And on the whole credit was freely extended. Business failures in the towns frequently could be attributed to excessive and uncollectible due bills.

The model of a town included things of the mind and spirit as well as material phenomena. Schools and churches are obvious cases, but in addition there were newspapers, lecture series, amateur dramas, and lending libraries. Speeches by itinerant politicians, occasional concerts or plays presented by traveling artists or piano teachers were prominently announced and reviewed in the local papers. Culture made the difference between the wilderness and civilization, however personally philistine the town promoters might have been.

But cultural opportunities were usually later developments. Many towns began with a bar-saloon that provided refreshment for the railroad workers and local cowhands, followed by a small general store and perhaps a hotel. In Rudyard, during the first six years of the town's life the major facilities were established in the following order: railroad stops and station, post office, saloon, general and hardware stores (one each), hotel, elementary school, cluster of three specialty stores and services, two or three churches, newspaper, electric light plant. This order would vary somewhat from town to town. In a country village the store would be first, and the electric plant might never appear. The post office might be third or fourth if the town was not designated by the railroad as a station stop.

Agreement by the federal governments would bring the post office in due course, since the rail company needed a place to receive messages. Moreover, the homesteading operation required a post office somewhere in the neighborhood if the community was not large enough to support a land office, since the post office supplied the necessary information and officials for making claims. Newspapers were an early necessity, at least in the United States, because by law homestead entries had to be given public notice; such entries were compensated, supplying a subsidy for publication.

Rudyard, Montana: Starting Up

RUDYARD: BORN AND BOOSTED

The birth of a new town in Choteau County is indicated by articles of incorporation filed in the County Clerk office today by the Rudyard Townsite Company, with a capital stock of $40,000. The incorporators are Roswell S. Miner, of Havre; Martin O'Malley and Anthony J. Sanford of Inverness. Rudyard is a railroad point about 20 miles east of Chester. (*River Press,* Fort Benton, 30 April 1910)

A town is "born"; but we also learn that it is incorporated, a company. Where? At a "railroad point" about 20 miles east of Chester, and (though this is not stated) about 35 miles west of Havre; that is, about midway between these two principal Hi-Line division points established by the GNR. A railroad point was often nothing more than a telephone and an old box car, not a division point, with sidings, depots, warehouses, repair facilities, and so on—those things were at Havre and Chester. Inverness, another small railroad point, was much closer to Chester, too close to become a major town. This was something Messrs. Sanford and O'Malley apparently knew, so they decided to put their money on Rudyard. According to some writers Rudyard was named by Scots-Irish railroad workers after Rudyard Kipling, the English author and poet.

Rudyard's site had been known for a while, perhaps a decade, thanks to the railroad crews who worked their way across the plains toward the mountains. And no doubt thanks to some old trails crossing there. In almost every instance these little railroad points that eventually became stops had some presettler use as a place of meeting or movement. Havre, the major town and division point on the central Montana Hi Line, was once known as Bull Hook Crossing, a key low-water point on the Milk River.

The land between Havre and Chester is an enormous rolling plain 100 miles north and south, and 60 miles east and west, drained by the Milk River and Big and Little Sage Creeks. Up to 1910 it was rangeland, used for grazing by the assorted cattlemen along the Milk River and its tributary streams and by some of the Canadian (or American-Canadian) ranchers in the north, since international boundaries were not always honored in the nineteenth century. The land was made available to homesteaders in 1909, and the first settlers found little in the way of facilities. "We were among the first to settle north of Rudyard in the Fall of 1909. At that time there was nothing at Rudyard. J. T. Frazers and us were the only neighbor families that winter north of Rudyard. No school until 1910. We went to Inverness for our mail and groceries. Then things began to grow and people began to come" (Mrs. J. W. Chapman, p. 33).

But progress moved quickly, and by the spring of 1910 Rudyard could provide many basic services and amenities to the townsfolk. "P. D.

Reed, manager of the townsite of Rudyard was in the city on business Wednesday evening. He says that Rudyard is not only 'on the map' but is forging to the front in a very optimistic manner. Since the townsite was platted a lumber yard, two stores, a livery barn and two restaurants have been established there, with other business places in contemplation. Mr. Reed feels quite proud over the outlook for his young town" (*Havre Promoter,* 29 April 1910). All of these establishments were vital for the incoming homesteaders, and acquiring them was therefore an easy way to make profits. The major incentive for the individual entrepreneur was commercial, and many of the promoters invested in more than one town, since it was not always easy to determine which one was going to become a center for population and services. During its first decade, Rudyard attracted investors and entrepreneurs from nearly every major town in northern Montana.

By October of 1910 Rudyard was already attaining a civic identity, as a column called "Rudyard Doings" in the *Chester Signal* attests:

> Geo. Case and G. Afflerbaugh are finishing their business places for the winter with galvanized siding, quite an improvement over board siding.
>
> Herman Robinson returned this week from Lethbridge [Alberta] and other western points. He says he likes Uncle Sam's side of the line best. Strange isn't it?
>
> Warren Simpson brought a real pig to town Tuesday morning, weighed 450 lbs. Mr. Ulmen was the purchaser. This truly shows that hogs can be raised and fattened in Choteau county.
>
> School commenced again Monday with Charles D. Coy as teacher. The trustees have surely made a wise choice in securing Mr. Coy, as he has had both experience and success as a teacher and professor.
>
> The basket social given Friday eve was a decided success. Every one present seemed to enjoy themselves hugely, and it was worth more than the price of a basket to see Bruce Beagle eat fried chicken and we never had any idea that H. S. Robinson was such a lover of pie, until Friday eve.

And the settlers kept coming. "There have been 32 cars of emigrants unloaded at Rudyard so far this Spring. Pretty good showing, isn't it? Enough that we should have an agent at once" (*Joplin Times,* June 1911). "Agent" means a railroad agent, to help make Rudyard an established place of homestead entry; "we" refers to Rudyard's promoters, who, lacking a newspaper of their own, had to publish in the little news sheets of other station stops. And the town itself was mindful of its own destiny. "At present Rudyard is the only town between Chester and Havre that can give deeds to the lots that are purchased. People ought not to stand back now but if they are thinking of investing in town lots they should do so while they are cheap" (*Joplin Times*, 15 July 1911).

Rudyard claimed growth potential, and it did grow slowly, according to need, but growth also was a commodity vigorously sold to the public. More than building lots were being promoted and marketed, and some of the real estate dealers got into legal trouble promoting prostitution. There was nothing unusual in such activities in these little towns on the railroads, despite dubious moral and legal implications. These activities were lucrative.[2]

The growth pattern in Rudyard was steep during the first two or three years, in particular the rapid establishment of facilities for settlers. But things leveled off after a while, and after six or seven years the town promoters felt the need for a little more boosterism.

> BOOST FOR RUDYARD
> Let us all boost for the best little city in the state.
>
> It is very gratifying to note that the spirit of progress is very apparent in this town and if the present sentiment is continued, Rudyard will progress more in the next year or two than has been the case in the past. We have the most favored spot in the state for a prosperous town and with united action on the part of our citizens this will be the business center of the most prosperous farming section to be found in the state. . . . We have everything that goes to make a splendid town and we should not hide our advantages, but talk about them on every occasion. Let us have a boosters slogan: RUDYARD IS THE BEST PLACE ON EARTH TO LIVE, and it is if we make it so. (*Rudyard Dispatch*, 20 July 1917)

"It is if we make it so." That is, let's build some houses for people to live in. Stores, banks, services of all kinds, but few or no dwellings. Where did the early businessmen and storekeepers reside? In the first-floor rear or second floor of their places of business for the most part, a few even had shacks or tents in the back yards. Thus we discern a pattern. First, invite the settlers and sell them what they need to get out to the homestead; second, switch the message, and induce them to come and live and work in town. But at the same time you can't ignore the farmers. The article continues with a long list of names of farmers and concludes by complimenting them:

> [They] have all aided in the growth of the town, but its future depends chiefly upon the farmers of the surrounding country who—as the grain receipts at the elevators this fall will show—have been very fortunate.

So long as there were settlers to supply and goods to ship, the town's business was self-sustaining, but directed outward. Houses for town residents were one problem, the absence of a town chamber of commerce was another.

> We ought to get busy and organize a commercial club to help put our locality where it belongs. We have been in the rut too long. We have some of the most enterprising and energetic citizens to be found anywhere. . . . Why not get together and hasten things along. . . . We can double our population in a few years with prompt action. (*Rudyard Dispatch*, 17 July 1917)

So the booster spirit was also a cry in the wilderness: an indirect acknowledgement that towns like this needed more than the obvious business of selling things to transients, of catering to a national project—homesteading—that would soon be over. Boosterism was not only a matter of local patriotism or civic pride, it was a plea to start doing things for each other, to create a permanent town population and its institutions—something that would keep people at home, working for each other. Through the years, this would prove to be Rudyard's perennial problem.

Tracks, Trains, and Strains

The railroad created Rudyard by making it a station stop and thus giving the green light to promoters. But it was the habit of railroads to count on the natural selection process of town evolution and to invest in the community only if it served railroad interests. There were, in the first place, differences between the train service bringing settlers and picking up farm produce and the train service between the little towns and villages along the tracks. The latter need was often ignored until the towns began complaining that it was difficult to visit friends and relatives or conduct business if the railroad neglected its local customers. Even when the railroad complied with demands to run local service between towns, it was usually insufficient. Running trains for distances of ten to thirty miles to benefit a small number of passengers, however regular, was clearly a problem for the railroad, and the automobile soon supplanted such local rail traffic. By the end of World War II local passenger train service was almost entirely abandoned along the CPR and GNR lines in Canada and the United States; it was over by the 1980s, except for special tourist and excursion ventures.

The lack of tracks and crossings became an increasing burden for towns as their populations and businesses grew.

> RUDYARD MUST HAVE INDUSTRIAL TRACK
>
> The Great Northern Railroad had the plans completed early in the spring for the lengthening of the industrial track. Time passes and nothing is done. The crossing is often nearly blocked with cars and is a menace to every one crossing. Already one farm wagon has been run into and there is likely to be another accident at any time. It begins to look as if it would be necessary to appeal to the Railroad Commission to get justice. (*Rudyard Dispatch*, May 1917)

The dilemma was clear: On the one hand, the farm produce had to be picked up and the farm and industrial supplies unloaded; on the other, jamming trains into the middle of the town meant that people and automobiles had to wait for the long strings of cars to crawl through. The towns had been established on both sides of the tracks, with the station in the middle, but this design meant that as traffic increased the town was cut in two. Building more tracks and sidings was one answer, but in the larger towns the problem was eventually partly solved by the lopsided growth of the town mainly on one side of the tracks. This created the "wrong side of the tracks," often occupied by shanty towns, freight depots, and sometimes red light districts.

But the importance of the railroad was enduring. Without the line the towns would vanish. And as time passed, the railroad became increasingly conscious of its obligations to the citizens of the towns it had created. In Rudyard, station agents and their families were among the town elite; their children attended local schools and they patronized local businesses. Charitable contributions were made by the railroad, and during wartime the railroad made its land available for home gardening. Much of this activity was a matter of public relations, and while townspeople knew the railroad was a vital asset, resentment over its business practices flourished. The link between the grain elevator companies and the railroads was especially irritating, and in Canada it led eventually to the farmer takeover of the elevator system and the birth of new left-leaning Populist parties, including the Cooperative Commonwealth Federation of Saskatchewan and the Non-Partisan League of North Dakota.

Necessities and Amenities

It was one thing to plant a town along the railroad and open up stores, but quite another to establish the viable infrastructure of a modern community. The model for these towns was the settled urbanism of eastern and midwestern North American communities, and nothing less than that would do for the founders and builders of Rudyard, as well as for all the other homestead-railroad towns. The problem, of course, was that the necessities and amenities of town life cost money, money that could not be generated in ordinary commercial enterprises. You couldn't squeeze it out of the merchants in the form of taxes because they would simply move elsewhere, as so many of them did at regular intervals anyway. And since the town was trying to attract settlers it couldn't very well advertise taxes as the price of entry.

The booster spirit was exhortation, an attempt to persuade the initial population of commercial opportunists that the town was worth supporting and worth living in; that it was more than just a convenient location for making a little money off the settlers or the railroad facilities. It was difficult to create something permanent, something to permit continuity of community, out of a sparse and uncertain population of transients.

Water is the most important of natural resources, but if there is water in the ground, the individual can always drill a well and supply himself and add the well to the assets of the property when he sells out. Home wells and business wells supplied Rudyard with water for a long time—until 1947, to be exact: "Congratulations to the Commercial Club of Rudyard! While we here in Chester have laid down with the complaint, "can't," Rudyard has drilled a well to the depth of 960 feet and struck water. Watch out Chester, or our neighbors to the east will be making us look sick" (*Liberty County Times,* Chester, 20 March 1947). But this was not the end of the story. By 1955 the Federal government had completed a large dam on the Marias River and Willow Creek, streams running to the east of Chester, and with it created Lake Elwell, a reservoir sufficient to supply nearly all of the little towns between Chester and Havre with water. By 1965 the county had proposed a $9 million bond issue to pay for the installations. This project represented a further development in the collective consciousness as the several towns pooled their needs and resources. Self-sufficiency, at least on water supplies, was no longer a matter of individuals or of individual towns.

Electricity had a similar history. Until 1917 power for Rudyard was supplied by a small plant located in the rear of a hardware store, and uncertain current was delivered until 10 p.m. every night. In 1917 another store decided to buy a 50 horsepower lighting plant that furnished "25 kilowatts, sufficient to handle 2000 lights and a storage battery which will keep the lights steady night and day. There will be sufficient power to run wash machines, electric irons, and toasters. . . . Street lights will be of the 150 watt size" (*Rudyard Dispatch*, 24 August 1917). However, the promises took a long time to mature. It was not until 1929 that the town received street lights. Finally, in 1948, the federal government established a Rural Electrification Administration plant for the region, and Rudyard and its neighboring towns had a reliable and augmented service.

Roads and town streets were more problematic. While larger government investments, at county and federal levels, were eventually available to supply water and electricity at adequate levels of supply, transportation arteries had to depend on local resources almost entirely. In the early days any individual might be able to drill a well or install a small engine to generate current, but streets and roads had to be collective responsibilities from the start.

Roads outside of town presented an especially difficult problem, since Rudyard could do little or nothing about roads in county jurisdiction. Townspeople insistently pressured the county commissioners to improve the situation, but shortage of funds and equipment made it difficult for them to meet the demands presented by every little town in the county. The papers published accounts of serious accidents caused by dangerous and deteriorated roads.

The most important stimulus to road building was the automobile, and cars were available in Rudyard almost from the beginning of the town. The first automobile sales agencies were in the livery barns, where horses and high-wheel autos competed for space. While draft horses were used on farms well into the 1920s, tractors had supplanted them by the early 1930s; horses used for buggies were gone by about the same time. Rudyard was really born too late to have been involved in the full horse culture of livery stables, hitching posts on the main street, wagon makers, harness shops, and the like (Lingeman 1980:264).

Were telephones necessities or amenities? Both. An amenity when the population was small and there were few pressing needs for communication; a necessity as time passed and the growing complexity of the regional economy and society, and especially its increasing need to deal with the external world, required more frequent and insistent communication. In 1917, the year when so many innovations appeared in Rudyard, a local telephone company was established to serve the town and several neighboring districts and villages. The company had recurrent financial problems through the years, but someone generally stepped in and bought the lines, keeping the service open.

Telephones keep people in touch. They are needed not only for business transactions but for all kinds of social communication. Newspapers have a similar function, but they have the advantage of creating a permanent record. And record is precisely what newspapers on the U.S. homestead frontier were supposed to do: to fulfill the legal requirement of publishing homestead entries, provings up, and relinquishments, as well as to serve as town and country directories. Newspapers were essential. As soon as the settlers started arriving in numbers, there was demand for a paper, and since the government paid the editor a small fee for each entry notice published, the sheet had a modest built-in subsidy that would increase as the number of incoming settlers increased. This gave the paper, of course, an added incentive to encourage the booster spirit.

Newspapers had another important function: their printing plants to furnish the community with printed forms and the merchants with throwaways, to make greeting cards for the public, posters for sports events and dances and all the activities of the town and its country districts. A print shop could be seen as a symbol of the up-to-dateness of the area; there is nothing like the printed word to convey the aura of civilization. Newspapers were important. Their editors took themselves very seriously; they were well aware of the value and meaning of "the press" and often reprinted homilies to that effect from other local papers.

Editors of small-town papers struggled to maintain a delicate balance between informing the community (and telling the truth) and on the other hand avoiding offense and unpleasant revelations. The *Rudyard Dispatch* was no exception. On 10 August 1917, in response to a series of indignant letters concerning a news item, the paper published the following article:

DISPATCH ASKED TO RETRACT

The article in the Dispatch last week relating the story of Mr. Anderson's accident seemed to interest some of our readers very much. Mr. Wm. Goffrier, George Goffrier, Charles Zuege, and L. Hall came to the Dispatch office and demanded that we retract the article.

Some people seem to think that the only news we ought to publish is to tell who goes to Havre and who goes visiting on Sunday. As long as we live and publish the Dispatch we will continue to stand for law enforcement and stand with the law abiding people. Several different persons had spoken to us about the speeding on the streets and thought that we had ought to give them a "write up." We had delayed hoping that no accidents would occur although we were daily expecting there would be one. It had become so that women and children were afraid to cross the streets. The state law says: SPEED SHALL NOT BE GREATER THAN IS REASONABLY SAFE AND PROPER UNDER CONDITIONS EXISTING AT POINT AND TIME OF OPERATION, AND SO AS NOT TO UNREASONABLY ENDANGER THE LIFE, LIMB, OR PROPERTY OF ANY PERSON ENTITLED TO THE USE OF THE HIGHWAY.

We do not wish to do any one an injustice nor print anything that is untrue. However, we are at a loss what to retract. The only statement we made in the article is that "T. Anderson was run into by an automobile driven by Albert Goffrier," and that seems to be a fact that many people can swear to. The article goes on to say "WHO IT IS SAID was driving up and down the street at great speed." . . . We did not say they were driving at great speed; we said that other people told us so. As we wanted to be absolutely fair to all we published both sides to the question, so we do not see where there is any cause for complaint.

Here is a newspaper editor, trying to be a progressive, truth-telling, informative servant of the people, who discovers that some of the people would prefer that certain things are kept off the public record. The episode is a microcosm of the small-town newspaper world celebrated in literature and movies, a time when boilerplate or canned news and ads hardly existed, and the columns had to be filled with firsthand reports on "doings," politics, events. By the 1950s most of this intimate newspaper culture had disappeared, and the paper suffered the fate of most small-town sheets, becoming a medium for announcements of sales, picnics, official reports, government notices, and syndicated state and national "news."

The general store is another prime symbol of settlement on the homestead frontier, or, for that matter, over the entire rural landscape of the United States and Canada from the Atlantic Coast to the Rocky Mountains and beyond. It was a unique institution, rare in Europe, where in the villages small family-owned specialty shops were the rule. The North American general store came about as the result of several circumstances. It was a sedentary conversion of the frontier peddler, who carried an amazing variety of wares in his wagon or cart. This all-purpose, traveling variety-store kind of merchandising was necessary in a partly settled wilderness with inadequate roads, limited sources of supplies, and a transient population following a variety of occupations. When settlements did appear, the concept gave rise to the general store, whose objective was to provide everything the settler needed, at reasonable cost and credit.

Sanvik's store was one of the biggest on the Hi Line, although it was not the earliest general store in Rudyard. Ole Sanvik, from Norway, bought out an earlier store, Tracht's, in 1928 and continued its tradition of service to the entire surrounding community. In the 1960s the Chester newspaper interviewed Robert Sanvik, son of Ole and inheritor of the business, inquiring into the secret of the store's success, in the face of the decline of businesses in Rudyard.

> He believes they've been able to keep up with the times because they adapted as quickly as the market shifted. He saw the first hoola hoops back east at a convention; sent Selmer [his brother] four dozen. "Selmer didn't know what they were—thought I'd gone off my rocker. But he sold 'em before I got home. You've got to keep up or you've had it."
>
> Bob and Selmer Sanvik were more than just good businessmen. They were builders. They represent a vanishing breed of men who believe hard work is the solution to most of the problems facing a community.

These sentiments are more than just Protestant-ethic sloganeering or chamber of commerce hype. For a small town in a region of sparse and transient population, they represented the simple truth of business success: personal business, business in direct, face-to-face contact with its customers on a daily basis, and a business that must develop cordial, friendly relations with its suppliers in order to insure a steady flow of goods. And credit was the name of the game, credit from friendly suppliers and credit to friendly customers. The problem was to maintain a delicate balance between credit and profit; one was always paying off somebody, or keeping somebody on the books, with the surplus one managed to accumulate.

Dixon Brothers, located in Maple Creek on the CPR line, was a similar enterprise. The Dixon store, like Sanvik's, weathered the storm, outlasting the parade of competitors, finally closing its doors in the mid-1960s (Sanvik's lasted into the 1980s). The Dixons followed the same formula: Keep up with the times and work like dogs to keep the store going, the merchandise fresh and attractive, and the customers happy. As the years passed the energy and vision deteriorated and the bills piled up. By the time the store closed for good, about 1960, when the son of one of the original brothers (both deceased) retired, it had thousands of dollars of unpaid customer bills and unpaid debts to suppliers.

The local newspapers on the Montana Hi Line and along the CPR tracks in Canada contain histories of these enterprises, with the emphasis on the operators, who are presented as benefactors of their communities and guardians of tradition. "Ole Sanvik has been named a member of the reception committee which will greet the Crown Prince and Princess of Norway when they visit Helena on May 29" (*Liberty County Times,* 1939). Ole was county assessor, writer of a column in local newspapers, candidate for railroad commissioner, and the proprietor of the "finest store on the Hi Line." The Dixons in Maple Creek had similar careers. One was mayor for years; both brothers met the Queen of England on her railway journey across Canada in the 1930s.

Doctors, Death, and Burial

> Dr. Buisson, the dentist, will be in Rudyard October 25th and 26th to do your dental work. He will be at the Spannuth Hotel. (*Rudyard Dispatch,* 15 October 1915)

> The Dispatch leased the building north of the Dispatch office to E.A. Hawkins of Big Sandy last week. Mr. Hawkins will put in a stock of drugs and run a first class drug store. He also expects to bring a doctor to town. This is what Rudyard needs. (*Rudyard Dispatch,* 9 June 1917)

Three things stand out. First, outside specialists, like dentists and optometrists, would spend a day or two in Rudyard, then move on to the next town. And this was not simply due to frontier conditions; the procedure has continued along the Hi Line and also in western Canada in spite of provincial and national health insurance. Second, general practitioners were hard to get; the promises, given in editorials and news columns, of one coming to town recur for years, as doctors would try it out for a few years, then move on. Bills were hard to collect, and practice was limited to fairly routine illnesses. Third, so far as the *Dispatch* was concerned, doctors and drugstores were part of the business life of Rudyard, a sign of a forward-looking community. Most little towns eventually acquired resident physicians, usually aging and often semiretired doctors whose interests were broader than medicine. Real estate, club activities, town government, hunting and fishing, farming, investments in town businesses —are all on the record for such men. Reports on the professional skills of these "medical fixtures," as one local history writer calls them, are usually mixed, and often dramatically so.

Town newspapers regularly reported (and still do) deaths in the region in the form of obituaries of varying length, depending on the importance of the deceased in the history and affairs of the locality. These obituaries describe funeral arrangements as well as biographical details. Severe illness and death are also covered indirectly in the personals columns of these small-town papers, when the family writes a note of appreciation for services given by medical professionals, relatives, and friends. Whether the attitudes expressed represent the "real" sentiments is hard to say, but some standard patterns are evident.

Perhaps the most obvious is the view that death and illness are to a considerable extent concerns of the community. Since the town populations are small, most everyone would hear about illness and death through word of mouth and newspaper items. But there is more. The personals column of the newspapers contain reader-written items memorializing death and expressing gratitude for favors, expressions of sympathy, and just about everything else. These items seem to be more frequently published in the papers on the Saskatchewan side than in either Alberta or Montana, which corresponds, perhaps, to the dominant small-town British-Ontarian strain in Saskatchewan culture and its emphasis on intimate social interaction. The custom, however, is still observed in all western and midwestern small-town papers in both Canada and the United States.

Death and illness, then, are public events in the town-country community that is served by the local newspapers. It is important to let your readers—your neighbors—know that you are grateful for care and attention and for services rendered, and the paper is willing to turn some of its expensive space over to this reader-composed material. Some papers charge for this printing, others do not, but the charges are always nominal and the compulsion to publish these notices is very strong. Families and individuals who neglect to thank the "community of caring," or simply anyone who contributed a valued service of any kind, are faulted; they are people who "don't care very much," in the words of one editor with whom we discussed the custom.

The dead had to be buried. Where did they put them on the frontier? In the country it was a matter of finding an appropriate place under a tree, in a coulee at some distance from the homestead, or, if a country church existed, in the church burial ground. A few of these still exist on the prairie, but most of the dead were moved when the churches were re-established in town. Sooner or later the towns had to create their own cemeteries. In Rudyard the local cemetery began in March 1916 with a petition and an assessment of $3.00. A short time later, in May, it was dedicated—an apparently successful example of local action.

"Doings" and "Happenings"

Small town newspapers everywhere in North America, regardless of how active the editors may be, have an obligation to carry detailed reports on the experiences of their constituents. This is especially the case for the northern plains, where populations are small, dispersed, and organized into intimate networks of kinship, friendship, and civic affairs. The accepted format for reporting the activities of neighbors is a separate column or section, often called, as it was in Rudyard, the "doings" of the community, with separate columns for the town and relevant or distinguishable country districts. To group the material this way also signals, and reinforces, the local identities of districts and neighborhoods. Here are samples of typical "doings" in Rudyard and environs for 1916 and 1917:

> Several new residences were started in Rudyard this week. Joe Simon is building a house on his lots in the Rogers addition. A. H. Griffin has concrete foundation for his new home completed. Mr. Claypool is building a house in the north part of town. W. J. Ledin will soon start the erection of a house. Harry Hill has bought two lots in the Rogers addition and will erect a modern up to date residence on them soon.
>
> Ben, J.H., S.H. and Edwin Crandall bought tickets for Belton (West Glacier) Friday. They expect to bring the winters supply of meat with them on their return.

On Thursday evening a number of neighbors and friends gathered . . . to surprise Mrs. John Danielson, who was leaving for the east for an indefinite stay. The evening was very pleasantly spent in playing games and conversation. Before going home, Mr. Halfpenny, with a few well chosen words, presented Mrs. Danielson with a purse from the company. Mrs. Danielson was almost overcome by their kindness but managed to thank them in a few broken sentences. The party lasted until well after midnight.

The Misses Anna and Elizabeth Dittrich and C. L. Stark and Joe Welliver went to Havre Thursday, March 28 and returned the same day. The roads were almost impassable, but they passed many cars on the road that were unable to get through the mud and reached Rudyard in the evening. They had some slight trouble with their car so stayed at the Spannuth Hotel until Friday morning.

Mrs. G. J. Wicks is very ill with pneumonia. She became very ill Saturday evening and is in about the same condition at this writing. No change is expected for several days.

Peter McCowan went to Havre Tuesday evening to secure his citizenship papers.

A Salvation Army lassie was in town Monday collecting for the heathen at home and also in foreign lands.

Peter Isaacson has sold his farm and purchased Mr. Paulson's Chevrolet. Carl Paulson has purchased a new Overland.

War has started in Rudyard: On Monday afternoon two prominent farmers in Rudyard got into a heated argument over the war and finally the line was passed and this so angered the defender of the flag that he struck at the other and it looked as if there was to be a battle to a finish but the combatants were parted by friends.

"Happenings," another Rudyard newspaper concept, refers to two classes of events. The first, and most numerous in terms of published items, comprises the activities of organized groups, of which these towns had plenty. The happenings in the second category were events of a miscellaneous nature: accidents, tornados, visitations by dignitaries and entertainment troupes, economic news of importance, and so on. They fall into one large, miscellaneous category because they are, in the main, not controllable or were not planned by the local people, or did not necessarily result from deliberate actions by residents of the town.

Places to Stay

These homestead towns always had hotels of one kind or another, places to stay, to room and board, to stop overnight, or to live there for months and even years. The towns were always full of transients—homesteaders, new businessmen, salesmen, railroaders, newspapermen, hunters, government officials. While the first businesses probably were bars for the railroad workers, the first commercial buildings were boarding houses or "hotels." The first Rudyard establishment called a hotel was a large frame house built in 1909, where travelers could get a room and meals. With the homesteaders due to arrive in Rudyard in numbers in 1910, a hotel was a likely proposition for people with money to spend on construction. A series of hotels followed.

The first was the Case, built in 1910 by one of the pioneer town families. It was a small affair, with five or six rooms and a dining room managed on the American plan, which meant meals went with the room charge—a glorified boarding house. The second was the Spannuth, a real hotel with ten rooms, a large lobby, and a dining room on the European plan. This opened the facility to parties, lunch meetings, annual Christmas parties, occasional square dances, church and Sunday school services. The Spannuth functioned for a while as a community hall, a facility that all these towns lacked in the beginning, since it was more important to provide facilities for travelers and prospective settlers than for townspeople, many of whom were temporary residents.

The Case went out of business in 1917, and the Spannuth promptly built an addition, but competition appeared immediately in the form of the Grand Hotel, built by a new immigrant family. This family went bankrupt in the early 1920s, and the hotel passed through the hands of three owners before it, too, gave up the ghost. But the Grand became a Rudyard institution, a hotel specializing, more or less, in service to local people. Country mothers and children stayed in it over the winter months, while the kids went to the town school; town teachers lived there, as well as young women who had lost their husbands; doctors had their offices there; a beauty shop occupied part of the lobby for several years; and country children were welcome at all times to stay there if the weather made it hard to get home.

Halls: City and Community

The multifunctionality of the hotel was echoed in the structures erected for government and social functions. These facilities appeared from five to ten years after the business blocks and other important buildings were erected. During those years dances, town meetings, committee meetings, and other activities took place in the hotels or second floors of store buildings or garages. There was no dearth of such affairs; the towns simply found it difficult to raise money to construct buildings for purely official or civic uses. Usually the campaign to raise money to build halls sought to get donations from—or to sell shares to—businessmen, town leaders, or retired ranchers living in town, and often the land for the structure was donated, in whole or in part, by one of the early town settlers who had bought lots in order to get a corner on the market.

Rudyard's city hall project began in 1916. A committee of businessmen was formed to plan a building and to set up a stock company to finance the structure. Since city halls by themselves do not produce income, the building was planned as a combination opera house and city hall: "Up to date there has been about $2000 worth of stock sold in the proposed City Hall. As winter is coming on, we think it would be a good idea to get started on building the hall so as to have it ready" (*Rudyard Dispatch,* 15 September 1916). And so they did. The building was furnished by Thanksgiving, when there was a "big dance, show, and turkey supper." The opening "was a complete success in every way. Two hundred and twenty five tickets were sold, making receipts of $562.50." The "size of the floor space was 40 × 100 feet."

Two years later the Rudyard Opera Company organized another stock company with $10,000 capital stock to accommodate local drama and musicales and finance traveling entertainment. The building served the town well until 1963, when it burned to the ground, taking two other buildings with it. Then the fire jumped across the street and burned down two major business blocks. Rudyard never fully recovered from this disaster.

Service Businesses

Rudyard had the full complement: automobile and farm machinery dealers, garages, lumber yards, hardware stores, cafés, beauty parlors, carpenter shops, electric shops, clothing stores, and so on down the main street. The types and numbers of services grew slowly over the years, and they were often of short duration. Mrs. Langel's materials, covering a few years in each decade from 1910 to 1940, notes twenty businesses closing, of which half were sell-outs to new owners, and ten or so second attempts by owners to open businesses in lines that had failed at least once. The larger and better established stores, like Sanvik's, retained their identity, but there were periods of decline and then revival under new management.

This fluctuation in service enterprises is characteristic of small towns in the West. Rudyard experienced rapid growth of its business life in the early years, a decline as the homesteading population thinned out, a modest revival in the 1920s, another decline in the drought-and-depression period of the '30s, revival again after World War II, decline again in the 1970s. Each period of business decline coincides with a dip in population or national economic difficulty. In addition, the booster spirit over the years created an impression of economic growth and progress that belied the uncertainties of the grain-and-cattle economy influenced by drought and price fluctuation. In all but a few of the businesses, like the general stores and the automotive and machinery dealers and repair services, the trade was rarely sufficient to support a family and a modern enterprise for more than a few years before decline set in. Capital for revival was not easy to obtain in most years.

Investment in town businesses by outsiders was routine, especially in the early years. In a sense, all investment was made by "outsiders" since all settlers were outsiders. But there were special cases, where outside interests had resources the town needed. An example are the lumber companies. There was always one dominant one in Rudyard, although there were periods when two tried to make it. Since there are no good sources of lumber in the northern plains, contracts with timbered regions had to be established. The first lumber yard in Rudyard (1915) was substantially financed by a Minnesotan who owned forest tracts and lumber mills. Two or three local men supplied the money for the yard facilities. Two years later the Minnesotan sold his interest to Mr. Tracht, of the family who also owned the first general store, and returned to Minnesota. The business went through three more owners in subsequent years, and the yard and buildings were heavily damaged by fire in 1970. A fourth owner took over in 1977 and rebuilt the facilities.

Small service businesses like bakeries, dry cleaners, beauty parlors, shoe repair, or restaurants changed hands regularly:

> Geo. Case has leased his hotel to Mr. Mitchell from Strathmore, Canada. Mr. Case will move his family out on his fine farm, 1½ miles south of town. (*Chester Signal*, 20 June 1912)
>
> Luther Eller closed his dry cleaning shop in Rudyard. (*Liberty County Times*, 2 June 1949)

> Rudyard Electric operated by Clarence Een the past two years has been sold to Charles and Walter Cross. (*Liberty County Times,* 14 April 1949)

Such turnover was one result of population movement, people coming in, trying out business opportunities, then leaving for greener pastures. Another cause was the dual nature of many occupational careers: A farmer would invest the proceeds of a bumper crop in a town business, run it a few years, then move back to full-time farming. The constant changes gradually became an accepted phenomenon. So long as the service was being performed by someone, the change was not a mark of failure or economic decline. On the contrary, the fact that the businesses were usually taken up by someone else and the service continued was considered a sign of economic vitality.

Genuine, "secular" decline set in after World War II; that is, a net loss of businesses that could not survive with the increased automobile traffic and general prosperity, which led people to shop in larger towns. Improvement of the main highway, U.S. 2, which parallels the Great Northern tracks along much of the Hi Line, also encouraged more automobile movement. During the 1940s all general stores save the Sanvik emporium disappeared, never to return, and even Sanvik's had its problems. Restaurants and cafés hung on and still persist, because people need a place to sit, drink coffee, and catch up on town gossip.

Celebrating Eternity

If small towns last forever—well, almost forever—as new functions and services are found to give them a new lease on life, then this persistence needs ceremonial recognition. And recognition is given, at regular intervals, to commemorate founding dates and other great events in the history of the community. Rudyard has several, but the big one, attended by over 3,000 people, was held on 20 June 1960 and was written up in the *Liberty County Times,* since by that time Rudyard no longer had a newspaper.

> OVER 3000 ATTEND 50TH ANNIVERSARY IN RUDYARD
>
> Over 3,000 people gathered in Rudyard to help the community celebrate its Golden Anniversary over the week end. . . . The huge throngs of people that witnessed and participated in the celebration were kept constantly occupied as the well organized event was kept rolling smoothly throughout its duration.

The permanent population of Rudyard at the time of the anniversary celebration was less than half the number who returned for the festivities. Even so, this small number meant that Rudyard was still a reasonably viable town as viability is defined in this region. On the other hand, Robsart, Saskatchewan, on the CPR main line, celebrated its seventy-fifth anniversary in 1989 as a ghost village, with only two families, although over a thousand people attended the occasion. Such demographic disparity is even more noticeable in reunions in country neighborhoods, where the number of remaining farm families may be as little as 5 percent of the original settlement population.

But the relative loss of population in these communities is an impetus to celebration and reunion, not something to forget. Loss of population is understood as an inevitable consequence of the experimental nature of the settlement process. The fact that people departed is not a confession of failure; it is only one facet of an experience with many dimensions. The experience of settlement, of living together, lives in memory. But each celebration tends to attract fewer people, as the population ages and subsequent generations find it increasingly difficult to remember the past. Most of the returnees in Rudyard's celebration were second-generation offspring of the original settlers. In 1960 those people would have been in their 50s or early 60s, and many or all of them would have lived in Rudyard at least briefly. But by the third and fourth generations, like the folks who came to Robsart in 1989, the nostalgia incentive might be weaker, and one might expect a smaller turnout. However, such predictions are tricky: there is a cyclical pattern of decline and renewal in the towns and communities, and also in the memories of people. The size and prosperity of the town or district is not the issue; it is the place itself—the place where the memories begin, and where they can be renewed or captured by people who never really experienced them. And they are simply fun: the concerts, ball games, art exhibits, and dancing make for a day or two of sheer enjoyment.

Critics of the settlement of this section of the U.S. Great Plains, with its difficult climate, marginal resources, and remoteness, have their point. No doubt the region could have had a more carefully planned settlement, based on better knowledge of the environment and its economic potential. And the railroads probably created too many towns, but since most of them were planned in the 1880s it was not possible to foresee the automobile age.

Most of those small towns died on the vine, so to speak, a couple of generations later. And there is no doubt that, from certain perspectives, the whole homesteading venture in the northern plains was a "mistake"—a mistake paid for with hardship and loss of community in later years. But on the other hand, the whole effort produced remarkable human beings, a wealth of participant-produced experiential and historical literature, and a valid footnote to the history of North America.

Chapter 12

Lives: Town Builders

The people who built or developed towns on the homestead frontier were determined to make them up-to-date, integral parts of the larger urban world. But since the towns were rooted in the agricultural economy of the countryside, they also had to maintain a rural profile. The term "hick town" was common in both Canada and the United States, but it had more of a bite in the States, since the town builders and investors there were more aggressively boosterish in outlook, with backgrounds of lively capitalist activity in the Midwest, Texas, and the Central Plains, where "progress" was already well established.

The pace of development in the Canadian towns seems to have been a bit more leisurely, the tastes less flamboyant, and the emphasis on kinship, solidarity, and family ownership greater. Many of the town-builder types had rural backgrounds themselves, hailing from small towns and country villages in eastern Canada. At the other extreme, the big entrepreneurs of the cities, such as Calgary or Winnipeg, derived from elite families in Toronto or England. The well-known Galts of Lethbridge, Alberta, exemplify the entrepreneurial family in Canada (see den Otter 1982). Founded by brothers Alexander and Eliot Galt, the company developed coal mines and built short-line railroads to move the coal, established irrigation companies and a major real estate company, and built part of the "Turkey Track," a narrow gauge railway connecting Lethbridge and Great Falls, Montana. They eventually sold the line to Jim Hill and the Great Northern. In 1901 all Galt companies were combined in a giant holding enterprise, Alberta Irrigation and Railway Company, which in 1912 was bought by the Canadian Pacific. The Galts built Lethbridge's first general hospital, the building that now houses the Lethbridge Historical Society and Museum. A comparison of the Galt history with the saga of the Conrads (e.g., in Murphy's 1983 biography of C. E. Conrad, the Montana and Missouri River basin trader and entrepreneur) reveals some of the differences in the entrepreneuring spirit in Canada and the United States: the Conrads come off as tougher, more energetic frontier characters, while the Galts project an image of decorous British frontier elitism.

Presenting accurate biographical materials on town builders and their adventures in small entrepreneurship presents a problem in the writing of local history. Financing and building a quasi-urban economy on an undeveloped frontier, even under the most equable conditions, required a good deal of energy, ambition, and a willingness to make sharp deals and eliminate opponents. If the historian is in a mood to celebrate progress, the activities of these town builders are presented as constructive and beneficent. Their questionable deals, exploitative energies, and substantial profit-taking, which had to be large in order to raise capital and to uphold their facade of prosperity and reliability, are ignored in most of the authorized biographies. One must locate unofficial or later journalistic accounts produced by outsiders in order to discover what really happened. Moreover, most of the businessmen and investors who established towns projected an aura of gentility, a celebration of middle-class values presented as a means to assure prospective investors who might be frightened of the frontier. They represented the passing of the frontier and the coming of orderly, bourgeois civilization. They were at the opposite pole from the remarkable characters of the early frontier, people like Mike Connelly, a refugee from potato-famine Ireland who in his lifetime was a logger, drover, freightman, boatman, Benton trader, butcher, rancher, and horse thief and who fought in some of the Nez Percé battles, visited Sitting Bull at Fort Walsh, rode as a cowhand with Charley Russell, and served as Chouteau county commissioner (for a family history, see LHB 78: 80–88).

But while the businessmen were taking over, the local culture of the earlier frontier was in the hands of large numbers of single men without kinship or locality ties, adventurers, cowhands, highwaymen, professional women, barkeeps, and the like—people who supplied the work force and the entertainment industry for both the towns and the country, but who hardly possessed a genteel lifestyle. As time passed, this older, rougher behavioral style, featured in the national entertainment media, came to characterize the Wild West, the lusty culture of the frontier. Attitudes toward this culture were and are ambivalent. Just as classic Western movies portray, for instance, the local bankers first as unscrupulous villains and then as models of rectitude, so the local historians alternate between praising the local capitalists as solid citizens and the local desperadoes as culture heroes, or depending on the attitudes of the particular writers, vice versa. These themes emerge in some of the biographical sketches we have culled from the local history literature.

Some Secondary Capitalists on the Hi Line

"Secondary capitalist" is the term Dave Walter, a historian and librarian at the Montana Historical Society, uses to refer to "a phalanx of unrecognized, influential Montana entrepreneurs arrayed in the background twilight" (Walter 1989:34). Walter notes that the standard histories of Montana feature men like Marcus Daly, the "Copper King," and others whose national recognition was due to extreme wealth and flamboyant exploits—building fantastic frontier mansions or acquiring wives who wound up as professional entertainers. But the locally produced histories feature a different breed of entrepreneur variously called "founding fathers," "pioneer town-builders," or "chief benefactors." These were men who brought the first significant capital into the small community and used it to establish businesses, construct buildings, and donate money and institutions to the community. These men and their wives seemingly were satisfied with a smaller arena of success, the big frog in the small puddle was the aphorism in use at the time. Why did they decide to limit their scope of operations or fame to the locality? Possibly because of the timing of their operations. They came early, settled in a new town, invested in what seemed to be a sure thing, tied up their assets in local real estate and political connections, and found it easier to stay and enjoy the puddle.

Walter's article on secondary capitalists features one of these men: Simon Pepin, a classic type of the Canadian-American West. Born in Quebec in 1840 in a "large French-Canadian Catholic family," he left home at fourteen and headed straight for New England, then to St. Louis, and by 1863 he was working as a teamster on the Oregon Trail. In Utah he joined a party of gold-seekers and wound up in Virginia City, Montana, with about three thousand other men and a few women. Gold was not for him. Pepin invested in wagons and teams and became one of Montana's "most reliable wagon bosses" by the 1870s (Walter 1989:35). Surplus cash went into supplies for trading posts and general stores; people who couldn't pay bills in cash did so in cattle and land, and so Pepin became a cattleman supplying beef to military posts and miners. The U.S. Army was in the midst of frontier post construction, and Pepin took contracts, becoming a principal builder for three posts in the 1870s and '80s. Ranching became his major business as land suitable for range became available and Pepin had the cash to buy it. By 1887, when the GNR track moved across northern Montana, the Pepin family was able to sell land and water sources to the railroad. This meant they were able to control the location of railroad division points, of which Havre was the most important. And this led to the next turn of the commercial wheel: retail business. The Broadwater-Pepin Mercantile had branch general stores across northern Montana and ranches in the Alberta section of the Cypress Hills and in the Bear's Paw Mountains. Pepin built his fourteen-room "mansion" in Havre; it was modest compared to the huge houses built by the mining, cattle, banking, and trading entrepreneurs of Helena and Fort Benton, but imposing enough for the locality.

Pepin's philanthropic efforts took many forms: loans to businessmen whose establishments were injured in town fires; a regular program of personal loans at modest interest rates to small ranchers; donations of land to the Catholic Church and to town parks; donations for church construction; and financing for town office buildings. By 1901 he wound up as the major stockholder in the First National Bank of Havre, and eventually he negotiated a merger with the Security Bank, becoming president of the new enlarged business. He died in 1914 with a total valued estate of $1 million, peanuts compared to the mining and cattle barons but substantial for a secondary capitalist on the Hi Line.

Heading about thirty miles east on the Hi Line we come to Chinook, Montana, another GNR stop and the headquarters of many of the early Bear's Paw Mountains ranching enterprises. Pepin's analogue in Chinook was Andrew S. Lohman, and we can quote part of his biography:

> Andrew S. Lohman was probably influenced in his choice of a home territory by the stories which his father told concerning his own days in the Far West. Soon after he had completed his schooling, he headed west, in the early years, where he remained until 1879. His subsequent travels took him to Leadville, Aspen and San Juan, Colorado, then to Arizona, Mexico, and ultimately New Mexico.... He then traveled to Mexico and thence to Alaska, arriving in the northern territory in time to sign a petition changing the name of the

> capital from Harrisburg to Juneau. At that time there were only one hundred and forty-eight white people there. . . .
>
> On coming to Montana in 1889, he and Mrs. Lohman first located at Chinook, where they opened a store that same year. Later Mr. Lohman purchased some sheep and acquired ranch acreage, where he built up his holdings to twenty thousand head of sheep. With the assistance of his capable wife, he then opened another store in the town named Lohman in their honor. They helped in many ways in the development of this town. Andrew S. Lohman had an honorable record of mercantile transactions. In his many years in retailing, with extensive credit advances to settlers and prospectors at all times on his books, he never once resorted to the law to collect a debt. Mr. Lohman sold his big store in 1900, when he built the Lohman Block. The herd of twenty thousand sheep which he built up he disposed of at the time he turned his attention to the banking business. It was in 1916 that he founded the Lohman Farmers State Bank at Lohman; and realizing the need for another such institution in the region, he established the Lohman State Bank at Chinook years later. . . . It was Mr. Lohman who promoted the construction of the electric light and power plant at Chinook, personally paying the costs of its building out of his own finances along with a few other men. In addition to the honor of having the town of Lohman named after him, he was elected the first mayor of Chinook in 1901. (Burlingame and Toole 1957, 3:135)

This was a substantial citizen, who "never once resorted to the law to collect a debt" (one wonders how he *did* collect his debts). To get into banking he sold 20,000 sheep. We also learn that he financed the power plant, but one supposes that he got a fair return on his investment, since he eventually sold the town lighting system to the Montana Power Company. Mr. Lohman was also a director of the old Stockman's Bank in Fort Benton, a financial center for the local livestock industry.

The Lohmans, like other small-town entrepreneurs, brought urbanized tastes with them to the frontier. Lillian Miller, the wife of one of the Bear's Paw ranching pioneers, came with her family from Iowa but grew up in Chinook and lived for the school months with the Lohmans. She described the first Lohman house in her memoir "I Remember Montana." The Lohmans at the time were operators of one or two general stores and had come to Chinook only a few years earlier.

The Lohmans lived above the store. A long stairway led up to these quarters from the back of the store. There was also a door to the street at the bottom, so you could go outside without having to go through the store itself. At the top of the steps was a large room which served as a store room. Furniture of all kinds, mattresses, dishes, kitchen utensils—almost anything needed in a house could be found there. From this store room two doors led into the four-roomed living quarters, one to the kitchen, the other to the parlor. Our bedroom with two beds, Lillie's and mine, was back of the kitchen and had to be shared with the house keeper. The other bedroom was Mr. and Mrs. Lohman's, opening into the parlor, so if we ever chased each other as children do, we could race from room to room, through the store room and back to the kitchen again.

In those days [mid-1890s] furniture was very ornate. The large mahogany bed in the Lohman bedroom was beautifully carved, chairs of mahogany or walnut had carvings on their high backs and the seats were covered with brocaded satin. The mahogany clothes wardrobe which held their clothes had doors which were also richly carved.

Thick, flowered axminster carpets covered the floors and full-length Venetian lace curtains fell to the carpet below. It was all very elegant to me.

The kitchen and dining room, combined, was just an ordinary everyday kitchen but it was a busy center presided over by the house keeper. There were seven to cook for, since the clerks took their meals there, and they ate in shifts, so there would always be two clerks in the store at all times. The housekeeper . . . had to do the cleaning as well as the cooking. The washings and ironings were sent to the little Chinaman, Lee Cum, who had a laundry across the street.

Mrs. Lohman, herself, dressed meticulously and, perhaps, even a little more elegantly than we, now, would think proper. She was a beautiful woman, with soft, dark, naturally wavy hair which was always perfectly groomed. Her complexion was clear and she used no makeup, which at that time would have been considered vulgar and common. . . . She was postmistress of Chinook and the post office was located in one corner of the store. This was a popular place. . . . In addition to these activities she was the official bookkeeper for the store, and their private business as well. She knew prices in every department and Mr. Lohman relied on her for everything. He would occasionally remark, "Well, I had never had the education Lily had." He had been a miner in Butte . . . where they had been married and lived before coming to Chinook.

The Lohmans did it up brown. When they completed a large warehouse near the depot, they gave a huge ball to which the entire community—townspeople and country folk—was invited. Mrs. Miller tells us that "Everything was to be free so naturally crowds gathered from near and far." The new warehouse was the ballroom, and the Chinook Band supplied the music for the called quadrilles. Mrs. Lohman, we learn, "engaged a seamstress who came to the house to make her gown. It was a lovely creation of canary-colored brocaded satin with a long train." Thus the Lohman family became part of local history. "The death of Andrew S. Lohman occurred on October 8, 1930. He will be remembered as a kind, industrious, and intelligent man, who was never too busy with the important commercial and civic interests of his community to give a friendly greeting, or to help a less fortunate person in need. His generosity manifested itself in many charitable things he did to help his fellow men" (Sanders 1913:136).

H. Earl Clack was another secondary capitalist who wound up in Havre. He was born in Texas, the son of a Confederate veteran and rancher and judge, whose hegira northward to Montana is reminiscent of the journey that forms the basis of Larry McMurtry's novel *Lonesome Dove* (1985). Family members came and went between Texas and Montana for several years. At the age of eighteen, Earl left Texas and joined his sister, who had married in Havre, and after a trip or two back to Texas he moved to Havre and never left. He had enough cash to buy a wagon and two horses and had, according to his biography (Burlingame and Toole 1957, 3:421–23), "plenty of self-confidence." His brother Philip soon joined him and became a prominent Hill County rancher. The Clack business expanded into feed and hay, and by this time (1905) the homesteaders were beginning to produce grain, so Clack established the first grain elevator on the GNR tracks. Plowing back his profits from grain, feed, hay, and cattle as a sideline, Clack in 1913 decided to enter the pioneer oil distributing business, in recognition of the growing importance of the automobile. Becoming the local agent for Continental Oil, he soon established his own business and developed about 200 sales agencies for various petroleum products. Meanwhile his grain and feed business prospered in the expansion of farming and ranching. His elevators and mills also carried complete lines of hardware.

Earl Clack built business blocks in Havre, financed hospitals and irrigation companies, and gave to local charities. He was a member and officer of several fraternal organizations, and served, as did Andrew Lohman, in numerous civic and political appointed positions. Clack retained ownership of several farms and experimented with hybrid corn before it became a major commercial undertaking. In the 1950s his oil company merged with Husky, a national refiner and distributor, and with this venture the name of Earl Clack became known in financial and business circles well beyond the Hi Line.

The wives of these capitalists also played important roles in town-building. Mrs. Lohman helped to found, finance, and manage a Catholic-Indian missionary school for the then-landless Cree-Ojibwa Indians camped in the Bear's Paw hills south of Chinook (now the Rocky Boy Reservation). She was active in various church groups and clubs and was also the brains behind at least some of the business. Mrs. Clack participated in a variety of women's organizations and Presbyterian church groups, and was active in parent-teacher organizations and was chairperson of the regional Girl Scouts Council. She helped to found, and for a number of years directed, the local H. Earl Clack Museum and Havre's historical society. She served as a district president of the Montana Federation of Women's clubs. Both women had pioneer backgrounds, and both were brought up in small towns, Mrs. Lohman, née Martin, in Butte; Mrs. Clack, née Turner, in Texas.

In most of the town-based entrepreneuring families, both husbands and wives had cosmopolitan interests, and while most of them operated farms and ranches, they did so because their business depended on the country industries and because their financial base included land and stock taken in trade. It was this mixture of industries, an automatic diversity of investment made necessary by the very nature of the frontier development economy, that contributed to their success and at the same time helps explain their devotion to their locality.

The situation was much the same on the Canadian side. Each of the towns along the CPR had local capitalists who worked hard to create an economic and infrastructural base for the community. In Canada, mercantile enterprises seem to be somewhat more common as the basis of business life. There were fewer opportunities for the development of local private finance because of the domination of business by eastern Canadian banks. Large, often British-financed family companies, such as the Galts in Lethbridge and the Burns family in Calgary, sometimes established and controlled town enterprises, but there was still room for home-grown "secondary capitalists" on the Canadian side.

Storekeepers: The Dixons of Maple Creek, Saskatchewan

The bills of the Dixon Bros. Store in Maple Creek bore this heading in 1909:

> DIXON BROS.
>
> Wholesale and Retail Dealers in
> DRY GOODS, GROCERIES, PROVISIONS, BOOTS AND SHOES, CLOTHING, STATIONERY, HARDWARE, LUMBER, ETC.
>
> Interest at the rate of 10 per cent. per annum charged on all overdue accounts.

The store was opened in 1883, the year after the CPR tracks came to Maple Creek, and by 1909 homesteaders were flocking in, getting off the CPR "settler specials" by the dozens every day. The business changed from a modest country store to a general emporium and business practices also changed. If the Dixons had actually charged 10 percent interest on all overdue bills they would have closed overnight. Few of the settlers could pay in cash; the majority had to use credit, repaying whenever they could. The Dixons not only eased up on interest but were lenient about repayment, and when the store finally closed in the 1950s it had thousands of dollars in uncollected bills and thousands in debts to suppliers.

Note the "ETC." in the bill heading. There was hardly anything in the way of consumer goods and farming or construction equipment manufactured in the nineteenth and early twentieth century that the Dixons did not sell. Their suppliers, as can be seen by looking at the annual letter books from 1886 to 1900 in the Saskatchewan Archives, were spread over eastern and midwestern Canada and the United States. Photos of the store during the height of the homesteading period show farm machinery, tools of all kinds, tents, furniture, automobiles, dishes, yard goods, ready-mades, tarpaulins, milk bottles, and harness and saddlery equipment, although by 1910 the town also had specialty stores retailing most of these items. The Dixons stocked or ordered these diverse items simply because they had the trade and because it was convenient for a country customer to shop for all his needs in one place, pile them into a wagon, and take off.

Throughout the history of the enterprise, family members played important roles, and the complete family history book runs to 200 pages. Two Dixon brothers, John and Isaac, married the Dawson sisters in Oshawa, and the women joined their husbands later in 1883, after their children were born and could withstand the shock of moving. Isaac's son Alfred later operated the store and other family members worked there as clerks and bookkeepers. One nephew, a Dawson, was sent to Bottineau, North Dakota, to open a branch store and to look for gold in the Sweetgrass Hills of Montana (he failed to find a significant deposit). The many relatives back home in Peterborough, Ontario, were visited frequently, and younger members of the various families were accustomed to spending holidays in the respective western or eastern homes. The children of the original brothers married ranchers, farmers, businessmen, and professionals in Maple Creek and other western towns, and from time to time extended family reunions were held in the old three-story frame house (which some time later became the Maple Creek Community Hospital). At the height of the Dixon saga, about 1910, as many as eighteen people lived permanently in the house, along with a rotating assortment of visiting relatives.

Like other merchants of the period, the Dixons took a lot of stock in trade, horses in the early days, cattle later. The family established two ranches south of town, and from time to time they farmed other properties they had bought or traded. Profits from the lucrative settler business in the first decade of the century had accumulated to the point where the Dixons felt they could branch out into the booming raw materials industries springing up all over western Canada, so they bought into a venture called Alberta Clay Products Co. This organization was an American-Canadian scheme, set up on the basis of interest shown in clay and ceramic products by a consortium headquartered in Saint Paul, Minnesota. A stock company was formed, with shareholders from Alberta along with the Dixons, and a plant built in Medicine Hat to make use of the extensive clay pits in the vicinity. John Dixon apparently owned a controlling share, and other members of the extended family seemed to have had some as well. Dixon became vice president of the company, and he hired an American as manager of the plant. Other shareholders accused the manager of inefficiency and attempted to discharge him. Dixon defended him and, as events seem to indicate, justifiably.

The Dixons then bought out most of the other shareholders and established a Canadian board of directors. However, this board soon forced out the manager. Eventually another Minnesota company bought some stock from the Dixons, but acrimonious disputes over the management and operation of the plant continued, and eventually the Canadian board members tried to take control of the company from the Dixons. The Minnesota company defended the Dixons and tried to stop the Canadian takeover. The international quarrels went on and on, and eventually the

Dixons sold out at a loss. The correspondence, available in the Saskatchewan Provincial Archives in Regina, suggests that John Dixon lacked the aggressive competitiveness usually associated with these early development companies and was unable to fight off rapacious businessmen determined to take control. The letters suggest that Dixon was aware of the machinations of these people, but was too trusting to fight them on their own terms.

Trouble also developed inside the family. A third brother, Albert E. Dixon, a lawyer, had stayed in Peterborough to manage the financial property and business of the Whites, the family of their mother. This man kept no books, paid no bills, was eventually sued by creditors, and left town. The estate had to be liquidated in order to pay the creditors. The correspondence in the Saskatchewan archives gives a picture of a well-meaning man, anxious to placate his brothers and to do his best but unable to handle complicated financial dealings. The chief problem seems to have been his willingness to accept unregistered mortgages as security for loans and other hand-shake transactions, and because his bookkeeping was badly managed he defaulted on payments to mortgage-holders and failed to pay bills and to record insurance premiums. John Dixon eventually went to Ontario and arranged with a law firm to liquidate the Ontario business.

The Dixon brothers appear to have had a working relationship in which Isaac—and later his son Alfred—operated the big store in Maple Creek and John handled the investments of surplus proceeds of the retail business. The Alberta Clay venture was the largest of these investments and the only one in which John tried to run a business outside of Maple Creek. But he held securities from several companies who were suppliers for the store, dealing in candy, meat, and canned goods. He also held stock in several insurance companies for which the Dixons acted as agents (it was common all through the West for local general storekeepers to write insurance policies and act as agents for various financial businesses). John was in charge of the extensive ranching business, handling transactions with the provincial government over leases, water rights, grain and feed companies, meat packers, and rail cattle shipment transactions.

The Dixons, like other secondary capitalist families, were deeply involved in the civic affairs of Maple Creek. They kept the books and supervised the management of the community hospital; for a time they managed the newspaper, when the editor and manager of the paper absconded with funds; they planned and managed the first public water system; and John for a decade was the local postmaster, since the post office was located in the store.

As the business gradually dwindled in the 1920s and '30s under the management of two second-generation Dixon brothers—Alfred and Dawson, both sons of Isaac (usually known to the family by his middle name, Chester)—the store business was all that was left. John had died in 1918 and most of the investments had gone sour or been sold off to meet bills and to provide cash to the family members according to the terms of his will. The limited activity of the store had to support, in whole or part, nine persons in three domiciles. During the 1930s the managers of the store managed to accumulate a small fortune in uncollected bills, which also meant considerable debt. Municipality taxes had not been paid for some time, and when Alfred died in 1966 the store was given over to the town in lieu of a cash settlement. The historic old building became a controversial subject in the town council, with several members campaigning to have it turned into a historical museum and the others eager to tear it down and sell the valuable property (on the main street, fronting the railroad) to commercial interests. The latter position won out.

The glory days of Dixon Bros. began in the 1890s and lasted until about 1920. Their main mission was to supply and launch the incoming settlers. Attempts by John Dixon to convert the business into a diversified financial and production business, on the model of other western Canadian family-owned development companies, all failed, and, as the retail business dominated, the assets were distributed among family members until nothing was left but a hulking stone building. Family was the secret of the Dixon brothers' early success, but in the end it was the cause of its decline and death.

There is, however, the issue of heritage. The Dixons represented the nineteenth-century old guard of Canadian emigration, the British Isles-Ontario-bourgeois component that became especially significant in the development of Saskatchewan society and politics. The Dixons came from this milieu and brought it to Saskatchewan, where it served them well as a replica of their original Ontario undertaking. As the frontier developed and more aggressive settlers began to dominate the trade, the Dixons made some effort to cope but ultimately found it too individualistic an effort. In Alberta and across the line in Montana the economic situation was in general more rugged and open. But of course the small-town storekeeper profile was present everywhere, and the Dixons are an especially interesting case because of their distinctive Canadian cultural patterning and unusually large family.

Shorty Young: A Recreational Entrepreneur on the Hi Line

Not all local capitalists in Montana were interested exclusively in "legitimate" business. One who wasn't was Christopher Young Jr., called "Shorty." Here are two contrasting biographical sketches:

> Christopher W. Young, Jr., one of three children, attended school in Buffalo, Rochester, and Syracuse, New York. When he was only thirteen years of age he went to Canada, and was employed by a friend of the family who was in the insurance business. . . . Mr. Young after coming west spent a short time at Fargo, North Dakota, before locating in Havre. In 1906 he bought a mercantile business which he conducted for several years. He put up the Montana Hotel. . . . Much of his capital has gone into real estate, ranch lands and mines. . . . He is president of the Bear Paw Mining and Milling Company and president of the Rocky Boy Mining and Milling Company. . . . For six years he was a member of the city council. He belongs to various Masonic bodies, and is also a past president of the Fraternal Order of Eagles. . . . He is a Presbyterian. (Raymer, ed. 1930:576)

> During his lifetime, Christopher W. Young was known as a gambling house and bordello operator with a reputation as a practical joker. Born in Buffalo, New York on April 1, 1878, he came to Havre around 1900 and owned and operated a number of entertainment establishments including the Mint, the Honky Tonk and the Parlor House. After his death in 1944, most of his property was put into a perpetual trust to be used for the "maintenance, care and education of the poor and needy of Havre." (Yuill and Yuill 1986:31)

In 1980 the Montana Historical Society arranged to have Shorty Young's house at 419 Fourth Avenue in Havre listed on the National Register of Historic Places. Shorty bought the house from a Great Falls brewer, who acquired it from a bankrupt former Havre mayor. It was, and is, an interesting house: a large one-story bungalow with hand-painted friezes, Japanese wallpaper, solid mahogany woodwork, and a garden courtyard.

Gary Wilson provides a detailed sketch of Shorty Young's persona:

> Shorty was "Shorty" because he was only about 5′ 2″. But he was well proportioned and wiry, almost as if he were a wrestler or an

acrobat. The blue-eyed, brown-haired Young always had a big cigar in his mouth. He generally wore suits and loved striped shirts. His most outstanding personality trait was his sense of humor, which never rested. Young was a rather quiet, polite person in public, but a complete extrovert among his friends. Shorty also had a strong, stubborn and cold-blooded side that knew no quarter. (Wilson 1985:10)

And Shorty Young was also a secondary capitalist, a builder and benefactor of the town of Havre; his charities, his investments, and, of course, his estimable services in providing recreation and entertainment for males in this Hi-Line railroad town in the early twentieth century won him a secure place in its history. No citizen of Havre is as well known, and his exploits have in some measure become a tourist attraction. Copies of his candid biography by Gary Wilson (1985) are best-sellers in local stores.

Shorty Young headed west after a brief sojourn in Ontario, where he apparently tried horse racing. His journey along the northern route was classic: New York-Minnesota-Fargo-Montana. He landed in Havre not by chance. Havre already, in the late 1880s, had a wide reputation as a hell-raising community. It was a kind of focal point for loose males. Fort Assiniboine, the major U.S. Army post in northern Montana, had a couple hundred young soldiers; the horse and cattle outfits in the Bear's Paw Mountains and elsewhere south of the Milk River supplied ranchers and cowhands; the GNR used Havre—created it—as a main division point. Assorted landless Indians, tribal Cree, métis wanderers, a few bandits, and other men interested in a good time outnumbered the small business class (people like the Pepins and several other French, Canadian, and American entrepreneurs). But there was money to be made in Havre, hell-raising town or not; it was a railroad center, a major crossing of the Milk River, a port for the settlers, and a service center for Canadian settlers beyond the boundary. Jim Hill, the railroad baron, did not live in Havre, but he visited frequently and had a vested interest in maintaining the community. From time to time he maneuvered its politics, installing reform mayors, instigating cleanup operations, and arranging business financing.

The story of Young's operations is a complex one, with numerous establishments opening and closing as the town worthies and reform mayors and sheriffs attempted to close him down. His principal establishment in the period between 1904 and 1910 was a large three-story frame structure called the Concert Hall or the Montana European Hotel or, more familiarly, the Honky Tonk (this was the "Montana Hotel" noted in the first of the two biographies). In contemporary photos, its interior looks like a Hollywood set for a typical western dance hall/bar/gambling joint/vaudeville palace: a large room with boxes and a bar along the sides, tables on the main floor, and a stage at the rear for performances. In the vicinity Shorty also operated a high-toned house of prostitution, the Parlor, and a low-rent version of the same called the Crib, shaped like one of the 1920's linear "tourist courts," with a girl in each room or two-room suite. Shorty also opened a classy bar downtown, called the Mint, which later became a regular vaudeville theater. The Honky Tonk burned down once and was rebuilt, then burned again, probably by arson.

Shorty's principal wholesale business interest was liquor. Bootlegging was a major activity in Havre after prohibition began in Canada in 1916. Shorty opened a saloon a few feet from the international boundary north of Havre for the convenience of Canadians who wanted a drink, but he also ran liquor into Canada. With the advent of prohibition in the United States in 1919, the direction of flow reversed, and Young became a major supplier of Canadian booze to Montana. The success of the bootlegging business in northern Montana was due in part to the Royal Canadian Mounted Police, who established depots on the Canadian side where the runners picked it up for the dash across the border. The liquor was pre-taxed—unbonded—and the RCMP monitored the operation in order to make sure no one redirected it back into the Canadian market. About forty miles north of Havre was Govenlock, a Saskatchewan village that served as the principal semi-official liquor depot.

Shorty was in and out of court, raided and re-opened several times. He operated a clandestine brewery producing fake Canadian beer in the tunnels and catacombs underneath the Honky Tonk. These premises also included a speakeasy, with secret exits and entrances. When the sheriff and his men tried to get into the known entrance, Shorty would usher his patrons out through one of the tunnels and sometimes confront the lawmen in front, coming around from the rear, asking what the fuss was all about.

Shorty used the money he made from his liquor interests and recreational establishments to invest in ranches, businesses, and town real estate. By virtue of his investments and wealth, and his undoubted philanthropic activities—Christmas baskets for the poor, and the like—it was hard for the town fathers to stop him. They nevertheless repeatedly tried, though Shorty always managed to start up again. His posthumous benefactions were genuine. His will created a trust estate on the basis of rents and other income derived from real estate properties. The money was divided among the several fraternal organizations of which Shorty was a member, to be used for various beneficial purposes: a swimming pool, playgrounds, hospital equipment, medical attention for children, and youth camps.

Shorty was married three times, although only two of his wives are identified in the local historical accounts. His first wife, Lillian Nichols, who appears to have been the principal tastemaker in the decoration of the famous house and was the owner of a white automobile, several horses, and an extensive wardrobe, divorced Shorty in 1919. Shorty then married Margaret Coughlin, a former waitress from Butte, also known as "Mag the Rag." The Youngs gave parties, using the basement ballroom in the big bungalow, but there was a social gulf between Shorty's crowd and the elite of Havre. Shorty joined the Masonic lodge in Chicago, since the Havre chapter would not permit him to enter it. After he returned to Havre a legitimate Mason, the local chapter still refused to let him take part in any of its activities. Nevertheless, Shorty named the Masons, along with his other fraternal lodges, as beneficiaries of his trust.

Christopher W. Young Jr. died in 1944. His life in Havre can be profiled—as it was in the first of the two biographical sketches—as that of a solid entrepreneur and town builder, and in one sense that is what he was. He brought capital into Havre, invested his own gains in the town, and participated in civic activities to the extent permitted by the town leadership. In the eyes of the elite Shorty sponsored and built the other side of the Christian, middle-class value system: "vice," masculine entertainment, the exploitation of women as objects of pleasure, games of chance, rumrunning. Shorty's career stands midway between the fast and loose days of the open frontier, with its gun-wearing, hard-drinking characters, highwaymen, gamblers, and unscrupulous land promoters, and on the other hand the organized, syndicated urban criminality of the twentieth century. His activities reached a peak after 1910 as the towns became urbanized and local capital had accumulated. He moved into the prohibition era with gusto, and his activities during that period are more reminiscent of Chicago than of a frontier town in Montana.

Shorty also presents an interesting problem in the writing of local history in postfrontier societies. He is now a kind of tourist attraction, something for the town to boast about, but always with an embarrassed grin in recognition of the conflicting values: Respectability is a virtue and the thing that makes a town civilized and responsible, but at the same time the old days were lots of fun and something that attracts attention. More has been written about Shorty Young than about any other early citizen of

Havre and the Hi Line, with the exception of Brother W. W. Van Orsdael, the colorful and adventurous Lutheran missionary and itinerant minister, church founder, and all-around inspirationist. In other words, the Line's two best-known citizens were a man of Bacchus and a man of God. The men of Mammon—the Lohmans and the Clacks—seem colorless next to them.

Chapter 13

Lives: Country Men and Women

The settlement of the Canadian-American West was a planned political, technological, and economic venture. But beyond all the bureaucratic involvements were the individual settlers who came to the frontier by themselves or in small family or neighborhood groups. The process of individual adaptation merged with the building of district communities and eventually towns, counties, municipalities, states, and provinces. In the autobiographical materials presented in this chapter we focus on the life trajectories of individual homesteaders and their lives with family and community.

The chapter contains portions of autobiographical documents for two men and three women who spent most of their lives in country districts and small towns. They were real settlers, although we have not used their real names. Three of the five crisscrossed the international boundary in search of their life goals, and participated in the Canadian-American rural cultural pattern. None of the writers displays any particular consciousness of ethnicity or nationality. Their social and economic positions vary: the first man, whom we call Fred Haas, was an odd-jobs worker who tried farming but failed at it or gave it up. The second man, Frank Adamson, was a homesteader who stuck to his farm and eventually made it pay, the kind of man for whom Fred Haas repeatedly worked. Sarah Evans was a working woman, as we call her; after an abusive first marriage she supported herself in various jobs—a kind of feminine analogue to Fred Haas. The other two autobiographies, of Elvie Jones and Kate Mills, are both by homestead farm women, but their experiences and approaches to life are quite different.

Our choice of documents was based mainly on the amount of detail included by the writers, and their ability to portray experience and feeling. Above all, we looked for descriptions of life events we considered typical for settlers after our reading of shorter accounts in the local history books and our own field research. Our selection was, of course, limited; most people do not write their life histories. People who write autobiographies do so for a number of reasons. They may feel a need to create a narrative ordering of their experiences over a lifetime or they may feel a need to explain their lives to others, and in the process to justify their actions to themselves. They may be encouraged or persuaded by others (family, social club, historical society) that their experiences are of particular value, in which case both inner- and other-directed goals are part of the autobiographical rationale.

Strictly speaking, an autobiography should have a sequential or chronological organization of the lifetime recorded and include some reflection on the meanings of that lifetime. We found very few that follow the conventional format of autobiography. The autobiographies we use begin with their own (or their family's) decision to emigrate, then describe the successive moves and the resulting consequences for themselves and their families. Maturation is connected with work, and a successful life is tied to their own or family members' capacity for hard work and the establishment of a family household and enterprise.

Autobiographies are usually written for a more or less conscious reason. In the documents we use, such reasons are indicated in three out of the five. Fred Haas states that he wants simply to get the record straight—for himself or for the shadowy members of his family he mentions from time to time but never really deals with in detail. As he remarks about his experiences during the Great Depression, "You Readers will think this is all made up, if you don't believe this just go out and try it for one year." Frank Adamson states that the encouragement given to him to write about his experiences by his family was an important incentive. Kate Mills recorded her experiences in response to a direct request from the Burdett Women's Institute. But Elvie Jones and Sarah Evans do not tell us why they decided to write, although the reader may find some hints.

We decided to perform some modest editorial work on the documents: slight rearrangements of passages and a certain amount of commentary and analysis. The amount of editing with respect to punctuation and spelling also varies, depending on the writing style; in general, we have done a minimum amount—enough to clarify passages but not enough to disguise the diction. The greatest amount of editing we did was to punctuate and paragraph the long autobiography of Fred Haas. His spelling and syntax is eccentric. Throughout his document Haas uses capital letters as a means of emphasis; for example, his closing sentence reads as follows:

> Now I am nearing MY seventy eighth birthday IN a few days, I look back over my life IT has been one struggle AFTER struggle BUT I HAVE enjoyed it all made many friends and lost some, I always made the best of things, some were good and some were bad.

We decided to use fictitious names since some of the people mentioned in the documents were alive at the time of research, but also to lend a kind of archetypical sense to the individual cases. We do not believe that any of the documents contain embarrassing material, and since the writers or their representatives donated the documents to public institutions, they apparently intended them to be read. The experience of emigration and settlement is something to be proud of, a record of a heroic era.

Country Men

Fred Haas was an itinerant laborer, a type the northern plains had (and still has) in great number, mobile, single men: cowboys, lumbermen, railroad workers, teamsters, bartenders, gamblers, and farmhands, to name a few. The most remarkable thing about Fred's autobiography is that he wrote it, or that a man with his limited education and hard life found the time and repose to do so. From internal evidence it might be guessed that since he wrote it after his retirement it represented for him some sort of culmination or capstone. Although Haas was a man on the fringes of organized society, he was aware that he had a life with a beginning, a middle, and an end.

Frank Adamson was the paterfamilias of a locally honored pioneer family; in short, he was everything that Fred was not. Frank was never Fred's employer, but he was very much the kind of man that Fred worked for repeatedly. And Frank displays many of the same attitudes that Fred found so exasperating: a lack of real understanding of the problems of the landless labor class, mixed with a degree of respect arising from the fact that without these men the farmer could not have done his chores. This relationship—the farm laborer and the farmer boss, the cowhand and the rancher—has been explored in novels and films, but rarely in serious scholarship. It is a strange relationship: men closely associated in hard work, in a degree of privation, fulfilling mutual needs and engaging in mutual exploitation, yet at the same time miles apart in social outlook and social status.

Fred Haas: Laborer, Farmer, Family Man

This account is recorded in a seventy-eight-page photocopy of a typewritten document in the Alberta Provincial Archives. Fred Haas begins with a few pages on his childhood in Iowa, then describes his move to Canada with parents and siblings when he was in his mid-teens. He spent the next sixty years in Canada—mostly Saskatchewan—going from job to job, trying to farm but failing at every attempt to establish a permanent occupation. He struggled with his tyrannical father, married and raised several children, and kept his family alive through the drought and depression with intermittent farm and construction labor jobs. He spent fourteen months in the Canadian Forces during World War II but was discharged before seeing active service, then continued through the rest of his working life in odd jobs. He returned to the United States after fifty-seven years in Canada, visited relatives, started traveling by bus and train across the States and Canada, returned to Canada and his life of temporary jobs, visited his sons and daughters, was hit by a car at seventy-six, recovered, and concluded his autobiography at seventy-eight: "I look back over my life it has been one struggle after struggle but I have enjoyed it all made many friends and lost some, I always made the best of things, some were good and some were bad."

The single young men who commonly moved from homestead to homestead were an essential source of manual labor on the agricultural and town frontiers. Without these men—and a few young working women, most of whom eventually married—the frontiers would have been starved for laborers and service attendants. They represented a crucial resource, yet they are the least known and certainly the most minimally celebrated individuals. They appear in the local history books by name, warranting at best a paragraph or two, often nothing more than a sentence: "He came out here from Minnesota in 1905, worked around on the ranches and took out a homestead, but left in 1911."

In contemporary jargon these people were losers; they never belonged to the larger social fabric, never or rarely engaged in civic activities, avoided the settled farming, ranching, or town societies, bankers, and businesses. Their friends were others like themselves, who quarreled with employers, worked hard but never for long in one job or locality. Yet many of these people, like Fred Haas, married and had families, struggled to keep them alive and well, and often witnessed their offspring's modest successes. Tragedy, accidents, privation, disappointment, and exploitation were their constant companions, yet many of them, like Fred, came through.

The Beginning: At Home in Iowa

> I was borned in the u.s.a. moving to canada before I was ten years old. I cant remember much of my early life, up till I was three or four years old my father was a labour worked at different jobs first in the wagon factory, then he went wheeling coal at the brick yards, unloading coal to dry the brick with. After two or three years of this work, dad decided he could make more money working for one of his brothers out on the farm. As dads brother was up in canada with his steam plowing outfit breaking up new land for the settlers, then he needed some one to look after the farm back in the states.

Fred's father started as a laborer, a farmer without a farm, a man who accepted opportunities as they came, whose main goal in life was to make a little money and keep the family eating. His first job was to look after his brother's farm, and he did so for three years, until Fred was six. By this time Fred and his brothers were ready for school, so his Dad notified his brother (who didn't like it) that he had to look for a place nearer the school. Dad found a job as general farmhand on a place with 500 hogs and 240 acres of cropland, and the family moved there.

> But dont forget it we came in for our share of the chores. We had to carry in wood and coal and the water pails had to be kept full as in those days there was no water in the house. . . . There was no inside toilet or hot water tap to turn. Our bath tub was mothers big wash boiler and tub. . . . In the winter we had to carry in large blocks of snow melting for soft water to wash with.

And they stayed in this "job," as Fred called it (not "home"), for two years. Then Dad quarreled with the owner about wages and the behavior of the boys, who seem to have taken to cutting off pigs' tails. Fred's father had secretly made arrangements to move to another, similar live-in job with the owner's son several miles up the road. So, when Fred turned six years old, they moved.

Fred's memory begins to work. He tells us a string of anecdotes about a young boy's life on an Iowa farm: falling out of the hay mow and knocking himself out on the barn floor, mule and horse runaways, chores and discomforts, and fun with his brothers and sister. In 1910, when Fred was nine, Dad decided he wanted to move to Canada, where his brother was making a living doing custom plowing for the incoming homesteaders. Uncle came down to help the family move, and they packed two freight cars full of farm machinery, horses, cows, and baggage. They apparently went up the old Grand Trunk north-south line through North Dakota, crossing into Saskatchewan at North Portal and staying for a few days in a little town, possibly Estevan.

> What a dismal place to call home, as it was snowing and blowing and cold that is what they called a blizzard. As we arrived in the morning we didnt have to go to school until afternoon what a school it was. When we got to school that afternoon we was treated as though we was from far away Russia and yet we had only travelled 1500 hundred miles we was called every thing they could lay their tongues on even the teacher called us immigrants, ask me what grade I had been down south, I told her grade seven well she said you haven't the brain of a six year old kid so why do you come up here trying to make out you are so much smarter than the ones borned in canada, then the teacher put me in grade one what a deal.

The two cars arrived a couple of weeks later, and the work of trying to make the farm near the town into a home for two families began. It lasted two years, and then "there was trouble amongst the two women," so the brothers agreed to split up. Uncle found Dad a half section of land to rent in the vicinity, and they divided up some of the stock and machinery. And so began another series of stories about a boy's life on a farm, this time in southern Saskatchewan. Fred says that "whenever anything happened at home I was always blamed, as I was the mischief maker around the house." In several incidents Father blames and punishes Fred for routine hijinks (although hijinks on these farms could be dangerous: spooking horses so his brother was thrown, being chased by a mean old cow, wrecking hay wagons). But Fred was strong and gradually took over much of the important farm work.

> While dad did the flunky work, such as building fence and he helped Mom in garden and with the milking. Some day he would tell me he would go drive the outfit as I had been a good boy, his idea for that kind of talk was just to make me feel important, he just wanted to see what kind of job I was doing out there. . . . he ask me if I wanted to get on the binder while he carried out the back swath, as that carrying out was pretty tough work for us little boys [Fred was about 12]. I got to run that machine quite a lot as dad liked to stook. . . . One time he ask me to help stook some oates but my back was too sore to stook so I told him, but it wasnt too sore when he caught me riding one of his steer calf, then I was in deep trouble. He took me with the strap and worked me over good.

Fred's mother enters the picture as the protector and socializer. She plans birthday parties, takes him to neighborhood dances, and comforts him after Father's punishments.

And so Fred comes into his eighteenth year, still on the rented farm in Saskatchewan. His Dad continues to boss him around; he leaves home for brief periods but always returns. The "Spanish flu" in 1917 decimates the neighborhood: his mother catches it and loses all her hair; his brother almost dies, but Fred escapes it.

> Now I am almost 19 years old and would be staying home to work with dad again I didnt relish that but someone had to help. If Mother hadn't been there I would of went long ago. I was always a momas boy so I stayed just for her sake. . . . Dad had told me before we started to farm he would pay me the same wages as the rest of the farmers was paying which was about fifty dollars a month with board but I had to buy my own clothes. After I had worked for one month, he told me he didnt have any money to pay me with, but he would try to get it for me, but I knew damn good and well it would be after the crop was threshed before I would see any wages. So just for mother I stayed home as she was in poor health after her go around with the flu.

The passage continues with a complicated deal Father attempted to work on Fred, involving an arrangement to do custom threshing for a neighbor with one of the horse teams. The neighbor, however, preferred that Fred use the team to haul water for the steam engine powering the threshing rig. And so he did, earning $150.

> But that job didnt last only until I could get home as dad wanted to charge me two dollars for every day the team was threshing, said he had paid out my summers [and] that I owed him forty dollars and he needed it so he could pay out the balance of the thresh bill [he had contracted the threshing to another neighbor after he sent Fred off with the team to earn the wages Dad couldn't pay]. That was when all hell broke loose mother went up one side of him and down the other like a house on fire. What mother told him sunk in pretty good, then after the smoke had cleared he told me to keep goddam money but I wouldn't be there the next year as he would get a stranger then he could get things the way he wanted them. Mother went after him again. She told him I stayed at home and worked hard the last five years and took his b.s. Then she told him once he [Fred] goes this place will go to hell, as none of the other boys will put up with him [Dad].

This pattern is repeated several times: Dad makes a promise to keep Fred on the farm, doing the important work, then reneges or cheats. The brothers left one by one, often taking horses or machinery with them that they felt they had title to. By 1921 Dad was sick and doing little work, and the sixteen-year old youngest brother was left with Fred to run the place. Fred began to sell stock in order to get the cash to operate the farm, keeping a few dollars for himself in lieu of wages and giving the rest to his mother to buy clothes and household necessities. During this period Fred became interested in rodeo and organized a rodeo committee among the local farmers and ranchers in the district, including, apparently, some from over the line in North Dakota. In his very first rodeo, on 2 July 1922, Fred rode a bronco and got thrown, breaking an arm and separating a shoulder joint. "When I got over that mess, no more broncos for me not as long as I live as I had learned my lesson."

> Now we are starting 1923 after a bad winter, the snow is going real fast and we have a lot of work to do but it will be the same old drag as the years before, look at a bunch of old hay burners, fight weeds, flies and the heat for the next six months without a break maybe the odd dance or base ball game.

In 1923 the younger brother left home and went to work for a neighbor. So Fred did it all alone, taking whatever jobs Father could give him. "Dad would tell me that calf or that cow was mine but when it came time to sell either one he did the selling and used the money for something else." Fred worked through the summer of 1923, but that winter he had his last fight with Dad, over an overturned hay bale wagon. So Fred, in deep snowdrifts, got his pony out of the barn and left home, getting a job with one of the neighbors. Fred was twenty-five years old.

Fred on His Own, with Wife

Here was a mature young man who had worked essentially as a hired man without regular wages for a difficult father for most of his life. He had virtually no possessions, no money, and no special knowledge other than what he had learned in farming a small, unproductive rented grain-cattle operation. Fred started as his father did, taking whatever job came his way, working for small farmers, trying to establish a close relationship with a farmer employer, leaving when the man could no longer keep his promises, trying out other jobs, going back to farm labor but also managing to homestead a single quarter, at the urging of the neighbor he was working for. Meanwhile his father and mother had left the rented farm and moved north into the newly opened land near Prince Albert; they asked Fred to come up and visit, which he did. His father again tried to get him to do the hard work—this time pulling the glacial boulders off the fields—but Fred refused and took the train:

> Back to the prairies for the summer this young lady [he had first met her on the trip north] again got on the train going to Saskatoon this time she was willing to visit [talk with Fred]. She ask me if I wasnt the young gent that had been on the train the Fall before, I told her I was we hit up quite a chatter she told me she had a brother living in Saskatoon she ask me how long I had to wait for my train out to Regina until the next morning.

Two years later he met her again, on a train to his next job on a farm west of Saskatoon. She asked Fred to come home with her and meet her brother. "What an afternoon that was, her brother kept the old coffee pot boiling. Little did I think I was bound for the wedding bell but that didnt come for over two years."

His work life continued to follow the routine: farm labor, moving dirt for construction projects, caring for cattle, having accidents, recovering, moving on to another job. Finally, in 1929, he met his young lady again, this time as a housekeeper for a farm family he got a job with, and in August of 1930 they got married.

> But what an up hill climb, the dirty thirties struck, prices went to hell, no work we had to go on relief to get something to eat. When the dirty thirties hit [1931–32] I was working for a machine company setting up farm machinery for two bits an hour they couldnt sell their stuff so the company had to close their doors. Then they laid off all employees, no more work. Now what are we going to do no money, and we had to live. I took a job delivering coal for one of the coal dealers in the city at thirty five cents that is better than nothing I thought. Then I fell across the top of the coal box hurting my back quite badly. That lasted six weeks, when I was able to go back someone else was driving my team, so once more I am out of work.

The "dirty thirties" were, for Fred, simply a continuation of the same: itinerant labor, moving from hard manual jobs back to farming, then back to hauling rocks, digging dirt, loading bricks, and so on. Crisis moved to crisis. No food in the house, no money, then a job for a couple of weeks and enough to "feed up." 1931:

> When I did get back to the city there was a letter from my sister, telling me her husband could use me if I was there as he was farming but couldnt get any help. She told me if I would bring the family [by now there were two young children] they had a house for us to live in but where was our car fare coming from. So I went to the city telling them I had a job out on a farm, that we needed car fare. The Relief officer gave me a voucher for two tickets so we could make it to the nearest rail center. Then my brother in law meet the train with a team and a wagon for a trip of about twenty miles. The next day we had to go down to my dad's old place and get his furniture so we could keep house. This house we were to live in was a homesteaders shack, built out of green white spruce lumber insulated with saw dust it wasnt the nicest place in the world to live but it was alive we had company every day and night, bed bugs. They were so bad one could hear them fighting at night, by grinding their teeth.

This didn't work out, either. The brother-in-law started lending Fred to his relatives for odd jobs, and the usual rigmarole began all over again:

employers promising good wages and then not delivering, or paying the agreed-upon price and then doubling the amount of work. Fred didn't take pushing easily; he reached a point with employers where he couldn't take any more and told them so. The document contains six or seven incidents of this type in his life, jobs that might have become relatively permanent but which were exploitative in Fred's view. But there was work all through the depression for casual laborers, people willing to do jobs for a few days for minimal wages, and Fred became one of these people—but not in his own mind. He was always a young man with a young family trying to make it, able to choose his job and his conditions of work. And for thirty years Fred managed to feed the family, retain the loyalty of his wife, and raise several children.

In 1934, in the depth of the depression:

> Well we made it through the winter but it was tough going trying to live on five dollars a month. Some days we had something to eat now we are going to carry on the best we can, one of the neighbors has taken us to his place to cut wood as he sold wood to the neighbors. I would get up in the morning do chores, then have breakfast, go out into the woods and cut a couple of loads of pole these poles was the full length tree measuring 30 or 40 feet in length. They was dropped in rows so they could be easily handled on to a sleigh, for each load of wood, this neighbor got two dollars a load and I got our board. One night after we had been there a month, we had gone to bed, I told the wife we was moving back to our own house, as these people was using us for suckers as they were selling this wood and getting the cash for it and not giving us only what we could eat. Beside the wife had to do the house work, while the old lady and her daughters roamed the country. The wife wasnt feeling too good as she was expecting another baby. When I told them we was moving back to our own place they wanted to know why as it wasnt spring yet and we would starve to death [if] we moved back to our own house. Then the guy came and told me they was going to start the baler again as he had got another contract for fifty tons of hay that meant a month work. Then by that time there would be farming to do as I had ask a farmer about a job for the summer, he told me when it dried up so we could farm he would let me know. One night him and his wife came over, he told me they was going to start seeding the next day and he could use me just through seeding, he would pay me one dollar a day with board. As he didnt farm too big the job lasted only

two weeks. . . . well he paid me for the two weeks that was the biggest fourteen dollars Id seen in along time. . . . when I got home and showed the wife my dreams vanquished, as there was soon to be another little one on the scene, so that meant another mouth to feed. . . . one day I was in town there was an old fellow wanted to know if I was the guy north of town on a certain place I told him I was he said he had a quarter section out there he summer fallowed he had the outfit but he wanted someone to drive it. What an outfit that was an old fordson tractor with two bottom plows. After I had seen this outfit I thought this must be the outfit Noah had in the Ark when the world was created. . . . One day he came along started to give me static about getting nothing done. I crawled off that wreck and told him to do his own plowing, that I was going home.

And so on through the dirty thirties: a job here, a job there, little or no cash, but always a little something to eat; and so the family got raised.

In 1937, after several months working in a lumber camp, Fred went back to his father's place. Dad made the usual promises about farming, but soon departed for a job in a lumber camp himself. Fred and his family (five children) stayed on the home place with Dad coming and going, often broke, rebelling against exploitation, moving on, coming back home.

War and Postwar

Now this is the starting of 1940, it is the same old story, not much change from the years before, only work work work. But the pay was nothing only starvation, on one side and hell on the other side. As I was trying to build up someone elses homestead, with the understanding the place would be mine when the title was obtained, which never happened as the other guy got the title and I got what the little boy shot at [reference to a joke about how a boy out hunting shot at animal feces].

The wife gave me my lunch with two slices of bread, lard for butter coffee made out of burnt wheat. I got this wheat ground for porridge, as we had no coffee the wife would roast some of this wheat for coffee.

So they "struggled along until January 18, 1943," and then he went to Regina and enlisted in the Canadian Forces. Fred didn't tell his wife, just said he was going to the city "for a holiday she told me she knew what I was going to do." After some transfers he wound up in Maple Creek, Saskatchewan, in a small Army training camp. During the next three months he was moved from camp to camp, getting special training—truck driving, mechanics, cooking. He was finally sent to Ontario for preparation for overseas service, but after some further moving he was told he would be discharged. Meanwhile, his family had moved to Saskatoon with his wife's relatives. Two or three times during his fourteen months of service he managed to visit them, usually on the way through Saskatoon during his movements from camp to camp.

After one or two temporary jobs, Fred was hired as a fireman in a power plant for a new meat packing plant. He worked there the next four years. He gradually became a valued employee, a kind of straw boss for the boiler room, doing much of the important work. He earned "fourth class papers" as a boilerman, and decided to apply for first-class engineer papers, partly in order to get a supervisory job away from the hot boiler room. He failed the tests because of, he says, his limited third-grade education. After one more year of boiler work, in 1947 he decided to leave the job. In this case, as in so many of his jobs—lumbering, farming, construction—he would approach a level of expertise and then could not or would not move on to a fully skilled performance.

From boiler firing he moved on to bricklaying and steel and concrete work, still in the Saskatoon area, while he and the family lived with his wife's relatives. Time came for the break, and they sold their possessions and bought five acres of land and tried to raise sugar beets, a project that failed but established a useful job connection with a beet mill. Next came a job in an elevator construction company; after that he became a hand for "some ranchers," haying and feeding cattle. By 1950 things had pretty much come to a survival crisis, and his wife thought she should return to her relatives, at least for a time. Fred agreed, and urged her to take a "rest as she deserved it as I had been away most of the summer working." So Fred stayed home, took care of the kids, looked for a job in town.

Fred Alone

His wife came down with cancer of the liver in 1950 and died in 1953, leaving Fred alone with the children. The eldest daughter was married and apparently lived at home (although this is the first we hear of the arrangement—Fred gives almost no details about his children and their fates). However, the daughter soon moved out.

> Now what am I going to do with the kids how will I make out, I still had my [illegible] I kept on hauling coal, my dad said the little

> one could stay with him until I could find a place for her. The only place I could find was in the kindergarten, and the woman was very good about that told me to leave the little one at her place when the others went to school, then they could pick her up when they went home at noon and night. I ask her what she was going to charge me for her trouble with the little girl, she said I could plow her garden, when it was ready when the garden was ready she asked me to come and plow it, then she had other work to do clean up the yard haul the rubbish away. Then she wanted to pay me for my trouble but I wouldnt let her pay me as she was good enough to help me when I needed help her husband was a cripple as he was in a wheel chair. Now there was a young divorced woman she was jealous of this elderly woman she thought I should come and help her as she had five kids. . . . I should bring the stuff and she would bake out bread for us, so I took the stuff to her, told her that when that was finished to let me know and I would bring more.

During the 1950s the employment routine continued: changing jobs every few weeks or months, returning to earlier positions and leaving them again. But Fred always managed to keep the family alive. One by one the children left and found jobs of their own. Fred seems to have become increasingly aggressive with employers as the pressure to support the family lessened. By 1962 he was beginning to complain that he was "getting on in years thought it was about time I was looking for something easier," which meant tractor driving on the farms. His last farm job lasted two years and marked a reversion to his very first employment as a farmhand. All those years and jobs, and back to the beginning. Time to relax.

Traveling

So Fred wrote his brother in Iowa that he wanted to come down and join the family reunion in August 1962 (although he does not tell us how he knew there was one—obviously Fred kept track of his relations).

> But we had finished the work [on the farm] so I took off but I was a week early, I didn't know where I was going so I went to desmoines Iowa, I phoned my brother from there he came on the phone he ask me what I was doing way out there I told him I was looking for him. We he said you are about three hundred miles from me going the wrong way. . . .

But he made it, getting lost, backtracking on trains, arriving at 2:30 A.M., with his brother there to meet him. The next few days various "cousins and more cousins" and an aunt or two took him around the countryside (Newton, Iowa) while he recalled incidents from his childhood.

> We went on down the road into a hamlet here was the first school that I went to still standing, two churches and their cemeteries. We went up to where the store was but it had burnt years before but a new one had taken its place.

Then the reunion: Haases from all over Iowa and Missouri and Illinois. Fred thought he ought to "get back to Canada" since the harvest was coming up and he had promised his farmer that he would be back for it, but the relatives wouldn't hear of it, and they continued to take him on tours around Iowa. He went to a house where he had lived with his mother and father and talked to the lady who lived there. "I told her I have lived up in Canada and been up there ever since we left back in 1910, I dont think she believed that as she told me she thought I wasnt over 35 years."

He worked another year in the States, then at age sixty-five decided to collect his Canadian "oldage pension," and off he went to Canada. He ends his autobiography with travel itineraries, interspersed with details about buying train and bus tickets and arguing with agents and talking with people he met. For the next several years he seems to have gone on trips two or three times a year, crossing Canada and the United States from coast to coast, having a ball. In 1974 he visited his son, a government employee, in British Columbia. The son died the next year, and Fred had the body shipped back to Saskatchewan, to be buried next to his mother. Fred had one last accident before he closed his autobiography. In 1976 he was hit by a car in Saskatoon, where he had been living for the past decade, and thrown "for over sixty feet." The incident terminated with another confused failure. He sued for damages, but "the lawyers got most of the damage and I got what was left." He gives the reader advice: don't be in a hurry to settle, pick your witnesses with care, and make sure your lawyer is not in cahoots with other people in the case. "Had I known the witness was a lawyer I would have went to him for advice, as the lawyer I went to was related to the insurance adjustor. So between the two I was beat out of a lot of money, and a bad back." This is his last anecdote, typical to the end.

Frank Adamson: A Farmer in Minnesota and Saskatchewan

The author called his typewritten autobiographical manuscript, in the collection of the Saskatchewan Provincial Archives, a "booklet." After working with this manuscript we discovered a typeset, lithographed version, privately printed and copyrighted. Comparisons indicate that editorial work had been done for the printed version. We decided to stick with the original. The document contains 107 double-spaced typewritten pages that describe a series of reminiscences, presented in interrupted chronological order, of a lifetime on the northern plains. The manuscript consists mainly of anecdotes about local events and happenings, accidents, farming, social relations, activities of the Royal Canadian Mounted Police, and natural disasters, all framed by autobiographical passages. We have selected those passages bearing on childhood and young manhood, since these are more detailed than those for his later years. The man we call Frank Adamson states at the beginning that his wife, "Grace," a schoolteacher, helped him with the writing, and its general literacy suggests that she was responsible for the spelling, punctuation, and syntax. Grace also contributed an eight-page reminiscence of her own toward the end of the manuscript, mainly recounting her experiences as a teacher.

This is mainly a story of a man whose parents supported his aims and helped him establish an agricultural career. Born in North Dakota in 1898, he moved with the family to Minnesota as a young child, thence to Saskatchewan in his thirteenth year. There the family stayed. Both parents were born in Norway. His father emigrated to the United States in his late 'teens; his mother came with her parents when she was eight. "I don't think my parents had much education but they did know both Norwegian and English and could write and speak both languages. They both had a lot of good common sense and were the best of parents."

The Adamson family history is typical of a great many immigrants to the Canadian-American West. The first generation comes from northern Europe, settles in the northern United States, moves one or more times, searching for promising locations. Finally, in the Canadian land rush around 1910, they move to Saskatchewan where they stay and where the second generation grows up. Migration for this family was a two- or three-stage process, extending over two generations, during which time the children had ample opportunity to become accustomed to the compromises necessary to establish settlement. Frank's growing up consisted of watching his father and mother slowly construct a permanent existence, all the while training their children to accept the roles that life on the rural frontier could provide. The mother took in sewing and taught school; the sisters worked out; the son worked with his father, farmed with him, accepted his help and encouragement to take out his own homestead and to buy his own land near his father's place.

These were people who, unlike the family of Fred Haas, were members of organized rural society, prepared to work hard, defer gratification, accept the modest existence of northern plains farmers, and slowly accumulate the stake that would eventually permit establishment. The Adamsons, in fact, were the kind of people that Fred Haas often worked for. Here is the way Frank Adamson describes a landless farm worker like Haas during the Great Depression:

> The year was 1934 and the times were pretty hard, money was scarce and workers were plentiful. The government had a scheme in which they helped the workers and the employer farmer. If you would keep a man for the winter they would pay you $5 per month and they would also pay the man or girl a monthly $5. I had agreed to keep a fairly new man to this country. He was from Norway. By name Haakon Busat. There weren't too many chores but I wanted to do some trapping that winter so it was nice to have a chore boy. . . . Haakon didn't have much chance of finding a job as money was very scarce. I had plenty of work as I was farming three quarters with a six horse outfit. . . . I told Haakon if he wanted to stay on for the summer I'd pay him $10 per month and if the crop yielded more than 10 bus. per acre and if I got more per acre I'd pay him $1 more for every bus. over ten, that is $1 per month more. A yield of 12 would give him $12 per month. He was glad to take me up on that as he had no other place to go. This made it nice for both of us.

So, as several employers did with Haas, Adamson took off, on a camping trip, leaving Haakon in charge. Haakon worked for Frank a number of years, but Frank does not describe his personality or Haakon's feelings about the arrangement. We cannot characterize Frank as an insensitive man, but the social and personality differences between people with land and those without were very great on the plains, and there was little communication—and always tension—between them.

Frank's Childhood

Although Frank was born in North Dakota, he tells us that his memories are indeed dim. Therefore we begin his life story with his childhood in Minnesota.

In 1904 my Dad got the fever of pioneer and we all moved to Minnesota. We homesteaded on some land six miles out of the little town of Northome. It had four saloons, two stores, post-office, livery barn and a lumber yard. . . . The woods in the district was real heavy, in fact it was logging timber without any open spaces except a few small meadows along the creeks. There was spruce, balsam, pine, elm, cedar, poplar, birch, oak, ash, maple and a few wild plum and willows. Dad taught me how to tell one from another. There were lakes of all sizes all through the woods. . . . Beautiful Island Lake was three miles long and two wide and full of fish. . . . We had fish all year round. . . . We lived in a frame house by the lake, the barn was log. Our school was also a log structure and it was there that I started to obtain an education when I was five years old. School was open all winter and we had long summer holidays, no doubt so children big enough could help at home. . . . Our teacher was a spinster by the name of Miss Hunter. She ruled with an iron hand. As I was a beginner she took me under her wing and I became "Teacher's Pet." I had a few things in my favor at that time, besides being a beginner and only six years old. They said at that time that I was kind of cute. (This to me now is sort of hard to believe.)

There were many saloons in most towns in those years. Logging was pretty well a winter job. A big part of the country was too swampy to get the logs out until it froze. The influx of lumber jacks brought business for the saloons. . . . This would be where Dad had to go when he was in need of more men in his logging work. They would be pretty well soused when he brought them out. . . . I was quite young at the time but it made me feel so disgusted that I decided I was not going to start drinking and I didn't. I hardly touched a drink until after I was twenty. . . . Dad never approved of drinking and mother was definitely against it. . . .

When I was about eight years old Dick [his brother] and I were assigned the job of digging potatoes. The crop was pretty good that fall and when they were all dug and sacked there seemed to be quite a few sacks to be carried in. . . . This was hard work and I wasn't much help. There were no horses available, so Dick came up with a solution. . . . We had a pretty sturdy hand sleigh. . . . Our milk cow was in the barn. Dick had found a small horse collar and a harness without a breeching. We put the collar on her scrawny neck and fastened the belly band. She stood patiently for all this nonsense but didn't seem to be pleased about it. He led up her up by the sled

> and held her while I hooked up the tugs. Dick pulled on the halter shank and Daisy took a step forward, the tugs tightened on the collar and the fireworks started. I guess she thought she was caught by the neck some way and she just plain exploded. She nearly wrecked the sleigh . . . and we had to get the spuds in the hard way anyhow.

Northome had a Fourth of July celebration, and Frank remembers the event fondly, a social gathering in which everyone was involved.

> Dad had promised this year that we could go. What excitement in our isolated lives. We all got dressed in our Sunday best. . . . I don't remember what all was on the program. They had run off a lot of the races on main street where the sides of it were lined with spectators. I had never seen so many people at one time before. Those some distance came in wagons but a good many walked.
>
> *The Move to Canada*
>
> It was a sunny day on July 15, 1911 that I got my introduction to the Canadian Prairies. We got off the train in Gull Lake, a small town in Saskatchewan [in the southwestern part of the province]. We took possession of the immigrant house, a building made of one ply lumber and unfinished but it was a shelter for those newcomers who couldn't afford to go to a hotel. It contained a stove, firewood, table and a few chairs. The rest of the necessary items we had with us. We could buy a few groceries at the store. We stayed there until Dad and Pete [another brother] would arrive with the freight cars. . . . In our case Dad and Pete had been held up at Portal, the point of entry into Canada and where the horses had to be checked before being allowed into Canada. Our best horse was condemned. He did not have to be destroyed but could not cross the border. Rather than leave him to be sold by the authorities Dad stayed a day or two until he found a buyer.
>
> . . . In the meantime, Jacob Aadland whom we had known before [in Minnesota] . . . had arrived to help us get ourselves and our belongings hauled to the homestead. When our cars arrived they were unloaded. They had contained a lot of lumber, three horses, two cows, two dogs, some chickens, ducks and cats and a wagon as well as trunks, boxes and furniture and other household goods. Dad managed to find a wagon and a single horse. With this and the one we brought and Jacob's we managed to pile it all on. The horses were

> hitched to the wagons, the cows led behind and we were off on our new venture fifty-five miles away.

It took them two days to get to the new place, south of Gull Lake and near the town of Shaunavon, on the Frenchman's River in southern Saskatchewan, not far from the Montana border.

> We arrived sometime after dark. Jacob had come earlier in the year so they were somewhat established. They had a sturdy sod house put up and a lumber barn. The house looked pretty crude from the outside but we were pleasantly surprised when we saw lumber floors and the walls were plastered with white mud from the river. . . . They took us in and between them and Jake's brother's family who were also pretty well settled we were given lodging and a home until our house was made ready. It was the way of our early people to help one another in those early years.
>
> On the first morning after our arrival Dad pointed out to us where our location was. If you can imagine a vast sea of rolling prairie with nothing but grass and sage brush. . . . It impressed us all the more, I suppose, because until now we had lived in the confines of wooded areas.

The necessities of life required pioneering activities. Fuel for the stove came from local deposits of lignite coal and brush from the coulees; native grass was cut for hay. "At first we nearly lived off the land as far as fuel and feed was concerned."

> We shot rabbit and prairie chicken but at that time there were a few antelope though we never had much luck shooting any. That was to come later. We always had enough to eat but not always the best. Many times when supply was low Mother cooked a sort of porridge out of water, flour, and a little salt. This was just thick enough so that it would spread out on your plate and then if we were lucky we might have a little sugar and milk on it. . . . A dab of butter, too, gave it a little better taste. As we became acquainted with the country we found we could get several kinds of wild fruit, Saskatoons, chokecherries, pin cherries, and black currants. . . .
>
> Those first years were very hard. There were no money crops to help until the land was gotten into production. No relief or Social

> Welfare; the only help was neighbor helping neighbor. Those who came in with some money had something to use to tide them over the difficult years. . . . I took in a bit each year in furs from trapping and hunting and I guess mother sold eggs and butter.

And at this point Frank gives us seven pages about winter weather and the great blizzards. The anecdotes are familiar ones: people getting lost, dying in the cold, finding a port in the storm, struggling with horses and sleighs, sleeping on the floors of cafés and stores in town in a bad storm, and so on. But the most important thing for Frank about winter weather was that it gave him his future wife. It seems that in 1937 the cold weather postponed the opening of school until February, so the teacher, whom we call Grace Schmidt, was marooned in a hotel in Gull Lake. Her permanent home was in Regina. Frank was asked to go into town and bring her back out to Aadland's, where she was to board. And so he did, having trouble with the team, at one point driving them on opposite sides of a telephone pole. And so the romance proceeded, down to 1939, when it finally led to marriage.

In 1912 Frank, at the age of thirteen, volunteered for military training. At that time, the Canadian Forces accepted young boys if the recruiting officer was willing to do so (the Forces followed the British regimental system, with officers in charge of raising their own units).

> The Captain was having trouble getting enough to join in spite of these fabulous wages 75 cents a day and all necessaries and so was scraping the bottom of the barrel. I was only thirteen, and just pint size then. He said I could qualify as batman, which involved looking after his horses, his needs, and his tent. . . . I was thrilled with the job and as Dad and Pete were enlisting and would be there, I would be well looked after. As I had been around horses all my short life and liked them, I thought I could handle it. In fact, compared to some of the city fellows there, who were plum green and hardly knew which end of the horse to put the bridle on, I felt like a real veteran.

The training lasted three weeks and, from the description Frank gives us, seems to have been a lark. There were nights out, consisting of striding up and down the short streets of Gull Lake, joking, yelling, and drinking more than was good for them. Frank went the second year, too, but not the third. His army life was over.

Frank goes on to tell us about his Saskatchewan school experiences.

> School life back in Minnesota was a sort of hit and miss affair, especially with the boys. We had our holidays in the roughest part of the winter and then in the spring and summer there was so much to do on the homestead. Tena [sister] and I went to school a little in the States and then the three of us here in Saskatchewan. I think Emma [sister] got along the best of the three of us [the two older brothers were already finished with schooling]. Tena found arithmetic hard, she was slow to catch on and then the teacher would get impatient with her. She'd get nervous and then couldn't learn anything. I liked arithmetic and I wasn't short on patience and so I would help her at nights. . . . I liked reading, writing, and arithmetic but the rest didn't interest me. History and geography confused me. It seemed to me they couldn't quite make up their minds who discovered America. As far as I was concerned the Indians had it pretty well discovered before the white man showed up. Where they slipped up was in not filing on homesteads right away. Now they accuse the white man of being claim jumpers, but in some cases nowadays, even though you have clear title and it is needed to put a railroad or highway through or to build a dam or to be under water because someone did build a dam your title isn't worth much and you can't do a darned thing about it.

The literary device appears frequently: the use of a reminiscence to lead into tongue-in-cheek social or philosophical observations about contemporary events.

In 1912 Frank "went to stay" with a bachelor rancher and thereafter spent a month or two with him for several autumns helping out with chores. The rancher was a friendly type and a good cook, and he let Frank ride, hunt, trap, and pal around with the cowboys. Room and board were free, and no wages were paid. The custom of farm or even town boys living on ranches for varying periods was common.

> While staying there I got to meet most of the local ranchers and cowboys and I just loved to listen to the ranch and cowboy talk. Some of them named me Muskrat, when they came through, others just called me the kid. The second fall I was there Fred [the rancher] gave me the colt . . . for helping around the ranch. It was the first horse I ever really owned and I was pretty proud of it. I called him Bill and started training and breaking him right away. Now, I really needed a saddle. I spotted one in Eaton's catalogue that I liked. It weighted 25 lbs. and the cost was $28. I started saving every nickel and dime

> and it took a year to get enough to buy it. . . . I was riding Bill with my new saddle out east in the hills when I met a rancher that I knew. . . . I knew he had seen this colt when he was at Fred Ervin's and he recognized him right away. He said, "I got a bill of sale for that horse and I can claim him any time I want to. . . ." Sometime after that I was riding again and met a mountie we rode together for a couple of miles. He made some remark about my outfit so I confided in him. He said, "If that guy tries to take your horse you let me know."

Frank liked the Mounted Police, and the manuscript has a number of anecdotes about them, including one in which Frank helped in a search for an old guy who had a lot to drink and then wandered off. Frank and a friend struck out on their own, since they felt they knew the country better than other members of the posse, including the Mountie. They found traces of the old man's wanderings and told the Mountie. The body was found nearby on the following day.

Frank attended his first rodeo in Shaunavon in 1914. In Montana and Saskatchewan in those days a district rodeo was an annual event in which the local cowboys had a chance to show their mettle. The affair was attended by Indians who "wore their hair in braids. They didn't use bridles on their horses, that is their way of riding horses. They just used a light rope or raw hide for one rein." And then there were the cowboys from Saskatchewan and North Dakota or Montana: "They wore angora chaps of all descriptions and many sported silk shirts of various colors, also silk neckerchiefs. They were ready to go all out for one big holiday. The homesteaders came in single or double seated buggies, democrats, wagons or whatever was available to travel in."

During the 1910s Frank seems to have done a lot of moving around in the region. He worked at nearly every task in the farm and ranch roster. Like many homesteader youths, he was attracted by ranch life, but in his case he always returned to farming and his family.

> 1918 was a good year as far as crops were concerned. That summer Dad decided to build a new house—a long time dream of his was to build a really good house. This we never had at any of the places we lived before. It would be one of the bigger and better houses built at that time in the area. It was to be 20 by 26 ft. It was two storeys high with a porch to the east and an open porch to the south. The lumber was hauled from Shaunavon and local carpenters were hired to do the work. We moved in when the house was completed in late sum-

> mer. There were eight rooms so now we could each have our own room. This house was well built and now after weathering sixty-five years of severe prairie blizzards, hail storms and wind it still stands straight, square and strong. Then it seemed like a mansion to us.

In 1918 the great North American influenza epidemic hit the area, and Frank tells the usual stories about the tragic deaths and the heroic attempts to save lives. Neighbors all took turns nursing each other's family members. "It was mostly men that did the nursing, mostly only men were available and perhaps because of the water to be carried and chores to be done it worked better that way. . . . The arrangement was kind of embarrassing to the women and girls." Frank, his brothers, sisters, and mother all caught the flu, but everyone pulled through. Frank portrays his sisters as hard-working, cheerful girls, playing pranks, enjoying life, and each with a specialty: cooking, playing the organ, riding horses. The girls worked out as housekeepers before marrying.

About 1921 he decided to start out for himself and acquired a homestead farther south, a few miles north of the Montana border. He bought most of his supplies in a little Montana town.

> Now that I had my winter supply of groceries I wanted to take the democrat back home. I would then ride back and spend most of the winter on the homestead. These one roomed shacks were fairly snug if they were banked up good with dirt. It didn't take much of a fire to warm them up. The walls were one ply of ship lap and one of tar paper with a rounded car roof so they were not very high. That winter I spent getting acquainted with my neighbors and hunting and exploring the country around, on both sides of the border. . . .
>
> About fifty percent of the homesteaders in our district were young bachelors like myself and lived in small shacks. We did a lot of visiting back and forth. When I brought my stuff into the shack I discovered I didn't have a dustpan. Well they say that necessity is the mother of invention. There was a small cellar under the shack about four feet square and four deep. Above it in the middle of the floor was a trap door about two feet square. When I swept, I swept it in the middle of this door. Then I lifted the trap door with the dust on it and carried it out and dumped it outside. This had one drawback, the door opened to the south. I couldn't dump it as the wind would blow it right back in.

Frank had a good time down there near the border. The prairie and coulees were full of young men like himself, and there was also the usual assortment of odd characters; all of them get their due in his manuscript. He worked for some, others he helped, others he observed in town and on the range.

Coming of Age

In 1923 the homesteading venture was over. Frank found it was too far away from the home place, and he couldn't continue to help his father. So back he went, relinquishing his claim and buying another quarter section next to his father's place. In 1925 he harvested his first crop, and in December of the same year his father died.

> When Dad's will was read I found I was named executor of the estate. Like most young people, who at some time in their growing up period thought they knew everything—well I was no exception. In taking a good hard look at myself, I was surprised to find out how little I did know. I had done a little growing up along the way but I still had a long way to go. As far as stepping into Dad's shoes, that would be quite a chore and I knew I wasn't man enough to do that yet. I was 28 then and I would try to do the best I could.

His father's will divided the property among the children, leaving a substantial fraction to Frank's mother. The sisters and brothers began to move, acquiring their own places. Pete decided to move onto newly opened homestead land in the northern part of the province. Frank stayed home and managed the home place. He moved quickly into full independence, joined the new Wheat Pool, and became one of the solid citizens of the community.

Frank and Grace did not marry until 1939. In a short reminiscence inserted near the end of the manuscript, she implies that the reason for the delay was the depression. Apparently Frank felt he had to stick to the farm and see it through, make it pay; Grace taught school in various locations. Frank doesn't write about his wedding, although he mentions Grace frequently; he provides almost no information about their life together.

So Frank took over his father's homestead farm and combined it with his own land, totaling a full section or more, just before the Great Depression really hit. Many young men of the Last Best West emigration to the prairie provinces came into ownership of the family enterprises during this period. They often failed because the farms generally required refinancing and money was scarce. Frank was lucky; his father, with his children's (especially Frank's) help had put together a reasonably prosperous farm, one that could outlast both weather and economic decline.

Frank mentions the depression several times, and provides one detailed description in the latter portion of the manuscript:

> I don't believe anyone who never experienced these years could really imagine what they were like. We had a fairly good lot of years and then in the late twenties things began to get pretty bad. It would really be depressing if we only remembered the hard things of those years. There were good things about them too. For instance, everyone was in the same boat, resulting in deep community spirit. There was more time for recreational activities. . . . At this time there was also an overabundance of people looking for work. Unions were almost non-existent in the west and wages were very low. Everything was cheap, too, then, but it did not help much when you had no money. Some prices were as follows—eggs 2 to 10 [cents] per dozen, butter 15 to 25 [cents] a lb., beef 3 to 5 [cents] a lb. live weight, wheat went down to 19 [cents] a bushel. Wages for a man were as low as $5 and many worked for their board. A good watch cost $2.

These conditions were especially difficult for the landless: recall Fred Haas's experiences as one of those work-for-board people. Frank continues:

> Dust was everywhere, it came in clouds that you couldn't see across the yard or across the street. Sometimes you had to have lights lit in the middle of the day. Dust sifted through the house through cracks, you felt it between your teeth. Walking it would sting any exposed skin. . . . Farmers lost their topsoil and they had to try different ways of farming to try to stop this eternal soil drifting.
>
> Many small children hardly knew what rain was. Many families fed up with it all, heard of better places and moved out. What money people had finally dwindled away in dire necessity. Curtains, bedspreads, pillowcases, tablecloths, dish towels and even some underwear was made of flour sacks, which were made of good cotton material. Children's clothes were made over from the best parts of larger garments of older members of the family.
>
> There were times, that . . . the air seemed to be swarming with

> wings. Grasshoppers! and if they came down your crop, garden or whatever, if it survived, was soon demolished.

Frank stuck it out and eventually became a reasonably prosperous Saskatchewan farmer. Born into a good family, he married a hard-working woman, raised several fine children, and eventually sold out in 1971 to move into a little house in town where he lived out his days. In his last years he was largely bedridden, owing to the crippling effects of the many accidents he suffered. Before this he and Grace did some traveling, visiting relatives on both sides in Canadian cities: her folks, his siblings, and their own children. Members of the families came to see them after retirement to help with Frank's medical problems. Frank's final paragraph:

> Now, I have told some, not nearly all, the happenings in my life, but enough, I hope, to let my family know of the struggles, the joys, the sorrows, and the hardships that helped shape me into the person that I am. I am content to live out these last years here with my wife, knowing God has been good to us and that we will now enjoy whatever comes. We look forward to visits from family, relatives and friends and also to do what visiting our situation will allow. With this I bring this writing to a close although I think of more and more things that could have been included.

Country Women

The three women's autobiographies in this chapter were selected to illustrate the range of women's experiences on the homestead frontier. All three writers portray themselves as people who refused to let difficult circumstances hold them down; they exemplify the ideology of self-reliance, of making do, of the inevitability and acceptance of hard work. Two of the women, whom we call Sarah Evans and Elvie Jones, grew up on the homestead frontier and married there. Kate Mills came to southern Alberta as a young bride, fresh from city life in Scotland. A large portion of her autobiography records how she adapted to the frontier and learned to be a sheep rancher's wife. Because she was an early resident, prior to the large influx of farm homesteaders, her narrative also includes encounters with wandering bands of displaced Indians and horse thieves.

Kate Mills was a typical housewife in a nuclear family, with its classic division of labor between men and women. Elvie Jones, widowed with young children, lived alone, managing both the farm and the household.

Her experience typifies the lives of widows who homesteaded with their children in Canada and the United States, as well as women in any period who maintain the farm after the death or disablement of their male partners. Both Mills and Jones represent women who became a source of strength on the family farm and in the community during the hard years of depression and drought.

Sarah Evans's experience was different. Without responsibility for children she was more mobile and consequently able to make her own decisions. She does not say that she would have remained in her abusive marriage if she had had children, but certainly her childless status permitted her to enter the wage market and achieve a degree of financial independence.

Despite their quite different backgrounds, all three women held similar basic goals: marriage, children, and the maintenance of a nuclear family household. They probably held similar ideas about courtship, marriage, and sexuality. Such shared expectations and experiences were part of the women's culture of the time, largely independent of class and ethnicity. It is this shared ideology and similarity of experience that was partly responsible for the immediate comradeship between women in the homestead districts.

Sarah Evans: Migrant and Working Woman

The account is based on a 36-page typewritten manuscript in the Montana Historical Society archives. Sarah Evans begins her story with her birth near Spencer, Iowa, 7 March 1883, "one of six children," and ends with her retirement in a nursing home in Conrad, Montana. Written in 1967, when she was 84 years old, the narrative describes her experiences as a child on the homestead frontier and details the expectations held for young women and the need for children to contribute to the household economy.

Sarah Evans was a child during a time when homesteading was viewed as a good way to make a living. But seeking land required travel, cash, and a constant search for jobs. The saga of the Evans family is one of movement from place to place, job to job, and the breakup and reunion of the family unit. Despite the movement and interpersonal dissension, her family ties remained strong. Social and economic support for the family as a whole was a major factor in decisions about movement.

Sarah Evans's autobiography begins with the story of a girl growing up on the homestead frontier, but it also reveals how family and household relationships led to an early and abusive marriage. It describes how the roles for homestead farm women demanded that they function as producers, in contrast to urban, middle-class ideas that emphasized women as dependents. Sarah's story also illustrates how personal autonomy and individual choice were integrated into the wider kinship system of expectations in the frontier and postfrontier societies; and, finally, it depicts both the desire for opportunity and the acceptance of minimal material rewards.

It is tempting to compare Sarah's career as a working woman with Fred Haas's story. Haas lived out his life on the fringes of rural society, but Sarah was less isolated, more able to adapt socially, and eventually she became a civic functionary in her final place of residence in Montana. She remained associated with a strong kin group and worked for them as well as for herself, even after she left her marriage and supported herself. Fred Haas seems to have been concerned mainly with his own wife and children. Fred had an impossible father; Sarah had a better one. Fred was alienated from society, perhaps because he was alienated from his kin; Sarah accepted the social scene and made her way through it.

> *Sarah Evans's Own Story*
>
> I was born near Spencer, Iowa, on March 7, 1883, one of six children of Frederick and Susie Wolfe. There was myself, my sister Anna, and four boys: John, George, Edwin and Walter. When I was two years old my parents moved with my sister and me and brother John to South Dakota.

The family stayed in South Dakota for four years and then moved to Idaho, where the father found work in a sawmill. During this sojourn in Idaho they moved from their claim (which was traded for some cash and a "big gray horse") to a "log cabin with all kinds of fruits and flowers that we never had when we lived in Iowa." Sarah recalls this period as a "happy" one, and it is here that Sarah received her only formal education (through third grade). The family was doing well economically, and "dad had acquired some cattle, horses, and pigs."

> Then in 1893 something came to break up our little home. My dad's sister and family lived a few miles away from us and they never did like to stay in one place very long. He went to Alberta and took us a claim and when he came back he told my dad what a wonderful place Canada was. My dad became all excited and wanted to go too, so he put our cute little home up for sale. He had no trouble finding a buyer and sold everything except the horses and a few chickens and

got a covered wagon ready and packed our belongings in it and we were on our way to Canada. My mother and we kids cried when we left our cute little home. There were three families of us who were going—my dad's brother Frank and family and his brother-in-law Nate Nichols and family (Nate being the one who went first).

The group traveled by horse and wagon to Spokane and then by train to Shelby, Montana, and by wagon across the border to Canada. Upon reaching their claim at Beaver Lake they discovered it lay under water and returned to the States.

> When we arrived in the States we split up; Uncle Nate and family and Uncle Frank and family headed for Oklahoma and we were alone from then on to Iowa [where her grandparents lived]. . . . When we arrived at Glaston, N.D. dad learned that there was help needed in the Red River Valley [in Manitoba] as harvest was in full swing, so we went there and got a job right away. Besides himself, Dad hired the horses out to haul wheat. . . . We camped in an empty house while dad was working. . . . There was a well of water near the house; it was full of frogs. We did, however, have a new supply of groceries. Coming across the wild country from Beaver Lake we had coal oil for the lanterns and somehow some had gotten mixed in our flour, making it awful to eat but since it was all we had it was to eat it or do without. . . . Dad ate with the harvest crew while he worked in Red River Valley. When harvest was over we started for Iowa again, going through part of Minn. and by that time weather was pretty chilly. Farmers were good to us and let us sleep in their nice warm barns. . . . We finally arrived back again in Iowa near Spencer, where I was born, and stayed with some folks who were related to my Uncle Frank's wife. We were there for a few days and Dad bought some new shoes for me; I was so proud of them because they squeaked when I walked. From there we went on to Marathon and Dad got a job husking corn. There was a granary on the place, a well made building part of which was filled with millet seed, and we lived in the other part.

During the next three years Sarah's father worked as a farm laborer, and the family was helped by his mother and by her brother, who worked for a neighbor. The family broke up after the harvest; the children went with Sarah's mother to her parents to spend the winter. Her father stayed in Marathon, where the family joined him in the spring.

> The next spring dad put in a crop on that place and when the corn was ready to cultivate he had me ride on the tongue of the cultivator with a gunny sack for a cushion and drive the horses. I always loved to be outside working with dad.
>
> . . . That fall we moved again to a good farm but with only a small one-room house with an upstairs and a summer kitchen. We raised corn and wheat. Wheat was good in Iowa and made lovely bread.
>
> . . . My sister and I husked corn in the fall. Snow was on the ground and so very cold we wrapped our feet in gunny sacks to keep them from freezing. . . . Our western horses didn't know how to eat corn when we arrived—they ate cob and all, but soon caught on to eating the kernels off. My sister worked for a neighbor by the name of Linstrom and then she took sick so I had to take her place. I was only 13 but I remember Mrs. Linstrom said I was as good help as my sister.

The following year Sarah's Uncle Frank and Uncle Nate wrote from Oregon, telling her father to come join them.

> Dad was discouraged with Iowa anyway; he had raised a good crop of corn and the price was only 8 cents a bushel. We had so much corn we didn't have room in the crib so we had to pile it out on the ground and use a lot of it for fuel. It made a good hot fire.
>
> . . . In the spring of 1897 dad got busy and got two covered wagons ready for our Oregon trip. . . .
>
> . . . We were all happy to leave Iowa and dad painted on the side of the wagons on the canvas in big letters a foot high FROM HELL TO OREGON. People would wonder which hell we were leaving and would ask and dad loved to tell them. There were several other covered wagons to join us—the Doyle family; Mrs. Kittle and her son Billie, a grown man and not very bright, and their little hairless dog, Danny, who was always shivering in the hottest weather. They drove a one-horse shay and their belongings were in the Doyle wagon, and Doyles had a grown son, Walt, who had his own wagon. Then there was Charley Sprasey who drove a team and buggy and another woman and her grown son whose names I just cannot remember. They drove a covered wagon too.

After a series of accidents, illnesses, and periodic stops to earn cash (an effort to which the whole family contributed), the family arrived at the

Ground Round Valley in Oregon. They left for Viola, Oregon, the site of their first Oregon homestead, after a short time. The pattern of odd jobs continued and, again, the whole family worked out.

> We spent the winter in Uncle Frank's house and dad got a job cutting wood. Anna worked for a family near a saw mill and I worked for a lady in Viola. She was elderly but very active—both of her sons worked in the timber. I took care of four horses—one was my own buckskin mare—and too there was a cow that I milked. I cleaned the barn but didn't have to do much cooking, which pleased me.

At this time Sarah was courted by her future husband, some nine years older. She was invited to his family's farm (she notes that they "had a nice farm and a nice big house"), and she and Bruce began to see each other weekly.

> Bruce came to see me every Sunday and we usually went horseback riding and always took mother along when she felt like going as she loved to ride too. During the summer Bruce asked if he could take me to "raise." I thought it was a funny way to propose, however I said yes. Then one night I was getting supper after having baked a batch of cookies. I was frying meat and using a little table fork to turn it when I discovered mother in my cookies, so I playfully touched her with the fork on her rump. She flew into a rage and picked up a stick of stove wood. I made a dive for the living room where dad was and she threw the wood at me just as I went through the door. It hit the door casing and if it had hit me on the head it would certainly have killed me. Dad asked what was going on and mother told him that I stuck her with a fork and he asked her why she didn't knock me down. Just then a knock came at the door; dad opened it and there was Bruce. Dad asked him in and I excused myself and went to the kitchen to finish supper. While I was in the kitchen Bruce asked dad if he could have me for his wife and of course dad and mother gave their consent. I know I didn't hurt my mother—she just didn't like it because I caught her in my cookies. I was only 16 and too young to get married. During harvest that summer I helped Bruce's sister in the cookhouse for $1 a day. I made enough to buy myself some clothes and I remember Bruce giving me a $5 gold piece. He also gave me a cute little horse. Bruce was not very affectionate; the night my parents gave their consent for me to marry him when he got ready

to leave I went with him to where he left his horse tied and he kissed me on the cheek and said good night.

Sarah and Bruce were married on Christmas day, 1899; she was 16, he was 25. His mother was decidedly unhappy about the marriage, feeling that Sarah was too young. The young couple stayed with Bruce's family until spring. In their own house Bruce began to abuse Sarah.

> He would mount his horse and ride away and never tell me where he was going. He would spank me until I could hardly sit and would tie me up in an old cave in cellar where there were spiders, bugs and lizzards; he'd put dust down the back of my neck and then pour water on top of the dust so I'd have to take a bath and change all my clothes. More than once when I was washing dishes he took the pan of dishwater and threw it on the floor so I would have to clean it up. When we went to visit my folks we always rode horseback. I didn't have a saddle and rode sideways with a cirsingle and Bruce would ride behind me and whip my horse as if he wanted me to fall.

The marriage went from bad to worse, with Bruce drinking and fighting and continuing to abuse Sarah. She writes that her father supported her, but she "didn't want to go back there to live." There were no children, and for an indeterminate period of time she continued to live with him, though it is clear that the marriage was over.

> After that I had my own room and he had his, and we had our separate bank accounts so I saved money from my cows and chickens and made up my mind to leave the first opportunity that came along.

In 1923 she sued for divorce.

After Sarah's divorce she stayed with her mother, working in various places as a cook. This arrangement continued into her second marriage. We can assume it was a way to accumulate the cash needed to open a small restaurant.

> Then I worked at different places, met and married Mr. Evans and we came to Montana and brought mother along the first time and spent the winter with my sister Anna who had moved there. In the spring we took mother back to Idaho, then we came back to Montana and I cooked for Arbie Leech for three seasons during harvest.

> Then we went to Portland and bought a confectionary, lunch and fountain and were there for five years when the depression hit and business was bad. We just about gave our nice place away, bought a car and trailer, loaded up our things and headed for Montana. That was in 1934. We rented the Jones place and started a little dairy farm and raised chickens, turkeys, pigs and bum lambs. Times were bad—cream sold for 8 [cents] a pound—I went to work for the Harry Ellis family. Then we had a chance to sell our lease and our cows so we did and bought some lots in Dupuyer and built a house.

Her husband was appointed justice of the peace, and she was appointed beef inspector, but neither job paid very much. Somehow they got along with help from friends and other odd jobs. In the early 1940s Sarah's husband became ill; he died in 1945.

During this period she was appointed "judge on the election board," a job she held for the next twenty-two years. Sarah's siblings had rejoined her in Dupuyer and provided emotional support. In 1964 she moved to the Pioneer Home in Conrad, Montana.

> I've been here over 4 years now and I wish I had come sooner as I love this place. I have many friends here and don't have to do a thing—but I carry the mail [for] the residents from the mailbox outside to my nurse, who sorts it, and then takes it to the rooms. I also take the morning paper to the rooms. I will be 85 on March 7th [1968] and this is the best life I've ever had. I have Ruth Davis for a roommate now and we get along fine as she is a very nice person. I go to Dupuyer to visit my niece Lucille, and her husband, Everett, and my many other friends. Last time I was there I took sick and my nurse Helen Throckmorton and her office nurse, Agatha DeVries, came after me. I love to visit my old home and think of the years I spent there working in the cafes and other things, but I'm just as anxious to come back to my new home and friends. It's nice to be wanted by someone, and they do seem to want me.

Elvie Jones: Saskatchewan Farm Woman

Elvie Jones begins her single-spaced thirty-five-page typed "Recollections" with the family's move west. Her narrative includes homesteading data, identification of brands, and two long essays ("Dogs I Have Known" and "My Friend the Horse"). Unlike Sarah Evans or Fred Haas, but rather like Frank Adamson, instead of a full autobiography Elvie wrote a memoir of selected experiences of her family's homestead settlement near Ponteix, Saskatchewan, her courtship, first marriage, and widowhood. Despite the gaps, the memoir is a specimen portrait of courtship and marriage among young women who came to the frontier as children (she was five years old). Jones is also representative of farm women who assumed primary economic control of the farm due to widowhood or the disability of their spouse.

Unlike Sarah Evans, whose conflict with her mother led to an early and disastrous marriage, Elvie Jones's portrait of her parents and family relationships is seen as the framework for a successful life based on cooperation and mutual support:

> All our brothers-in-law, and sister-in-law are a happy addition to our family. We have always had friendship together that was an envy to some of our neighbors. Our parents taught us to include people and be together as much as possible, to look only for the good in others, and never to gossip and never to condemn. Mom came from a large family where each was willing to cooperate. I'm sure we just naturally did the same way.

Coming West

Elvie's mother had her fourth daughter just two weeks before the Moore family came west from Ontario to Buffalo Horn, a district south of Ponteix, Saskatchewan, in 1909. Elvie, the second eldest, was five years old. She recounts how everyone in the Hastings County (Ontario) area was moving west: "My uncles got the fever, as they called it, and went to Swift Current, Sask. . . . They returned in 1910 full of ambition to get all their relatives interested." Moore's family was a large Ontario clan with close relationships among in-laws and step-children; the close ties and friendships among family members are referred to numerous times. Other members of both sides of the family had already homesteaded and encouraged the family's move. Elvie writes about the reluctance of her mother to leave Ontario:

> Convincing Mom to leave her lovely comfortable home she had spent ten years of wedded bliss in, was no small item. However when her Dad (my Grandpa) said that if all his children were coming west, he would also. Mom reluctantly consented. . . . Aunt Mable was a newly married bride. . . . She and her husband made plans to travel with us and make it their honeymoon trip. He would travel with the

ladies, and Dad would manage his own and Uncle Alex's two cars of settler effects.

Elvie's paternal grandfather and his wife were left behind:

> The night before we parted we spent the night at Grandpa Baragar's. After supper we had a little party in grandpa's parlor. . . . Grandpa was a devout Christian, and would not send us away without putting us in God's hands. So we ended the party with singing "God be with you till we meet again." Then he read a chapter from the Bible and got us all on our knees while he lead in prayer.

Elvie Jones's narrative includes familiar details of the move west and the initial problems faced in settlement. In particular, she recalled the advice and support given by earlier settlers and the strong friendships among neighbors that lasted a lifetime:

> In 1913 we were on easier footing. Mrs. Condie (an earlier settler and close neighbor) showed us the rough places in the road to avoid. . . . She told us, the first fall, "Now put in seven or eight tons of coal and about seven one hundred pound bags of flour, plenty of tea, sugar (100 pounds or so), salt, yeast, baking powder, dried fruit and everything else you will need for seven months or so. Feed your family oatmeal porridge—it's good for them. And if you run out of anything, borrow it from me, return it later. I will do the same."

Childhood and Adolescence

The Condie children became important playmates:

> We kids all played together halfway between the two homes, which were ¾ miles apart. . . . Our very first play houses were those four square holes at the corner of each section of land, about one yard wide, long and deep, a complete cube, with an iron post traveling around. . . .
>
> . . . In the fall of 1913, in September, we had a new (and only) brother, Hubert, the Condies had a new sister, just six days apart. Again our Mothers had made plans. You keep my kids and I'll keep yours for the events. We kids were rudely yanked out of bed at daylight and taken to Condies, and we didn't know why. But I'm sure Dad knew why.

Elvie was eight years old when her brother was born. The practice of sending children to another house during homebirths and the secrecy surrounding sex was not uncommon.

Elvie writes about the experiences she shared with her sisters in the settlement district:

> Olive and I always paired off and went around together. Olive was busy making a "hope chest" and would often sit and crochet or embroider. I did some too, but not for any hope chest as I never planned on getting married. Olive was rather quiet natured, while I was a tomboy. I found it easy in school while she found it hard. . . . I often did her homework and mine too, while, if there was any mischief, you could be sure I was in on it. Mom would say, "Why don't you act like a lady?" I would reply, "I don't want to be a lady." One time Olive got a plain pair of pillow cases, crocheted along the hems and embroidered a big "O" on them, and placed a leaf on each side of it. I was good at drawing so when she wasn't around, I made it into a sick calf's head, using the leaves for ears. Was she ever wild because she couldn't get it off. Mom would say, "I don't know what will become of that girl." Then Olive met Glen Ferguson in the most fantastic way. Mom wanted some wash water, so Olive and me dressed up like a pair of scarecrows (my idea) in Dad's old clothes, hitched old Queen to the stone boat and went for a couple of barrels of water at a spring. When we got there, George Epp's tank man was hitting for the same spring for water for the team threshing outfit. Well, we would have hid if we could, but we had to face up to it. As we dug together, they started a friendship that ended in marriage. Then Janie and I paled around together. . . . She was a little bit flirty though, and got us into "situations".

The "situations" seem to have had something to do with relationships with young men that may have transcended what Ontario Methodists believed to be proper. With four daughters in their adolescence, the Jones family was an attractive place for young people:

> Mom and Dad got us a new organ, and got a lad to give us lessons; they also bought us all the musical instruments we were interested in. We made the rafters ring. It also got the neighbour boys learning to play something, and we all sang songs. Mom and Dad loved to see us go through a hymn book. . . . Catholic boys were right in there

> singing too. . . . We played parlor games, and cut up. . . . Then we finally started to dance. I did first, Mom cried at first but Dad said, "I used to dance, let them, they've got to have fun." So no-one said anymore, not another young person was kept at home; it wasn't the same as in Ontario where there were other diversions.
>
> . . . At one time there were 28 of us going to Buffalo Horn School. How the young teachers managed us all in one room, I'll never know, but they kept perfect control over everyone. Now other schools started coming up, one about every six miles in each direction. It meant lots of Christmas concerts, one every night of the week before Christmas, with dances after each one. Well, that week we slept in the day time. Dad and Mom found it hard to get used to the fact that people didn't pretend to work in this country in the winter, as in Ontario.

Such conflicts between parents' values and the reality of life on the homestead frontier are written about without anger. There is an implication that the differences were part of adaptation to the new life, that one must be tolerant of changes.

> I think the silliest style of dress in all known history was in the twenties. First the straight bob hair cut for girls, simply cut off like a horse's tail. Then the boyish bob with kiss-curls. I was the first one in the family to get a hair cut, and Mom almost disowned me; in fact I was afraid to go home after I cut it. One by one though, the rest of the family cut theirs, and finally Mom wanted to cut hers. Dad had been trying for years to persuade Mom to give her consent for him to shave off his huge mustache, so he said, "If you cut off your hair, I'll shave off my mustache." So that stopped her for a while, then every feminine living soul in the district had her hair cut, so Mom had hers done too. Dad didn't say a word, he just cut off his mustache and refused to let it grow.

Harvest time and the seasonal appearance of threshing work crews remain one of the most frequent themes in reminiscences by both men and women; however, generation and age characterize what is remembered and what is emphasized. Women recall threshing crews as a time of overwork but also as a rather welcome change from a routine of food preparation for the family. Threshing experiences recorded by men emphasize their function as a rite of passage—the way the experience was important in their growing up as men. Elvie Jones presents the young unmarried women's view:

> As the local boys were interested in the new school marm, so were the girls interested in the new threshermen. They came from all over on the harvest excursion with special rates, which gave them a chance to see the country. We had a great variety of boys; we found the U.S.A. boys the most reliable, as they farmed as we did. A lot of the college boys from eastern Canada and English boys from England came out west; they hadn't the least idea of how to begin to harvest. . . . It was the harvest excursion that brought in the man who later became my husband. To me, he was the most wonderful guy in the world.

Marriage and Children

Elvie Jones married at age nineteen; her husband, Cliff, was twenty-one. She wrote little about his background except that he played hockey, worked for a printer, and, of course, did farm work. There is no record of how her parents regarded him.

> We bought a run-down farm nine miles from home [the prior owner had left it in "dispair"], the first year, Cliff got it in shape, and had a fair crop. The next year, 1927, our first daughter was born, and the crop was hailed out. Then a bumper crop in 1928, followed by the ten years of the dirty thirties. . . . My first home as a bride was a ten by fourteen bachelor shack. . . . In a couple of years we acquired a bedroom 8 × 10, built on the end, and later managed two more built on rooms and a path. It was my fairy castle, tho furnished by hand-me-downs and home made furniture. It was a joy to live in, even with not enough of anything to work with. Here our friends met, and our three beautiful wee daughters, Iona, Lorraine and Adoree were born. . . . One night as we stood in the dark and gazed across the prairie we saw a house light, and even the buildings, of which we knew were ten miles away, shining in the moonlight. Cliff said musingly, "This is where Jim Flanigan lived," and I said, "Yes, he left it, but we won't." He said with pride in his voice "You've got the guts kid, but for your guts I'd leave it."

As with other stayers, Jones sees particular strength of character in the settlers who remained.

> We also had a variety of doctors, plumbers, butchers, barbers, nurses and jewellers. All tried farming for awhile, then when they saw what it involved they left for parts unknown, quite often leaving their places by walking away with a suit case, having shut the door and left all gear and horses behind them. It seemed to be only the poor, and poorly educated who remained and by sheer determination and grit, sweat and blood, they built up homes to be proud of, raising their families to be courageous, honest and hard working. The pioneer farm had no place for a weakling. . . . You were in it sink or swim with no crying on anyone's shoulders, they had their own troubles. However, in times of sickness or calamity, every one took his team and did a man's seeding or harvesting without pay.

In her last chapter, entitled "Hopes Deferred," Elvie describes the depression years during which her husband became an alcoholic and committed suicide.

> How can I describe the hopes in the spring, only to be so disappointed later on, year after year, dust storms, horses dying with sleeping sickness, grasshoppers, wire worms, army worms, no money, relief cheques which were a mere pittance and had to be coaxed, begged and wrung out of the authorities. . . . Cliff would sometimes put in 200 acres of crop, and a three day blow would send the sand flying and cut off the small tender blades. He would walk from window to window crying, with his lungs full of sand that he had breathed in while seeding. . . . Many a time he would have just quit, if it had not been for my boundless faith in him.
>
> . . . When our first crop in ten years was showing up, along with fourteen years of debts, he said he was afraid to have a crop, for fear he would drink it all. Then one day, after a big drunk, he . . . shot himself.

After two weeks, Elvie returned to the farm, paid off the debts (with the aid of her family and her creditors), and raised her children. She remarried, but writes nothing about that marriage. Despite all of the hardships she endured, her narrative ends on a positive note: "Over sixty years can bring to memory a lot of living, but Dad was right—it was a great place to bring up a family."

Kate Mills: A Pioneer Ranch Woman

Kate Mills emigrated from Scotland in 1905 to marry her fiancé, who was already in Canada.

> From 1901 to 1905 the West was being advertised everywhere. "Come to Canada where wealth awaits you." . . . Like many others I had given my promise to come and help build a home in the Great West. . . . The fateful day arrived, and we all seemed in my old home as if afraid to make a noise. . . . The cab arrived which was to take me to the ship, and only then did I realize fully the step I was taking. . . . Down in my cabin I found friends, who like myself were going to join those who had started the home. They were all having a good cry so I was able to give full vent to my feelings. One of them asked how did my mother take it, and when I thought of her sad face as I clasped her hand in farewell, I said, "If this ship stops at Greenock, I'm going home"; but I felt better by that time, and so came to Canada.

Unlike Elvie Jones and Sarah Evans, Kate Mills was raised in a city; she had no experience on a farm or ranch. Her autobiography is, to a great extent, an account of her personal adaptation to rural life. Throughout the eighty-three-page, double-spaced typewritten manuscript (written in 1938) there is little self-pity. Her ignorance of sheep and sheep ranching and her failures in baking bread and in cooking are recalled with wry humor. In her ignorance Kate Mills is representative of the numbers of other young women who learned to adapt to the rural frontier. Kate's learning provides a useful comparison with the skills Evans and Jones learned growing up on the agricultural frontier and took for granted.

Another point of contrast is that Evans and Jones grew up surrounded by family and kin who provided economic and emotional support. In the early period of her marriage prior to homestead settlement, Kate was primarily dependent upon her husband. Two important themes in her autobiography are the need to become accustomed to isolation and, nevertheless, the important emotional support offered by other women in her life.

> When I got back to my home after my first Summer in a camp wagon, my husband told me he would have to go across the Line for Rams, and would be away for six or seven days. He took a team and wagon, so that he could return all the sooner. All the company I had, was a cat, and that was little comfort on the lonely prairie.
>
> After the first three days I would take the cat in my arms and

> climb the coulee bank every afternoon and look away to the South to see if I could see anyone coming, but no matter which direction I looked in, I could see neither a house, nor even a tree, nothing but bald Prairie. On the afternoon of the sixth day I had climbed the hill as usual, but saw no sign of anything, so I returned to the house and sat down to have a good cry. I had my head on the table and did not hear the door open and when I felt a hand on my shoulder, I did a silly thing, I fainted. It was my husband, and he had been below the hill just as I climbed it, and I did not see the wagon. He got as big a fright as I did, and said he would never leave me all alone again.
>
> . . . I got to visit my first neighbour, Mrs. Slawson, seven months after my arrival here. I meant to ask her how to bake bread, but could not summon up enough courage. She was a German and spoke quite broken English and I did not understand her very well at first. The week following, I visited another of the early settlers, a Mrs. Clark. She was a young woman with a tiny baby, and I managed to tell her all my trials. When we met we ran to each other, and put our arms round each other's neck, and just had a good cry. All the hunger and longing we each had to speak to a woman, and had stifled for so long, gave way, and we felt better after our cry.

Kate Mills's reminiscence has familiar material. She recalls maintaining an open door for strangers, the problems women faced with childbirth and accidents, the never-ending daily grind of household work, the absence of help and, above all, exhaustion and breakdown. Over eight months pregnant, exhausted by the trip to Lethbridge to make arrangements for the birth, she made a ten-mile trip to the ranch in a torrential rain.

> By the time we reached our home after driving ten miles in the rain, I was thoroughly soaked and very cold. When I went into the house I found one of the windows to the North was broken, and the rain was pouring in on top of the trunk where I had the clothes for my new baby. There was water all over the floor, and no dry kindling to make a fire. When I looked round and saw the back bedroom turned into a sheep pen, I just gave up and bawled. . . . The hired man had moved the furniture out, and put the sheep in.
>
> My husband ordered me to bed while he managed to get a fire started and mercifully I fell asleep and slept for several hours. When I got up, the sheep were gone and the hired man was washing the floors. The sun was shining again, so the sheep were all right outside.

Kate did not make it back to Lethbridge for the birth. A local woman who "acted as midwife for all the women who had babies at Grassy Lake, Burdett and Winnifred" delivered the child. Kate writes the next child was born in Lethbridge, her third child was born at home, and the fourth was born on a visit to her family in Scotland. In her narrative Kate recalls the toys and entertainments she developed for her children and a potentially serious accident:

> We had all the sheep in the large shed and from there to the dipping vat there were little pens where we put some sheep before putting them through the chute and into the dipper. As each lot was dipped one of the men would bend down over the dipping vat and remove the grass or straw floating on top of the dip. My children had to come with me so were watching the men. My second girl, aged four, went into the corral. She had watched the men clear out the grass so when they went to chase some more sheep into the pens, she bent down to clean out some grass which had been left, but as the side of the dipper was slippery, she went in head first. The sheep were making so much noise that no one heard her cry, but luckily a neighbour was passing in his buggy and saw her fall in, so he jumped the fence and pulled her out. You can imagine how I felt when he carried her in to me and said, "I found her in the dipper, Ma'am." She was quite sick for some time as she had swallowed some of the dip, and for a long time we could not get the smell of dip out of her hair.

Above all, Kate Mills emphasizes learning to be a ranch wife:

> It was during this first lambing that I got my first lesson in midwifery. When a ewe could not lamb herself, perhaps by reason of the lamb coming wrong or the legs twisted, my duty was to assist, as I had a smaller hand. Many times I took a piece of string with a noose on it, and after pushing back the lamb, I would feel for the forefeet, and slip the noose over them, then help the head forward, and the shepherd did the rest. Instead of the ewe trying to run away, she seemed to know that we were helping her and did her share by lying still. It was seldom that we lost either ewe or lamb.
>
> . . . I should tell you of my experience shooting at coyotes. While I was out at the sheep camp we were very much troubled by a lame coyote coming into the band almost every night, and very

often the remains of a lamb would be left to show us of his visit. My husband showed me how to use the shot-gun if he showed up during the day. . . . One day when I saw him coming I put a kitchen chair in front of the camp wagon door and rested the gun on it. Just as the coyote got opposite I pulled the trigger. I did not know what happened, but I landed at the back of the bed, and the coyote went merrily on his way. I did not know the gun would kick so much, but time and experience taught me a lot.

Eventually she did shoot the coyote, recalling the incident with pride.

Didn't I feel proud that I was proving I could do something as a sheepman's wife, but I still have the notion that it was not good guiding, but pure luck.

Kate Mills learned to cope with cold and blizzards, to round up sheep and drive a wagon and a team. Learning to become a sheepman's wife also included learning to be part of a larger community.

For a good number of years, Grassy Lake had a little excitement to look forward to as shearing came along. There were generally four or five bands of sheep sheared just South of the village, and as the shearing crew was quite large, together with the flock owners, the place was quite busy. They even managed at that time to hold a celebration on the first of July [Canadian Confederation Day], with sports of all kinds, horse racing and bucking horses, so that I had some idea of what the wild and wooly West was like.

. . . We [Kate and her sister-in-law] had wondered what to wear at a stampede and imagined it would be a dressy affair, so we both wore light dresses, ground length, large picture hats and sunshades, all the relics of city life back home in Scotland.

Everywhere we went we heard people saying, . . . "Oh, they are the sheepmen's wives." We were feeling rather foolish as the other women seemed to be wearing print house dresses. It was a lesson to us and we did not forget it.

Aside from the anecdotes, the most valuable material in Kate Mills's autobiography is her recollection of social relationships in the emerging district community.

The first real sorrow that I shared in was the death of a little baby boy, the first child of a young couple from Ireland. The child was never well from birth, and everything that could be, was done to save him. Towards the last we took turns at sitting up at night to allow the parents to rest, but in spite of all the care, little Tommy passed away. All the neighbors for miles round came to the funeral. We had no cars, they came in wagons, democrats, and buggies, and drove to Burdett for the burial. We had no minister these days, so when the little white coffin was lowered into the grave, one neighbour said to us, "Neighbours, we have no minister, but let us sing, 'Shall we gather at the river', and then repeat the Lord's Prayer."

Several anecdotes in her autobiography concern the gender division of labor.

For a number of years after the country was homesteaded we had the local farmers come to shear. Many of them had never sheared before and after supper each night they would go to their own homes, so my job was to turn the grindstone while my husband sharpened the shears for the next day. I would turn and turn until my arms were so tired I could have cried, but if I said one of the men might do it, I got the answer that sheep shearing for a whole day was no play boy's job and the men were tired, so as mother's work is never done, I turned and turned.

Kate's attitudes reflect the hard work of men and women in agriculture as well as the tension between men and women about the way tasks were divided. For Kate the hard work resulted in a satisfactory life, yet she ends her piece with a plea for women:

We have seen a great many changes down through the years. The younger generation are taking over and many of the old settlers have passed on.

We cannot pass however, without thinking of the many happy times we had and hoping that the kindly spirit of the early settler will not have entirely passed away, but that the younger ones will carry on. They too can do a light to brighten the lives of others, if they will only try.

I believe this is where the Women's Institute can do a lot of

> good. If we can only reach the farmers' wives and bring them in amongst us.
>
> Some of them live from day to day, going through the same routine of work, cooking, washing, milking cows and feeding chickens, and the only time they get to sit down is when something has to be darned or patched. No wonder many of our women look tired. If we could infuse a little happiness into our meetings, we would be doing something worth while.

On all frontiers the roles played by men and women naturally differ, but, at the same time, frontier society requires modifications in traditional roles and activities. On the homestead frontier women were offered opportunities for self-determination, risk, and achievement denied them in their late nineteenth- and early twentieth-century homelands. The men writers tend to emphasize technical achievements, the details of their work, and their engagement (or, in the case of Fred Haas, relative nonengagement) in community-building. The women, on the other hand, are more concerned with private experiences and social relations. But the women's emphasis on home life is also necessarily an emphasis on work, and their social relations share, to a considerable extent, the space of community-building. Thus, autobiographical writings provide individual perspectives on a complex social process, the details of which in the later local history books are often omitted or reduced to either matter-of-fact or formulaic statements.

Chapter 14

The Political Aftermath

This final chapter deals with some ideological and political consequences of the agrarian settlement of the northern plains. We have seen how the homesteading and town-building policies of the government and railroads brought thousands of unprepared settlers to a region with specialized resources. The region, however, did not yield sufficient capital to provide for demographic and economic stability, or to weather the financial storms engendered by the growth of North American society. Arriving with expectations of economic success, the settlers—both town and country—soon discovered that the land of milk and honey was in reality a difficult and unforgiving land. The majority of initial settlers departed, but those who stayed did a reasonably effective job of it, with the help of government agricultural facilities and funds. The portrait of homesteading and community-building in the documents we researched is based on their memories, not the negative accounts of those who left. This means that a majority of the documents tend to feature benign remembrance of the past. Hardships are described in ways that suggest they were less painful than they might have been.

The reasons for this disparity involve the promiscs made by the promoters of settlement. We noted that much of their promotional literature glossed over environmental and economic deficiencies in an effort to "get the people out there" (a remark in a letter from a politician to a railroad official) so they could realize returns on their political and financial investments. The land was the chief carrot; there is no doubt that of all the motives for moving west, the promise of "free land" was the most effective. "Be your own boss" was number two.

When the promises turned out to be false or overly optimistic, the political consciousness of the population took an immediate rise. The common theme everywhere was a feeling that the farmer and the country people generally had been left behind, swindled, exploited. Land values rose, inviting sales and exodus but making it difficult for the stayers to expand their holdings in order to keep up with constantly rising costs of operation, or to cushion the rise and fall of speculative grain and livestock prices. Poor crop yields due to drought might coincide with low prices due to an economic depression, or high crop yields might come in a period of low demand; either case brought low prices to the farmer. If the demand for beef dropped, ranchers might have to sell off their surplus stock at prices lower than the cost of raising them. And so on. Contingencies like these became the stuff of life all over the Great Plains and especially in the northern plains. And when the producers were not getting what they needed, town merchants and suppliers suffered as well.

Economic insecurity associated with these fluctuations got steadily worse, as the economy of the plains became increasingly dominated by the economies of the two nations, and by the brokers and entrepreneurs that controlled costs and prices. By the 1930s, a decade of disastrous drought, it became clear that the region simply could not be managed on a modest scale of farm production; individual producers could not even count on growing their own food in times of serious drought. So wholesale desertions occurred. However, leaving the homestead was by no means new—abandonment had characterized most homesteaded districts from the beginning. The community history books of a lot of these districts contain many more names of families than actually were present in the district at any one time, a result of the constant turnover of settlers.

Most of the conditions stimulating unrest and abandonment of farms and towns had been operative since the 1870s in the settled parts of the United States. That decade saw the beginnings of a diverse political movement generally labeled populism.[1] A form of social and economic protest in rural areas, it began in the U.S. South, where merchants had developed a scheme for taking crop liens as credit advanced to farmers. The proceeds from a high percentage of the crop were required to repay the loan, resulting in debt peonage for thousands of small farmers. From there protest movements spread into the Midwest, the central plains, and Texas—wherever rural people felt they were at the mercy of "the interests," as the merchants, bankers, grain elevator companies, railroads, and politicians were called. Populist movements began developing into political parties, and senators and congressmen began bringing populist grievances and strategies to Washington. Since the northern plains were settled very late, effective populist movements also appeared late. However, indigenous related forms of economic mobilization were strong in parts of Western Canada where many of the settlers from the British Isles had been involved in the famous pioneering Rochdale Cooperative movement in England. But the cooperative movement in the North American West often made an effort to avoid being co-opted by these political movements. (Cooperatives have generally shied away from aggressive political action; for the most part, they have made their peace with "the interests.")

Western Canadian farmers' movements began in the 1890s, and the first effective organization was founded in 1905 by Henry W. Wood, an American farm-settler in Alberta. J. S. Woodworth, a Winnipeg minister linked to the social gospel movement of the late nineteenth and early twentieth centuries, was a second major figure. His writings became the initial protocol of the farmers' organizations that eventually came together as the Cooperative Commonwealth Federation (CCF). The principal issues in Canada stimulating agrarian protest focused on the collusion between the grain elevator companies and the railroads, and the corporate-dominated agricultural marketing system in general. Both resulted in controlled prices, to the detriment of the farmers. And there was the reciprocity issue in the 1890s and early 1900s: The United States had offered free trade in agricultural products across the boundary (an early precursor of the North American Free Trade Agreement, or NAFTA), and the western farmers and businessmen wanted to reciprocate since the old north-south ties and actual kinship bonds of settlers on both sides were strong. However, eastern Canadian conservative interests were opposed, and they won out over Liberal support of reciprocity in Parliament. Western Canadian interests became entwined in eastern Tory and Liberal politics, just as the "free silver" western populist movement in the United States became involved with Democratic and Republican politics.

Saskatchewan became the home of the CCF, the most elaborate and politically potent populist party. Farmer insecurity in Saskatchewan was the most serious in western Canada. This was a province that depended on agriculture for its entire income for most of the first half of the twentieth century. A plethora of farmer organizations appeared by the first decade of the century, but it was not until 1933 that genuine unity was effected and the CCF emerged as a farmer-led party. The most important of the precursors were the Saskatchewan Grain Growers Association and the Farmers Union, plus some of the cooperative associations and federations. In the depths of the Great Depression and drought in 1933, these groups met in Regina and formed the CCF under the Regina Manifesto (a protocol closely resembling the Omaha Platform of 1892, a populist coalition document produced in the United States that lacked the decisive party-organizing theme of the later Canadian effort). By 1944, the CCF was able to capture the Saskatchewan government, and it has had two or three losses and returns to power there since. The CCF also went national, in the form of the New Democratic Party, and it now represents the left minority in the Canadian Parliament, with programs resembling a somewhat further-left Rooseveltian New Deal.

In Alberta, radical agrarian protest and reconstruction did not have the appeal it did in Saskatchewan, possibly because of a more diversified economy and more decisive conservative American influence. The CCF and similar groups were active in the very dry southeast quadrant of the province, but populism as a provincewide movement took a demagogic form in the Social Credit Party, which emerged in the 1920s and has continued to play a political role ever since.

The Non-Partisan League (NPL) of North Dakota was the precursor of the CCF insofar as the Regina Manifesto was based in part on its ideology and platform, and as it became an inspiring example of moderate, left-wing political success. With the usual border-crossing spirit, Americans and Canadians had been active in each others' movements. Elements of California Citrus Grower Cooperative ideology appeared in the Regina Manifesto, since the principal organizer of that co-op was invited to Canada to advise on cooperative marketing.

The Non-Partisan League achieved its most effective form in 1915, following the waning of influence and vote-getting power of some of its precursors, especially the Farmers' Alliance. The League advocated public ownership of all grain storage and processing facilities, meat packers, and refrigeration plants; low-interest loans to farmers issued by credit banks operating at cost; government-operated hail insurance; and related measures. All of these issues, plus a few more, were also important for the Canadians. The NPL tried to ally itself with the Republican Party in North Dakota in an effort to capture the state government. This was something of a novelty, since U.S. populist political movements from the late 1880s had had a fluctuating alliance with the Democratic Party (especially during the William Jennings Bryan era). The NPL did manage to secure a significant number of offices in the state government. However, since the national Socialist Party of the United States sent workers into the state to help organize voters, it became easy for Republicans, and especially local bankers and businessmen, to tar the NPL with a left-wing brush. In fact, North Dakota bankers simply sank the party by refusing to purchase bonds issued by League-organized state-owned industries and credit banks.

Montana experienced populist episodes as a spillover from the NPL in North Dakota, but, as in Alberta, a less agrarian-dominated economy vitiated an aggressive majority farmer-oriented movement. Montana radicals were preoccupied with the Anaconda Copper Company's domination of the state government and economy, and much activity was directed toward labor issues and legislation to control the influence of the company. However, the eastern half of the state, with its dryland grain farming and ranching, supported an active North Dakota–derived NPL for a while, in addition to such related groups as the Society of Equity. This latter organization had its heyday but, like so many others, gradually withered as the issues changed, as agrarian prosperity emerged, or as Democratic administrations with sympathy for the farmer appeared on the national scene. Theodore Saloutos, co-author of one of the standard sources on agrarian discontent in the upper United States, concludes that these farmer populist organizations were "shaped more by local and regional than national issues" (Saloutos 1945:393). During its short life the Society of Equity (a branch of a larger Equity organization with chapters in a number of western states) developed close ties with several Canadian organizations, especially those promoting cooperative marketing schemes in fisheries, grain, and dairy products. The Canadian groups were moving ahead mainly because governments had given them loans to cover start-up costs and other things, but the Equity groups were unsuccessful in attracting financial support from the conservative mining-dominated Montana legislature, and the federal government did not support such programs until New Deal days.

Summarizing, the rise of agrarian populism in the Canadian-American West featured one enduring form, the Saskatchewan fusion of cooperativism, agrarian radicalism, and welfare-state liberalism called the Cooperative Commonwealth Federation; one moderately successful organization, the Non-Partisan League of North Dakota; and at least one failed version, the Society of Equity in Montana; and a later, derived form, the Social Credit Party in Alberta, which was concerned with financial rewards and handouts appealing more to tradesmen, small entrepreneurs, and ranchers. In other words, true left-leaning agrarian populism was effective in this region to the extent that the constituency had a predominance of farmers and small rancher-farmers, and also possessed a cultural heritage of cooperativism and other agrarian political-economic programs.

Rural Passivity and Political Consciousness

Virtually every author of a rural community study in North America comments on the tendency for the inhabitants of rural neighborhoods and small towns to avoid intergroup conflict, ideological differences, and divisive or competitive activities. Mayors of small towns can stay in office half a lifetime because no one wants to challenge them; quarrels, even serious ones, are settled quietly, out of court; friction between factions develops from time to time, but tends to fade away or be smoothed over before too many people are lined up on one side or the other. Paul Voisey (1988), in his study of a small town in southern Alberta, notes that these are the behavioral patterns of small population groups, of *Gemeinschaften,* where the daily face-to-face contact creates a necessity for at least the appearance of harmony.

There is considerable truth in this, although in our experience there is more open conflict and disagreement in small towns and rural neighborhoods than outsiders realize. One difficulty is that the observers' periods of observation are usually fairly short. There are really two separate issues: One is the existence of disagreement and conflict in small communities, and the other is the openness of their manifestations. With respect to the first issue, we should say that there is probably no more or no less dissension in small communities than in large; and with respect to the second, this dissension in small communities tends to be concealed or papered over more often than in large, accessible communities. And there is a third issue: the way the dissension may be related to external socioeconomic forces and political organizations.

There are cultural reasons for avoiding open conflict and especially socioeconomic class resentments. Most homesteaded settlements were recent; their populations had a history of rural mutual aid and self-help, and their cultures had accumulated a powerful residue of sentimental attachment to the past ("heritage"), expressed in a reverence and honor of the pioneers who had such hard—and noble—experiences in establishing communities against all obstacles, without substantial help from the outside. Most stayer settlers and their offspring were relatively cosmopolitan individuals. They had traveled, experienced several communities, and dealt with government, businesses, and the railroads. The formation of political consciousness and the willingness to engage in protest movements was thus subject to both impeding and facilitating forces. The nature of the community and its traditions acted as an inhibitor, but the severity of the hardships and the relative cosmopolitanism of the settlers functioned to promote participation.

We found in our documents a kind of historical process or sequence in the emergence of political consciousness and action. In the early days of frontier settlement the settlers were preoccupied with survival and with helping each other, but in the postfrontier stage, as communities became established and population fluctuation decreased, people had time to devote to the community: to petition for schools and roads, to deal with government agencies that held the keys to basic resources. The title of this chapter, "The Political Aftermath," alludes to a third stage of settlement, which emerged when residents began to look outside the community for causes of what they came to define as underprivilege or exploitation. In this stage, individuals began to seek office and leadership in spheres larger than the local community, and people began to register their discontent at the polls.

To translate grievances into political sentiment may require time to permit hardships to become grievances, to build a sense of outrage, and to visualize remedies. On the whole, the process is paced by a generational rhythm of kinship and family. In the Canadian-American West the first generation of adult emigrants were preoccupied with the tasks of settlement: establishing homes, farms, and businesses, working for wages, building country neighborhoods, schools, and towns. Success was something to be achieved with hard work, and energies were directed to that end. Hardships were expected and tolerated on the whole, and if things didn't work out in the first location, the emigrant moved on to another. And emigrants who retained property in the homeland could always return. Anxiety and despair were part of the game, but there was little inclination to blame the authorities for one's hard lot on the frontier. And the frontier lacked political leaders. The true charismatic personalities of the era were business entrepreneurs, proselytizing churchmen, men and women who devoted their energies to the little communities in order to build schools, persuade the railroads to build stations, or the government to establish a post office.

But the second and third generations—the people who grew up on the frontier—viewed the situation differently. They had witnessed the trials of their parents and grandparents. They were aware of the exaggerated claims and promises of the land promoters, and they had come to realize that the situation militated against easy or secure establishment. They moved into leadership positions at different times, depending on the date of settlement. For example, in the eastern and southern United States, agrarian protests began in the 1880s as the post–Civil War settlements in those regions came to maturity, and by the 1890s they took the form of organized political movements. Most districts of the northern plains did not reach this generational stage until the late teens, early '20s, and of course the '30s, when the droughts and economic dislocations demonstrated once and for all the basic marginality of the resource situation.

Settlers in southeastern Alberta, the driest part of the province—mostly range country that probably should never have been put to the plow—had an especially difficult time. The area began to be settled before the land survey, promoted by a pair of North Dakota real estate entrepreneurs who located themselves in Lethbridge in 1906 and accepted applications for homesteads on government land that was due to be given its definite survey in 1910. The son of one of the settlers wrote in a history of the crossroads village of Foremost near the settlement: "First we must bear in mind that at that time our Province of Alberta was only four years old and local government had not had time to do a great deal of development" (LHB 20:13). Foremost had no train service, and the roads were simply dirt tracks across the plains. The community had no doctors, no schools, no banks, no local government. Most of these facilities were not acquired until 1913 or 1914, almost a decade after the initial homesteading. By 1911 the first settlers were in severe economic straits. Acquiring additional land, vital to any kind of farming in this dry country, required purchase of pre-emptions (free in the United States by this time), and people had no cash reserves since crops had been poor. The settlers drew up a petition to the federal government, requesting that payments on pre-emptions be deferred, money already paid be refunded, and some other financial provisions made to alleviate hardships. No action was taken, and the community went back to work on its own affairs. "We had little money and much hope and ambition." The case illustrates the emergence of political action under the most severe conditions, but it took the form of a simple petition to the authorities rather than full political mobilization. This indirect type of protest was common in the frontier homesteading communities, and most efforts were directed toward organizations and agencies in control of basic resources: roads, schools, and railroad services.

The priorities were clear. First you managed to get what you needed to survive, or at least get through the first two or three years, and then if time and energies permitted, you got to work on political action. In 1918, recalls another writer in the same history book, "there was great indignation locally" at the withdrawal of the CPR train service to only one train a week. The railroad claimed it was serving the war effort, but residents of Foremost believed it had nothing to do with patriotism but was a purely economic concern—Foremost didn't generate much revenue for the railroad. The local protests became vociferous, and members of the Canadian government board of railway commissioners came to town to hold hearings. No change was made in the decision, but the matter did not end there. An important CPR official was quoted in the Lethbridge newspaper as saying that the Lethbridge-Foremost line was a "luxury." Eventually the railroad, after continual protests and criticism from Lethbridge business and news sources, restored the service to two trains a week. The episode, as reported by the *Lethbridge Herald*, included this echo of radical sentiment:

> Well, there ain't no luxury in paying three cents a bushel extra on wheat rates between here and Winnipeg, 20 cents a hundred difference on first class freight, 50 cents a hundred on express, and a day longer on the train if you want to go anywhere! By golly you're right, the other replied, and there ain't no luxury about this train that comes down here that I can see. The only thing for it is government ownership, and that right quickly. (LHB 20:113)

Whether this was an actual quotation is not known, but at least the *Lethbridge Herald* was on the side of agrarian protest or populist sentiment. And the sentiment exemplifies the way local deprivations led to the rise of agrarian protest all over the northern plains. Among people with intensive training in doing things for themselves, and who were operating on very close margins with recurrent climatic and economic uncertainties, populist tactics were a logical outcome.

In the course of these initial years of settlement, people like those of Foremost had to confront a series of issues based on needs not being met because the decisions were out of the hands of the population. Hail insurance, community hospitals, ambulance service, irrigation assistance, payments for crop deficiencies due to weather, fair freight rates, regular train service, improved roads and bridges, emergency cattle feed in periods of drought, high school construction, homes for the aged, farm loans, loans for farm building construction, trees and bushes to construct windbreaks on the plains—these and many other needs emerged within a decade or less after a homesteaded district had reached the permanent settlement stage.

The training settlers received in the early years included not only self-help but also reliance on help given by neighbors, which adds up to the benefits of community solidarity, of people coming together to supply needs and services. The collectivism learned by the homesteaders was not only from books and slogans, but from practical experience as well. A North Dakota family homesteading in Alberta experienced year after year of economic difficulty due to insufficient land and poor crop prices. They also had to take in four young children orphaned by tragic deaths in a relative's family. During the winters the family moved to a nearby town so that the father could work for wages to supplement their income. Each year, after moving back to the farm they had problems with water and more accidents and misfortunes. The account concludes succinctly: "In the summer of 1923 . . . Dad and Uncle Walt signed up as charter members of the Alberta Wheat Pool" (LHB 109:549). The big grain pools—cooperative marketing organizations—were the spearheads of populist politics in Western Canada and to some extent in the northern U.S. states.

Thus many mature settlers, and their sons and daughters in early maturity, joined populist-oriented organizations. This was often a family decision. The Baker families who settled the Nemiskam district of southern Alberta represented a typical Canadian pattern of activism, devoting considerable time to farm organizations such as local cooperatives and especially the cooperative Wheat Pool. A. T. Baker notes that without his wife to keep the family going during the years of drought, grasshoppers, and bad roads, helping with farm chores, getting the children to school, he could not have become such an active supporter (and later manager) of the Alberta Pool.

> I think it appropriate . . . to comment on farm organizations and the consequences of accepting elected office in them. Although the welfare of agriculture has been greatly enhanced by these organizations, few people realize the debt they owe the farmers and their wives who founded them and over the long years nurtured their growing influence and power. During the farmer's absence the farming operation suffered and the wife had to assume responsibility for the children, endure loneliness, and usually, the drudgery of looking after the farm and keeping it going as best she could. (LHB 20:216)

The passage touches on the roles and duties of men and women. Politics was, at least in the settling generation, the responsibility of men, but the activities of women's organizations often had a good deal to do with the power structure of local communities and towns, manifested as the ability to initiate civic and social reform projects. The men, on the other hand, were concerned with the basic resources required for the conduct of agriculture and how these resources could be acquired. Since ultimate control over resources is located outside the community, involvement in state, provincial, and national politics became necessary.

The populist activities of farmers everywhere led to government programs designed to alleviate uncertainty and hardship. In the United States the New Deal was particularly responsive. The Agricultural Adjustment Administration, the Farm Security Administration, the Soil Conservation Service, the Bureau of Reclamation, and a dozen or so other agencies, some of them antedating the New Deal, did much to stabilize agricultural industries during the drought and depression period. In Canada during the 1930s their various functions were combined under a single measure, the Prairie Farm Rehabilitation Act, but by the 1960s Canadians had produced separate analogues to most of the U.S. agencies at the federal or provincial level. All of these activities were designed to assist and encourage the market economy and in no sense could be considered radical in the classical left-wing sense, although their critics insistently apply the "socialist" label.

Farmers all over North America have been the despair of national party leaders, who cannot rely on them to vote consistently. Saskatchewan farmers, after a generation of populist protest and enthusiastic solidarity with the CCF, turned back in 1960 to the Liberals and the Progressive Conservatives after agricultural prices had regained strength and the CCF and federal governments engineered a few reforms. The CCF, in the guise of the New Democratic Party, came back in the 1970s. Farmers in the U.S. Great Plains fairly regularly swing between Democrats and Republicans. Farmers in both Canada and the United States in the 1930s were attracted in large numbers by demagogic movements like Father Coughlin's, or the Townsend Plan, or Social Credit. Farmers vote their pocketbooks and their position of security or insecurity, perhaps to a greater extent than manufacturers and small businessmen. The special case of the farmer is his proclivity to form movements; farmers are, in fact, better members of protest movements than reliable supporters of parties. Parties are urban phenomena; they need mass support, mass rallies, large auditoriums, big-city machines, large conventions. Ruralites may like to attend these affairs in the city, but the facilities to hold them in the country are usually lacking.

And the populist movements of the past century were also creations of scale. Farming, due to the homesteading process, was attempted everywhere, especially in the West, on too small an economic scale to permit adaptation to the rapidly changing technological and financial demands of agriculture and product marketing. The loss of farms has been a matter of serious concern and sadness to defenders of the family farm and traditional rural values. However, the loss has also been an economic necessity, since it permits an increase of scale among the remaining farmers, who can then farm on a basis that permits efficient machinery investments, computers, college educations, and the other requisites of large-scale production, of which agriculture has become a branch.

Some have argued that industrialization and capitalization of agriculture spells the end of farmers' movements and farmer-dominated governments. Perhaps. Certainly the increasing level of education in the Canadian-American West implies more farm and town participation in state or provincial and national politics, and this means that agricultural interests are more thoroughly heard and responded to. No longer can the financial and industrial interests of the East make policy without consulting rural constituencies. On the other hand, the residue of homesteading remains in the form of sparse rural population (which means fewer representatives to the legislatures) and certain cultural values (which contain a degree of disinterest in and disdain for Easterners). Most certainly, the problems of resource shortages and speculative fluctuation of prices will continue despite national economic support. Therefore we predict that the populist impulse—the need to organize and vigorously promote local interests—is not dead, only temporarily dormant. The heritage of self-help and cooperative action remains alive in the rural Canadian-American West.

Notes

Chapter 1. Locale and Approach

1. The book represents a final contribution of our research on the social and economic development of portions of the Canadian-American West. The original project was known as the Saskatchewan Cultural Ecology Research Program (SCERP). Fieldwork started in 1960 and continued intermittently until 1982. Bennett and Kohl 1981 contains a history of the SCERP project and bibliography.

2. For the most part, anthropological approaches to history stem from the fact that most ethnological research dealt with non- or semiliterate communities, requiring the analyst either to avoid history or to attempt "ethnohistorical" reconstruction. Such reconstruction requires the use of individual memories. See Vansina (1985: 161). Also see historians Collingwood (1946:295) and Lowenthal (1985:187) for further discussion of the relationship between memory, experience, and history. The social sciences do employ remembered events and experiences as data; see Yans-McLaughlin 1990 for a recent discussion of the use of personal documents. Some ethnologists have questioned the validity of such research on the grounds of inaccurate recall by informants; see Bernard, Killworth, and Kronenfeld 1984. As Myres (1982) points out, reminiscence is often unreliable because the writer's recall has been influenced by standardized interpretations. For example, Milner (1987) compared a diary account with a later reminiscence and found changes in "memory." In his example, the diary, a daily record of travel, rarely mentions the appearance of Indians. However, in the written reminiscence they appear daily and are presented as a severe danger. Milner suggests that the memoir is structured in terms of a developing

mythology about frontier hardships. Kohl (1989) analyzes the role of audience in what is recalled and told. Our experience tells us that much depends on the particular subject matter: Some topics are more reliably reported than others. Bradburn et al. 1987 provides a useful analysis of the function of "anecdotal memory" in responding to autobiographical questions in attitude survey protocols.

3. However, as time passes, and as trade between Canada and the United States intensifies and is increasingly regulated, boundary mechanisms become better organized, the customhouses are larger, the lines of trucks crossing the border longer, tourists more frequently searched. In the old days, odd things happened on the Canadian-American West boundary, including a good deal of rum-running. In November 1939, a number of American-made military aircraft were pushed across the line between Sweetgrass, Montana, and Coutts, Alberta, perhaps the most remote and underpopulated section of the entire international boundary. Pushed because it would have been a violation of the U.S. Neutrality Act to fly them across. At the time, only the local people knew it happened, and some of them took snapshots to be published later in a local history book (LHB 15:256ff., 299).

4. In order to familiarize ourselves with the community history literature, we developed a special research project based on the 105 books included in the bibliography as a sample from the "Heartland" region of the Canadian-American West. The project enabled us to document the fact that the history books are not exclusively local products but have become part of the continentwide local history movement, with its strong nostalgic emphasis and its connections to professional historical societies and to national and regional celebrations. We interviewed and surveyed forty-six editors of books from our Heartland sample, asking them how they planned the books and what things influenced their plans. The results indicated that despite the editors' goals for producing something unique and different, the formats and subject matter of previously published books influenced their conceptions of what should be included in their own histories. Publishers, particularly the big commercial houses such as Friesen Printers of Winnipeg, made available models of books and "how to do it" seminars for prospective editors. Instruction manuals offer advice to local historians, telling them how to collect and organize the data (see Felt 1976 and Peterson 1986). In other words, to an increasing extent, the community history book genre is a network phenomenon, not just a simple response of local people to a need to write their history.

5. In recent years the frontier thesis has received considerable criticism, much of it based on some fundamental ambiguities in Turner's presentation. Our experience with participant-produced historical materials from one section of the western frontier led us to distinguish three aspects related to Turner's thesis. (1) Turner seems to have been captivated by the open, frank, friendly spirit the frontier environment helped to induce in settlers (see Ridge 1986 for suggestions as to the way Turner's own childhood in central Wisconsin might have influenced his ideas). (2) He was drawn to the idea of individualism: the extent to which the frontier environment gave rise to a strong-willed human being, able to take

responsibility for himself and also work with other members of the community. That is, Turner saw the frontier as a society of cooperative equals. (3) Turner apparently ignored socioeconomic stratification on the frontier. Our data show that the early frontier homestead and town society was not stratified to any appreciable degree, since everyone had just arrived and most settlers came from similar socioeconomic backgrounds. Turner might therefore have been thinking primarily of this early period. The later, "postfrontier" society in both town and country was of course stratified as wealth and resources accumulated and were unequally distributed. However, Turner still had a point: Values and habits of the early egalitarian frontier persisted and still persist in the stratified society of the North American present. Egalitarianism became a cultural style, even if it is not fully manifest in social and economic organizations. Thus, the early frontier *did* have a powerful cultural influence on the subsequent social history of the United States. It had less in Canada, where the western frontier was more disciplined and influenced by eastern British-style order and elitism.

6. The term "adjustment" is also useful, since it can refer to short-term modifications in behavior or social relations to ease the pain of existence, while "adaptation" might be reserved for more basic, long-term changes.

Chapter 2. Settlement and Environment

1. For the history of political consolidation in the Canadian Prairie Provinces see Friesen 1984. There is nothing strictly comparable for the American side, i.e., a book devoted to the history of the region comprising the states of, say, Idaho, Montana, and North Dakota. Instead, there are interpretive histories of the West in general, often combining the Pacific Coast and the Great Plains (e.g., Paul 1988, which attempts to handle both in a fine single volume). Limerick 1987 is a critical assessment of western history and its cultural, social, and economic implications. For Montana the most convenient one-volume account is Malone and Roeder 1976.

2. For histories of exploration, see Billington 1956 for the United States and Morton 1973 for Canada. The major early expeditions for the U.S. side were all government-supported, e.g., those led by Lewis and Clark, Zebulon Pike, Stephen Long. Pike and Long were probably the first explorers to emphasize the aridity and other forbidding features (Hagwood 1967). In Canada the principal early travel account of the Canadian plains and mountains was David Thompson's (White 1950). In the second phase of exploration of both countries, detailed maps were made, like those in the report by U.S. Army officer John Mullan on building a road through the U.S. Rockies (Mullan 1863), or his later emigrant guidebook to the Northwest (Mullan 1865). For Canada, John Palliser's expedition, commissioned by the British, provided detailed information on the plains and mountain areas, with emphasis on aridity; Palliser gave his name to a large area of southeastern Alberta, northern Montana, and southwestern Saskatchewan—"Palliser's Triangle" (really a parallelogram)—that he considered to be too dry for cultivation (Spry 1963, Palliser 1859). Henry Hind (1860), on the other hand, challenged that pessimistic view of its suitability for settlement. An example of a third, or "scientific," phase was the work of botanist John Macoun (1876; 1880–

81), who pronounced the plains section of western Canada fit for cultivation, providing certain care was taken. On the U.S. side the expeditions of the biologist Ferdinand Hayden (1862) are exemplary. A pictorial representation of major explorations, emphasizing Montana, is Thompson 1985, which also contains a reproduction of a previously unpublished map of the routes and topography of the International Boundary Survey, a joint British–U.S. venture, in 1857 (see Northern Boundary Commission 1872–76).

3. Innis 1956 is a standard Canadian history; Chittenden 1935, a U.S. history. De Voto 1947 and Don Berry 1961 are narrative histories mainly of the American companies. Rich 1960 is a detailed study of the Hudson's Bay Company. For a treatment of the role of Native American tribes in the fur trade, see Friesen 1984, chapters 2, 3, and 7. See Van Kirk 1980 and Brown 1985 for useful material regarding the role Indian women played.

4. References to the north-south trail complex can be found in most surveys of North American history and geography. See Cushman 1966 for a history of the Old North Trail, McClintock 1923 for a description of Indian trails that includes material on the Old North Trail complex, and Sharp 1955 on the portion of the trail in our study area.

5. For histories of the railroads, see Berton 1972, Hedges 1930 and 1939, Peterson 1969, and Smalley 1883. For accounts of the local railroads preceding the Canadian Pacific and Great Northern and how these were incorporated, in some instances, into the big lines, see Lingeman (1980:244–50) and Hudson (1985, chapters 4–6). For the history of Fort Benton and environs, see Sharp 1955, Fooks 1983, and Overholser 1987. Lass 1962 contains a history of steamboats on the Upper Missouri; a bibliography of histories of river transportation is found in Haites, Mak, and Walton 1975.

6. For some historical and biographical treatment of ranching history in the Canadian-American West, see the following: Anderson 1988, Atherton 1961, Blasingame 1958, Brado 1984, Breen 1983, Burlingame 1942, Dykstra 1983, Kelley 1980, MacEwan 1962, Kohrs 1977.

The Canadian leases assigned to American ranchers created a constant run of trouble in the 1880s for the Canadian government, which administered them for the Northwest Territories. Lewis Thomas (1975:275–95) collected a series of documents written by ranchers, settlers, and government agents illustrating the problems. Ranchers complained about harassment from incoming settlers, and settlers about harassment from the ranchers; ranchers complained about squatters invading the leases; ranchers complained about each other, especially about invasions of neighboring herds on leases. Members of Parliament defended settlers, and other Members defended lease-holders. Both ranchers and settlers asked for help from the Mounted Police. The government tried to collect lease rent from delinquent lessees or persuade them to buy outright; departments charged with managing land and water resources complained about overgrazing and other destructive practices.

7. The differences in settlement timing and policies between the United States and Canada were not due simply to cultural and political differences, but to the

different land tenure situations in the western sections of both countries. Until 1871 nearly all of western Canada was "owned" by the Hudson's Bay Company. By the 1880s, substantial grants were owned by the developing railroads. Eventually some of this land was sold to settlers. Before widespread land surveying and homesteading could begin, control over land had to be clarified. In 1870, an agreement reserved substantial amounts for the Hudson's Bay Company in return for their consent to give the dominion government territorial rights to the West; and the railroads, in the 1880s, had received as much as 24 million acres. By 1905 Clifford Sifton, the Canadian commissioner of settlement, had acquired almost all of the railroad land for settlement, and the last of the Hudson's Bay lands became available in the 1910–15 period. In the United States, except for railroad grant strips, almost all of the land was in federal government control from the beginning, so surveying and homestead openings could begin sooner and more efficiently. And the U.S. railroads worked closely with the government from the beginning in order to realize a return from settlement.

8. For an account of the Nez Percé War, see Josephy (1971). Much has been written about Riel (see Woodcock 1975) and the Riel Rebellions (see Stanley 1960 and Howard 1970). Louis Riel was a creature of both countries, but a loner who got lost somewhere in the consolidation of nationhood and the institutionalization of an international boundary. So there are slight differences in perspective. Woodcock (1975) presents the story from the standpoint of Gabriel Dumont, Riel's chief lieutenant.

Métis had been moving back and forth across the international boundary for years, since most of the population lived by hunting, trapping, teamstering, and other frontier occupations. French names are common across the northern reaches of the United States from Minnesota to Montana, and many families have métis backgrounds. But many French-Canadian immigrants from Quebec as well as French colonials also moved south into the States. Any métis could decide to abandon Indian identity and culture if their appearance was not markedly Indian and if they were literate, and many, like Jerry Potts, the famous NWMP scout, were of "English métis" origin. For histories and accounts of the métis people, see the following: MacEwan 1981, Giraud 1986, Sealey and Lussier 1975, and Peterson and Brown 1985.

9. The best single source for an appreciation of what the NWMP were doing and how they felt about it are the reports made by the force to the Canadian government. These are found in the *Sessional Papers* of the House of Commons, included in reports to the department of the secretary of state but sometimes issued in the annual reports of that department and sometimes as separate reports of the Commissioner of the NWMP. All of these reports are dated during the 1880s, when the Mounties were in their prime. Also see Turner 1950, Chambers 1906, and MacCleod 1976.

10. For an introduction to the physical environment of the Great Plains and its implications for settlement and agriculture see Malin 1984, Allen 1976, Blouet and Luebke 1979, Caldwell, Schultz, and Stout 1983, Currie 1945, and Davies 1978. Webb 1931 is the classic book on adaptation to the plains, but many of its technical discussions are now out of date. For an economic approach to plains

resources see Clawson 1981 and East and Neil 1975. For some studies of the problem of water and water use in the northern plains, see Clawson 1981 and Rickard 1979. Smythe 1969 is the classic promotional statement for irrigation as the key to making the plains into an agricultural empire; Hargreaves 1957 is an authoritative study of the dry farming movement, which like irrigation was promoted as a solution to the moisture problem; Saarinen (1966) studies how plains farmers perceive drought, or rather their hesitance to accept the inevitability of recurrent drought. Davison 1967 is a summary account of all the myths and dreams of water characteristic of the nineteenth-century promoters of settlement, with special reference to Montana. Also see Henry Nash Smith 1947 and 1950.

11. Bennett's *Of Time and the Enterprise* (1982) contains historical materials on ranching and farming in southwestern Saskatchewan and on the methods developed by settlers for coping with the specialized resources of the Heartland region of the Canadian-American West.

Chapter 3. Settlement Patterns and Ethnicity

1. The following items concerning ethnicity and migration theory were particularly useful: Bentley 1987, Cohen 1978, Conzen 1980, Erickson 1972, Huel 1978, Luebke 1977, Saveth 1965, Vincent 1974.

2. For a sample of studies for particular religious settlements, see the following: Dawson 1936; Boldt 1979 on Mennonites; Degh 1980 on Hungarian folk religions; Evans 1987 on Hutterites; Jackson 1975 on Mormons; Kauffman 1953 on the Amish; Rochlin and Rochlin 1984 on Jews; Koch 1977 and Sallet 1931 on Russo-Germans of various denominations.

3. Studies of ethnicity in various ethnic and sectarian groups settling the Canadian-American West include the following, in addition to items cited in the text: Anderson 1982, Bennett and Sherburne 1992, Bjork 1974, Dawson and Younge 1940, Holmquist 1981, Hurd 1937, Kloberdanz 1980, Kovacs 1978, Loken 1980, Lovoll 1984, Lowell 1987, Morton 1938, Palmer and Palmer 1985, Sherman 1983, Shortridge 1988, Tracie 1976.

Chapter 4. Setting Out: Emigration as a Social Process

1. Despite persistent literary images of western settlement as an affair of adventurous individuals, it was, as Margaret Walsh (1981:61) puts it, "as much a family affair as a single person's prerogative." Darroch (1981) notes how family ties provided major social and economic resources for emigration and settlement.

2. In part this revision has been a natural extension of the increased attention to women in historical writing; it has also been due to the revision of the concept of the frontier itself. For a review of the sequential development of critiques about western women's history and different roles for frontier women, see Patterson-Black 1978, Jensen and Miller 1980, Faragher 1981, Myres 1983, Armitage 1985, and Armitage and Jameson 1987.

3. Some historians—e.g., Faragher (1981, 1988), Stansell (1976), and Fink (1992)—emphasize the privation, unceasing labor, exploitation, and victimization of women. On the other side of the debate, Bartlett (1974), Myres (1982),

and Silverman (1984) suggest that the interpretation of women's experience as unrelieved drudgery fails to recognize that, for most women, agricultural homesteading was a continuation, not change, of their previous routines and that women as well as men were committed to the search for new economic opportunity. Harris (1983, 1993) includes factors of time, place, the nature of women's economic role, and women's land ownership to analyze women's status and autonomy.

Chapter 6. Settling in: Family and Household

1. Five contributions portraying the experience of women in the history of western settlement illustrate some of the ways historians have looked at the impact of the frontier experience for women. See Jeffrey 1979, Myres 1982, Schlissel 1982, Silverman 1984, and Stratton 1981. For Silverman, Stratton, and Myres, the frontier settlement experience led to an expansion of women's opportunities and a lessening of patriarchal controls. Schlissel and Jeffrey find continuity. The different conclusions are in part a function of different goals of the authors: Schlissel and Jeffrey use the cult of domesticity as the dominant belief system by which westering women could measure change. Their assumption that this belief system was widely prevalent is challenged by Silverman (1985) and Bartlett (1974).

2. This pattern has been noted by historians of western European family history. See Anderson 1980, Laslett 1984, Segalen 1986, and Habakkuk 1955 for discussions of changes in family organization and structure accompanying changes in work opportunities and control over resources.

Chapter 7. Growing Up: Memories of Childhood

1. Two recent exceptions are Elliot West's 1989 study of childhood on the far western frontier, *Growing Up with the Country,* and Elizabeth Hampsten's *Settlers, Children: Growing Up on the Great Plains*. Discussion of the problems historians face in reconstructing childhood can be found in Armitage 1979, West 1989, and West and Petrik 1992.

2. In a review of more than 200 homestead reminiscences, Daniels (1986:xxxv) notes that the most general pattern found in reminiscences is one in which difficulties are passed over with emphasis placed on the positive outcomes.

3. For example, Elliot West, who has warned against generalizing from childhood memories, nevertheless does so. Making use of contemporary child development theories of separation anxiety, he suggests that leaving home and the trail experience were "designed to terrify children" (West 1989:33). Certainly children on the homestead agricultural frontier were anxious about death and feared the loss of their parents, but such anxieties did not form the bedrock for their subsequent character formation, as West suggests. As West himself notes (1989:40), "the great majority of children neither died nor lost a parent," and most children did not go the Overland Trail route. Such contextual features need to be included in an application of the model of developmental psychology.

4. For a general discussion of what is remembered over time, see the collected papers in Rubin 1987.

5. Socialization is a complicated process with many kinds of learning in many settings, taught by a variety of agents. Henry (1960) emphasizes not only the multiplicity of items that must be learned but the polyphasic character of human learning—humans never learn just a single item but absorb many other things, such as social values, in the process. In all societies the process of cultural transmission begins at birth, rooted in the infant's complete dependency upon adult caretakers. It is defined as "the process by which we learn the ways of a given society or social group so that we can function within it" (Elkin and Handel 1989:2).

Chapter 8. Coming Together: The Formation of the Community

1. For studies of community formation and life on the North American frontier, see the following works. Bender (1978) attempts to trace the history of the idea of community in the United States and also to examine the meaning of social theory for the study of community in American life; "community" for Bender refers mainly to the spiritual aspects of the term. Hine (1980) presents a history of key forms of community life at different periods, thus providing an introduction to the empirical meaning of "community." Hine subtitled his book "Separate but Not Alone," which echoes our emphasis in these chapters on the combination of highly individualistic achievement and equally significant community interaction and cooperation. Clark (1968) provides a somewhat comparable survey of the forms of communities developing in the various Canadian frontiers.

2. "Community" is a generic term with at least two principal meanings: the general spirit of association and fraternity, and a particular assemblage of people in a particular place who share the tasks necessary for reasonably continuous social life. But, as noted in the text, the structure and form of actual communities vary with cultural and social styles. A review of various concepts of community in urbanized industrial-nation societies, as they are presented by sociologists, can be found in Warren 1978 (introduction and chapter 1), Redfield 1955, and Sims 1920, a classic text reflecting turn-of-the-century communities.

3. There are a few studies of rural community formation in the Canadian-American West. For examples, see Voisey 1988 and Myers 1990. In the 1950s and '60s the Royal Commission on Agriculture and Rural Life to the Government of Saskatchewan published a series of reports (e.g., Royal Commission 1956, 1957), which led to the establishment of the Centre for Community Studies in the University of Saskatchewan. The center embarked on a series of follow-up researches on the society and economy (e.g., Abramson 1965).

4. A 1992 book edited by I. Altman and S. Low, entitled *Place Attachment,* contains a series of essays on how people become wedded to particular homes and homelands. The essays have interesting materials, but the bias of the undertaking is toward long-term occupation; it assumes that stable residence is the real or normative condition. Very few findings relate to populations on the move—people deliberately and frequently moving in order to seek out a home, or at least a place where they can make a living and raise a family. In general, "place attachment" is not a single, simple behavioral pattern but rather the result of whatever objectives and goals permit stability of residence.

Chapter 9. Institutions and Services: The Postfrontier Community

1. Perhaps the most famous of the itinerant pastors of the Canadian-American West was the Rev. William Wesley Van Orsdael, a Methodist missionary and minister to the homestead and town frontier in Montana and North Dakota (see Brummit 1919, Smith 1948, and Lind 1961). An Ohioan who witnessed the Battle of Gettysburg as a boy, Van Orsdael went West as a result of his childhood fascination with such characters as Buffalo Bill and apprenticed his way into the ministry. He never attended a regular divinity school, and the administrators of the Methodist mission church kept him in an itinerant role because of his style of preaching, with its storytelling and songs, his flamboyant western hat, and an occasional sidearm. He was proud of his friendships with the Blackfoot Indians and the cowboy painter Charlie Russell. Brother Van, as he was known to everyone, offered respite from drudgery and gave a sense of conscience fulfilled to his listeners. Eventually he was able to stimulate 40 or 50 communities along the Hi Line in Montana and western North Dakota to build churches, but Van Orsdael never really had a church of his own.

Chapter 10. Women's Organizations: From Country District to Nation

1. In Canada the founders and leaders of the women's farm groups were well-educated, middle-class women from eastern Canada, Britain, and the United States (Nicholson 1974:154–55, Wilson 1977). Susan Jackel (1982:xxiii–xxiv) hypothesizes that the preponderance of educated single British women present in western Canada at this time (1910–20), due in part to the loss of men in the Crimean War, played an important role in the development of suffrage forums and the formation of women's organizations. However, the social context of that time period from 1890 to 1920 cannot be discounted. See the collection of essays in Tilley and Gurin 1992.

2. The first convention of the Saskatchewan Homemakers was held in 1911; the Saskatchewan Women Grain Growers were organized in 1913 as a response to the "result of the growing awareness among farm women that their contribution to the farm movement was stifled within the men's organization" (Marchildon 1985:89–90). In Alberta the first Women's Institute began in 1909; in 1912 the government awarded grants to six local institutes. The United Farm Women, organized in 1915, restricted its membership to farmers' wives and daughters, as did the Women Grain Growers in Saskatchewan. Whereas the Women Grain Growers and the United Farm Women took an active political stance, the Homemakers and the Women's Institutes, with semi-official government sponsorship, were considered to be apolitical. In Montana funds for Home Economics Extension began with the passage of the Smith Lever Act in 1914. Local women's clubs organized earlier were incorporated into the Extension Home Demonstration programs.

3. The Women's Institute's opposition to Hutterite schools was part of a more general position on immigration and an interest in promulgating an English majority society and culture. Similar views were at the heart of attempts to recruit middle-class women from Britain (see Jackel 1982).

Chapter 11. Rudyard: A Railroad-Homestead Town

1. Our data for the towns along the CPR line in Saskatchewan and Alberta give a comparative picture. The patterns are substantially identical. Like the Montana Hi Line, the CPR line of towns was established by the railroad and by entrepreneurs anxious to take advantage of the transportation and the settlers. The Canadian Pacific generally preceded the Great Northern by about a decade in most stretches, so the towns are somewhat older than their Montana equivalents. But the patterns of growth, decline, and revival are similar, with a final general decline and shake-out after World War II. The dynamic of the towns is also the same: an early, rapid establishment of many businesses as a result of outside financing and entrepreneurship, then fluctuation in response to the pattern of boom and bust in the western economy, and for the majority of the original settlements, disappearance or stasis at a low level of economy. (For some descriptions of small towns in southwestern Saskatchewan, see Bennett 1969, chapter 2.)

By the 1950s many small railroad towns in Canada and the United States began fading as lines were abandoned or had infrequent trains. The CPR, under Canada's VIARAIL management, terminated all passenger trains on the main line across western Canada in 1989. The Great Northern continues to carry them as long as AMTRAK is supported.

2. See Butler 1985 and Petrik 1987 for the analysis of prostitution as an economic venture open to women. Writing about Havre's early days, Gray (1971) notes the links between early entrepreneurs, bootlegging, and prostitution.

Chapter 14. The Political Aftermath

1. For historical studies of political and economic development in the background of populist ideology, see the following: Bogue 1963, Gates 1969, Lang 1990, Lipset 1990, Malone and Roeder 1976, Marshall 1986, Peterson 1919, Saloutos and Hicks 1951, Shannon 1945, Smith 1950, and Toole 1950 and 1972. For the emergence of populist attitudes: Henderson and Small 1983, Low 1984, Parson 1981. For histories of the populist movement taken as a whole, with emphasis on the earlier, nineteenth-century phase, see Goodwyn 1978, Hicks 1931, Pollack 1967. See the following studies of populist movements in particular states and provinces. *Saskatchewan:* Bennett and Krueger 1968, Krueger 1968, Tyre 1962, Young 1969, Lipset 1950, Sharp 1948. *Alberta:* Dempsey 1981, Voisey 1988, Irving 1959. *North Dakota and Montana:* Lang 1990, Saloutos 1945, Bruce 1921. *Western Canada generally:* Berton 1984 (chapter 9).

Bibliography

Published Sources

Abramson, Jane. 1965. *A Study of the Effects of Displacement on Farmers Whose Land Was Purchased for Two Community Pastures in Saskatchewan*. Saskatoon: Centre for Community Studies, University of Saskatchewan.

Alderson, Nannie T., and Helena Huntington Smith. 1969. *A Bride Goes West*. Lincoln: University of Nebraska Press.

Allen, Richard. 1976. *Man and Nature on the Prairies*. Canadian Plains Studies No. 6. Regina, Sask.: Canadian Plains Research Center.

Altman, Irwin, and Setha M. Low, eds. 1992. *Place Attachment*. New York: Plenum.

Anderson, Alan. 1982. "Generation Differences in Ethnic Identity Retention in Rural Saskatchewan," *Prairie Forum* (Special Issue on Ethnic Studies and Research in the Prairies) 7:171–96.

Anderson, Boyd M. 1988. *Beyond the Range: A History of the Saskatchewan Stock Growers' Association*. Saskatoon, Sask.: Saskatchewan Stock Growers' Association.

Anderson, Michael. 1980. *Approaches to the History of the Western Family, 1500–1914*. London: Macmillan.

Archer, John A. 1980. *Saskatchewan: A History*. Saskatoon, Sask.: Western Producer Prairie Books.

Armitage, Sue. 1979. "Household Work and Childrearing on the Frontier: The Oral History Record," *Sociology and Social Research* 63:467–74.

———. 1985. "Women and Men in Western History: A Stereoptical Vision," *Western Historical Quarterly* 16:391–95.

Armitage, Susan, and Elizabeth Jameson, eds. 1987. *The Women's West*. Norman: University of Oklahoma Press.

Atherton, Lewis. 1961. *The Cattle Kings*. Bloomington: Indiana University Press.

Barclay, Craig R. 1987. "Schematization of Autobiographical Memory," in *Autobiographical Memory*, ed. David C. Rubin. Cambridge: Cambridge University Press.

Bartlett, Richard A. 1974. *The New Country: A Social History of the American Frontier, 1776–1890*. New York: Oxford University Press.

Bender, Thomas. 1978. *Community and Social Change in America*. New Brunswick: Rutgers University Press.

Bennett, John W. 1969. *Northern Plainsmen: Adaptive Strategy and Agrarian Life*. Arlington Heights IL: AHM.

———. 1982. *Of Time and the Enterprise: North American Family Farm Management in a Context of Resource Management*. Minneapolis: University of Minnesota Press.

———. 1990. "Human Adaptations to the North American Great Plains and Similar Environments," in *The Struggle for the Land*, ed. Paul A. Olson. Lincoln: University of Nebraska Press.

———. 1992. *Human Ecology as Human Behavior: Essays in Environmental and Development Anthropology*. New Brunswick NJ: Transaction.

Bennett, John W., and Cynthia Krueger. 1968. "Agrarian Pragmatism and Radical Politics," in *Agrarian Socialism*, ed. Seymour M. Lipset. New York: Doubleday/Anchor.

Bennett, John W., and Seena B. Kohl. 1981. "Longitudinal Research in Rural North America: The Saskatchewan Cultural Ecology Research Program," in *Anthropologists at Home in North America*, ed. D. A. Messerschmidt. New York: Cambridge University Press.

Bennett, John W., and Dan S. Sherburne. 1992. "Ethnicity, Settlement and Adaptation in the Peopling of the Canadian-American West," in *Migration and the Transformation of Cultures*, ed. Jean Burnet et al. Toronto: Multicultural History Society of Ontario.

Bentley, Carter. 1987. "Ethnicity and Practice," *Comparative Studies in Society and History* 29(1):24–55.

Bernard, H. Russell, Peter Killworth, and David Kronenfeld. 1984. "The Problem of Informant Accuracy: The Validity of Retrospective Data," *Annual Review of Anthropology* 13:495–517.

Berry, Don. 1961. *A Majority of Scoundrels: An Informal History of the Rocky Mountain Fur Company*. Sausalito CA: Comstock Editions.

Berry, Gerald L. 1950. "Alberta-Montana Relationships." Master's thesis, University of Alberta (Edmonton). (Published as *The Whoop-Up Trail: Early Days in Alberta-Montana*. Edmonton: Applied Arts Production, 1953.)

Berton, Pierre. 1972. *The Impossible Railway: The Building of the Canadian Pacific*. New York: Alfred A. Knopf.

———. 1984. *The Promised Land: Settling the West, 1894–1914*. Toronto: McLelland and Stewart.

Bicha, Karel Denis. 1965. "The Plains Farmer and the Prairie Province Frontier, 1897–1914," *Proceedings of the American Philosophical Society* 190(6):398–442.
Billington, Ray A. 1956. *The Far Western Frontier: 1830–1860*. New York: Harper and Row.
Bjork, Kenneth O. 1974. "Scandinavian Migration to the Canadian Prairie Provinces, 1893–1914," *Norwegian-American Studies* 26:3–30.
Blasingame, Ike. 1958. *Dakota Cowboy: My Life in the Old Days*. New York: G. P. Putnam's Sons.
Blouet, Brian W., and Frederick C. Luebke, eds. 1979. *The Great Plains Environment and Culture*. Lincoln: University of Nebraska Press.
Bogue, Allan G. 1963. *From Prairie to Corn Belt*. Chicago: University of Chicago Press.
Boldt, Edward D. 1979. "Mennonite Community and Change," *Canadian Journal of Sociology* 4:151–54.
Bolkhovitinov, N. N. 1962. "The Role of the Frontier in the History of the U.S.A.," *Voprosy istoril* 6:22–38.
Bosetti, Shelley Anne Marie. 1983. "The Rural Women's University: Women's Institutes in Alberta from 1900 to 1940," Master's thesis, University of Alberta.
Bowsfield, Hartwell. 1969. "Writing Local History," *Alberta Historical Review* 17:10–19.
Bradburn, N. et al. 1987. "Answering Autobiographical Questions: The Impact of Memory and Inference on Surveys," *Science* 236 (10 April 1987): 157–61.
Brado, Edward. 1984. *Cattle Kingdom: Early Ranching in Alberta*. Vancouver: Douglas & McIntyre.
Braithwaite, Max. 1984. *Never Sleep Three in a Bed*. Toronto: McLelland and Stewart.
Breen, David H. 1983. *The Canadian Prairie West and the Ranching Frontier, 1874–1924*. Toronto: University of Toronto Press.
Brown, Jennifer S. H. 1985. "Diverging Identities: The Presbyterian Métis of St. Gabriel Street, Montreal," in *The New Peoples: Being and Becoming Métis in North America*, ed. Jacqueline Peterson and Jennifer S. H. Brown. Lincoln: University of Nebraska Press.
Bruce, A. A. 1921. *The Non-Partisan League*. New York: Macmillan.
Brummit, Stella W. 1919. *Brother Van*. New York: Missionary Education Movement of U.S. and Canada.
Burlingame, Merrill G. 1942. *The Montana Frontier*. Bozeman MT: Big Sky Books.
Burlingame, Merrill G., and K. Ross Toole. 1957. *A History of Montana*, vol. 3. New York: Lewis Historical Publishing Co.
Butler, Anne M. 1985. *Daughter of Joy, Sisters of Mercy: Prostitutes in the American West*. Urbana: University of Illinois Press.
Caldwell, Warren, C. Bertrand Schultz, and T. Mylan Stout. 1983. "A Symposium: Man and the Changing Environments in the Great Plains."

Transactions of the Nebraska Academy of Sciences and Affiliated Societies, vol. 11 (Special Issue).

Careless, J. M. S. 1989. *Frontier and Metropolis: Regions, Cities and Identities in Canada Before 1914*. Toronto: University of Toronto Press.

Carter, Eva. 1944. *Thirty Years of Progress: History of the United Farm Women of Alberta*. Calgary: John D. McAra.

Chambers, Ernest J. 1906. *The Royal North-West Mounted Police*. Montreal: Mortimer Press.

Cheney, Roberta Carkeek. 1983. *Names on the Face of Montana: The History of Montana's Place Names*. Missoula MT: Mountain Press.

Chittenden, Hiram M. 1935. *American Fur Trade of the Far West*. New York: Barnes and Noble.

Clark, S. D. 1968. *The Developing Canadian Community*. Toronto: University of Toronto Press.

Clawson, Marion. 1981. "Natural Resources of the Great Plains in Historical Perspective," in *The Great Plains: Perspectives and Prospects*, ed. Merlin P. Lawson and Maurice Baker. Lincoln: University of Nebraska Press.

Cohen, Ronald. 1978. "Ethnicity: Problem and Focus in Anthropology," *Annual Review of Anthropology* 7:379–403.

Collingwood, R. G. 1946. *The Idea of History*. New York: Oxford University Press.

Collins, Robert. 1980. *Butter Down the Well: Reflections of a Canadian Childhood*. Saskatoon, Sask.: Western Producer Prairie Books.

Conzen, Kathleen Neils. 1980. "Historical Approaches to the Study of Rural Ethnic Communities," in *Ethnicity on the Great Plains*, ed. Frederick C. Luebke. Lincoln: University of Nebraska Press.

Council on Environmental Quality. 1981. *Desertification of the United States*. Washington D.C.: Government Printing Office.

Crowe, P. R. 1936. "The Rainfall Regime of the Western Plains," *Geographical Review* 26:463–84.

Currie, A. W. 1945. *Economic Geography of Canada*. Toronto: Macmillan.

Cushman, Dan. 1966. *The Great North Trail: America's Route of the Ages*. New York: McGraw-Hill.

Dale, Robert F. 1967. "The Climate of the Great Plains," in *Symposium on the Great Plains of North America*, ed. Carle C. Zimmerman and Seth Russell. Fargo ND: The North Dakota Institute for Regional Studies.

Daniels, Sherrill F. 1986. "An Index to and Bibliography of Reminiscences in the Nebraska State Historical Society Library." Ph.D. diss., University of Nebraska.

Darroch, A. Gordon. 1981. "Migrants in the Nineteenth Century: Fugitives or Families in Motion?" *Journal of Family History* Fall 1981: 257–77.

Davies, W. A., ed. 1978. "Nature and Change on the Canadian Prairies," *Canadian Plains Proceedings* 6. University of Regina, Canadian Plains Research Center.

Davison, Stanley A. 1967. "Hopes and Fancies of the Early Reclamationists," in *Historical Essays on Montana and the Northwest*. Western Press.

Dawson, C. A. 1936. *Group Settlement: Ethnic Communities in Western*

Canada. Vol. 7, *Canadian Frontiers of Settlement*, ed. W. A. Mackintosh and W. L. G. Joerg. Toronto: Macmillan.
Dawson, C. A. and Eva R. Younge. 1940. *Pioneering in the Prairie Provinces*. Vol. 8, *Canadian Frontiers of Settlement,* ed. W. A. Mackintosh and W. L. G. Joerg. Toronto: Macmillan.
Degh, Linda. 1980. "Folk Religion as Ideology for Ethnic Survival: The Hungarians of Kipling, Saskatchewan," in *Ethnicity on the Great Plains,* ed. Frederick C. Luebke. Lincoln: University of Nebraska Press.
Dempsey, Hugh, ed. 1981. *The Best from Alberta History*. Saskatoon, Sask.: Western Producer Prairie Books.
———. 1984. *Big Bear: The End of Freedom*. Lincoln: University of Nebraska Press.
den Otter, A. A. 1982. *Civilizing the West: The Galts and the Development of Western Canada*. Edmonton: University of Alberta Press.
De Voto, Bernard. 1947. *Across the Wide Missouri*. Boston: Houghton Mifflin.
Dryden, Jean, and Sandra L. Myres. 1987. "Homesteading on Canadian Prairies," *Montana the Magazine of Western History* Winter 1987: 15–33.
Dykstra, Robert R. 1983. *The Cattle Towns*. Lincoln: University of Nebraska Press.
East, H. R. and Neil, D. A. 1975. "The Swift Current–Gravelbourg Region of Saskatchewan." *Prairie Regional Studies in Economic Geography,* no. 24. Economics Branch, Agriculture. Ottawa: Queen's Printer.
Eggleston, Wilfred. 1982. *Homestead on the Range*. Ottawa: Borealis Press.
Elkin, Fredrick, and Gerald Handel. 1989. *The Child and Society*. New York: Random House.
Erickson, Charlotte. 1972. *Invisible Immigrants: The Adaptation of English and Scottish Immigrants in Nineteenth-Century America*. Coral Gables FL: University of Miami Press.
Esval, Orland Eittreim. 1979. *Prairie Tales*. Banner Elk NC: Landmark House.
Evans, Simon M. 1987. "The Hutterites in Alberta: Past and Present Settlement Patterns," in *Essays on the Historical Geography of the Canadian West: Regional Perspectives on the Settlement Process,* ed. L. A. Rosenvall and Simon M. Evans. Calgary: University of Calgary.
Faragher, John Mack. 1981. "History from the Inside-Out: Writing the History of Women in Rural America," *American Quarterly,* 33(1):537–57.
———. 1988. *Sugar Creek: Life on the Illinois Prairie*. New Haven: Yale University Press.
Felt, Thomas E. 1976. *Researching, Writing and Publishing Local History*. Nashville: American Association for State and Local History.
Fink, Deborah. 1992. *Agrarian Women: Wives and Mothers in Rural Nebraska, 1880–1940*. Chapel Hill: University of North Carolina Press.
Finnell, Eva Gorman, ed. 1980. *The Montana Years: Chouteau County, 1910–1926*. Montana Historical Society.
Fooks, Georgia. 1983. *Fort Whoop-Up: Alberta's First and Most Notorious Whisky Fort*. Lethbridge, Alta: Historical Society of Alberta.
Freeman, J. S. 1961. "On the Concept of the Kindred," *Journal of the Royal Anthropological Institute* 91:192–220.

Friesen, Gerald. 1984. *The Canadian Prairies: A History*. Lincoln: University of Nebraska Press.

Galbraith, John Kenneth. 1964. *The Scotch*. New York: Houghton Mifflin.

Gates, Paul W. 1969. *Landlords and Tenants on the Prairie Frontier*. Ithaca: Cornell University Press.

Giraud, Marcel. 1986. *The Métis in the Canadian West*, trans. George Woodcock. Lincoln: University of Nebraska Press.

Gjerde, Jon. 1985. *From Peasants to Farmers: The Migration from Balestrand, Norway to the Upper Middle West*. Cambridge: Cambridge University Press.

Glazer, Nathan, and Daniel P. Moynihan, eds. 1975. *Ethnicity: Theory and Experience*. Cambridge: Harvard University Press.

Goldring, P. 1973. "The Cypress Hills Massacre: A Century's Retrospect," *Saskatchewan History* 26:80–102.

Goodwyn, Lawrence. 1978. *The Populist Moment: A Short History of the Agrarian Revolt in America*. New York: Oxford University Press.

Gordon, Linda. 1976. *Women's Body, Women's Right: A Social History of Birth Control in America*. New York: Grossman.

Graulich, Melody. 1984. "Violence Against Women in Literature of the Western Family," *Frontiers* 7(3):14–20.

Gray, James H. 1971, 1986. *Red Lights on the Prairies*. Saskatoon, Sask.: Western Producer Prairie Books.

Gross, Renie, and Lea N. Kramer. 1985. *Tapping the Bow*. Brooks, Alta.: Eastern Irrigation District and Friesen Printers.

Habakkuk, S. 1955. "Family Structure and Economic Change in 19th-Century Europe," *Journal of Economic History* 15:1–12.

Hagwood, John A. 1967. *America's Western Frontiers*. New York: Alfred A. Knopf.

Haites, Erik F., James Mak, and Gary M. Walton. 1975. *Western River Transportation: The Era of Early Internal Development, 1810–1860*. Baltimore: Johns Hopkins University Press.

Hampsten, Elizabeth. 1991. *Settlers' Children: Growing Up on the Great Plains*. Norman: University of Oklahoma Press.

Hargreaves, Mary Wilma M. 1957. *Dry Farming in the Northern Great Plains, 1900–1925*. Cambridge: Harvard University Press.

Harris, Katherine Llewellyn Hill. 1983. "Women and Families on Northwestern Colorado Homesteads 1873–1920," Ph.D. diss., University of Colorado.

———. 1993. *Long Vistas: Women and Families on Colorado Homesteads*. Niwot: University Press of Colorado.

Harrison, Julia D. 1985. *Métis: People Between Two Worlds*. Seattle: University of Washington Press.

Hatton, Timothy J., and Jeffrey G. Williamson. 1994. "What Drove the Mass Migrations from Europe?" *Population and Development Review* 20(3):533–59.

Hayden, Ferdinand V. 1862. "On the Geology and Natural History of the Upper Missouri," *Transactions of the American Philosophical Society*, n.s. no. 12.

Hedges, James B. 1930. *Henry Villard and the Railways of the Northwest*. New York: Russell and Russell.
———. 1939. *Building the Canadian West: The Land and Colonization Policies of the Canadian Pacific Railway*. New York: Macmillan.
Henderson, Harley, and Lawrence F. Small. 1983. *Montana Passage: A Homesteader's Heritage*. Helena MT: Falcon Press.
Henry, Jules. 1960. "A Cross-Cultural Outline of Education," *Current Anthropology* 1(4):267–306.
Hicks, John D. 1931. *The Populist Revolt*. Minneapolis: University of Minnesota Press.
Hildebrand, David V., and Geoffrey A. J. Scott. 1987. "Relationships Between Moisture Deficiency and the Amount of Tree Cover on the Pre-Agricultural Canadian Plains," *Prairie Forum* 12:203–16.
Hind, Henry Y. 1860. "Report of the Assiniboine and Saskatchewan Exploring Expedition," reprinted in "British Parliamentary Papers."
Hine, Robert V. 1980. *Community on the American Frontier: Separate But Not Alone*. Norman: University of Oklahoma Press.
Holmquist, June Drenning. 1981. *They Chose Minnesota: A Survey of the State's Ethnic Groups*. St. Paul: Minnesota State Historical Society Press.
Hought, Anna Guttormsen, with Florence Ekstrand. 1986. *Anna*. Seattle: Welcome Press.
Howard, Joseph Kinsey. 1970. *The Strange Empire of Louis Riel*. 1952. Toronto: Swan Publishing.
Hudson, John C. 1976. "Migration to an American Frontier," *Annals of the Association of American Geographers* 66:242–65.
———. 1985. *Plains Country Towns*. Minneapolis: University of Minnesota Press.
Huel, Raymond J. A. 1978. "The Public School as Guardian of Anglo-Saxon Traditions: The Saskatchewan Experience, 1913–1918," in *Ethnic Canadians: Culture and Education*, ed. Martin L. Kovacs. Regina, Sask.: Canadian Plains Research Center.
Hurd, W. Burton. 1937. *Racial Origins and Nativity of the Canadian People*. Census Monograph no. 4. Ottawa: Dominion Bureau of Statistics.
Innis, Harold. 1956. *The Fur Trade in Canada: An Introduction to Canadian Economic History*. Toronto: University of Toronto Press.
Irving, John A. 1959. *The Social Credit Movement in Alberta*. Toronto: University of Toronto Press.
Jackel, Susan, ed. 1982. *A Flannel Shirt and Liberty: British Emigrant Gentlewomen in the Canadian West, 1880–1914*. Vancouver: University of British Columbia Press.
Jackson, Richard. 1975. "Mormon Perception and Settlement of the Great Plains," in *Images of the Great Plains: The Role of Human Nature in Settlement*, ed. Brian W. Blouet and Merlin P. Lawson. Lincoln: University of Nebraska Press.
Jameson, Elizabeth. 1987. "Women as Workers, Women as Civilizers: True Womanhood in the American West," in *The Women's West*, ed. Susan Armitage and Elizabeth Jameson. Norman: University of Oklahoma Press.

Jeffrey, Julie Roy. 1979. *Frontier Women: The Trans-Mississippi West, 1840–1880*. New York: Hill and Wang.

Jensen, Joan, and Darlis Miller. 1980. "The Gentle Tamers Revisited: New Approaches to the History of Women in the American West," *Pacific Historical Review* 1980:173–213.

Josephy, Alvin M., Jr. 1971. *The Nez-Percé Indians and the Opening of the Northwest*. Abr. ed. New Haven: Yale University Press.

Kauffman, Floyd E. 1953. "Amish in North Dakota," *Mennonite Historical Bulletin* 14.

Kelley, L. V. 1980. *The Range Men: The Story of the Ranchers and Indians of Alberta*. Toronto: Coles Publishing Co.

Klassen, Henry C. 1991. "Shaping the Growth of the Montana Economy: T.C. Power & Bro. and the Canadian Trade, 1869–93," *Great Plains Quarterly* 11 (Summer): 166–80.

Kloberdanz, Timothy J. 1980. "Plainsmen of Three Continents: Volga German Adaptation to Steppe, Prairie, and Pampa," in *Ethnicity on the Great Plains*, ed. Frederick C. Luebke. Lincoln: University of Nebraska Press.

Koch, Fred C. 1977. *The Volga Germans: In Russia and the Americas, from 1763 to the Present*. University Park: Pennsylvania State University Press.

Kohl, Seena B. 1976. *Working Together: Women and Family in Southwestern Saskatchewan*. Toronto: Holt, Rinehart and Winston of Canada.

———. 1977. "Women's Participation in the North American Family Farm," *Women's Studies International Quarterly* 1:47–54.

———. 1988. "Image and Behavior: Women's Participation in North American Family Agricultural Enterprises," in *Women in Farming: Changing Roles, Changing Structures*, ed. Wava Haney and Jane Knowles. Boulder CO: Westview.

———. 1989. "Memories of Homesteading and the Process of Retrospection," *Oral History Review* 17/2 (Fall):25–45.

———. 1992. "Generational Transformation: Continuities and Discontinuities in the Lives of Woman Settlers in the Canadian-American Northwest," in *Migration and the Transformation of Cultures*, ed. Jean Burnet et al. Toronto: Multicultural History Society of Ontario.

Kohl, Seena B., and John W. Bennett. 1971. "Succession to Family Enterprises and the Migration of Young People in a Canadian Agricultural Community," in *The Canadian Family*, ed. K. Ishwaran. Toronto: Holt, Rinehart and Winston of Canada.

Kohrs, Conrad. 1977. *An Autobiography*. Deer Lodge MT: Platen Press.

Kovacs, Martin L., ed. 1978. *Ethnic Canadians: Culture and Education*. Canadian Plains Studies No. 8. Regina, Sask.: Canadian Plains Research Center.

Krueger, Cynthia. 1968. "Prairie Protest: The Medicare Conflict in Saskatchewan," in *Agrarian Socialism*, ed. Seymour M. Lipset. New York: Doubleday/Anchor.

Ladd-Taylor, Molly. 1986. *Raising a Baby the Government Way: Mothers' Letters to the Children's Bureau, 1915–1932*. New Brunswick NJ: Rutgers University Press.

Lang, William. 1990. "Corporate Point Men and the Creation of the Montana Central Railroad, 1882–87," *Great Plains Quarterly* 10:152–66.

Laslett, Peter. 1984. "The Family as a Knot of Individual Interests," in *Households: Comparative and Historical Studies of the Domestic Group*, ed. Robert McC. Netting, Richard R. Wilk, and Eric J. Arnould. Berkeley: University of California Press.

Lass, William E. 1962. *History of Steamboating on the Upper Missouri River.* Lincoln: University of Nebraska Press.

Lehr, John. 1982. "The Landscapes of Ukrainian Settlement in the Canadian West," *Great Plains Quarterly* 2:94–105.

Leighton, Alexander, and Dorothea Leighton. 1944. *The Navaho Door.* Cambridge: Harvard University Press.

Limerick, Patricia Nelson. 1987. *The Legacy of Conquest: The Unbroken Past of the American West.* New York: W. W. Norton.

Lindgren, H. Eliane. 1989. "Ethnic Women Homesteading on the Plains of North Dakota," *Great Plains Quarterly* 9:157–73.

Lingeman, Richard. 1980. *Small Town America: A Narrative History, 1620–the Present.* Boston: Houghton Mifflin.

Linton, Marigold. 1987. "Ways of Searching and the Contents of Memory," in *Autobiographical Memory*, ed. David C. Rubin. Cambridge: Cambridge University Press.

Lipset, Seymour M. 1950. *Agrarian Socialism.* Berkeley: University of California Press.

———. 1990. *Continental Divide: The Values and Institutions of the United States and Canada.* New York: Routledge Kegan Paul.

Lobanov-Rostovsky, A. 1965. "Russian Expansion in the Far East in the Light of the Turner Hypothesis," in *The Frontier in Perspective*, ed. Walker D. Wyman and Clifton B. Kroeber. Madison: University of Wisconsin Press.

Loken, Gulbrand. 1980. *From Fjord to Frontier: A History of Norwegians in Canada.* Toronto: McClelland and Stewart.

Lovoll, Odd. 1984. *The Promise of America: A History of the Norwegian-American People.* Minneapolis: University of Minnesota Press.

Low, Ann Marie. 1984. *Dust Bowl Diary.* Lincoln: University of Nebraska Press.

Lowell, Briant Lindsay. 1987. *Scandinavian Exodus: Demography and Social Development of 19th-Century Rural Communities.* Boulder CO: Westview Press.

Lowenthal, David. 1985. *The Past Is a Foreign Country.* New York: Cambridge University Press.

Luebke, Frederick C. 1977. "Ethnic Group Settlement on the Great Plains," *Western Historical Quarterly* 8:405–30.

MacCleod, R. C. 1976. *The North-West Mounted Police and Law Enforcement: 1873–1905.* Toronto: University of Toronto Press.

McClintock, Walter. 1910. *The Old North Trail; or Life, Legends and Religion of the Blackfeet Indians.* London: Macmillan.

———. 1923. *Old Indian Trails.* Boston: Houghton Mifflin.

Macdonald, L. J., and J. Macdonald. 1964. "Chain Migration, Ethnic Neighbor-

hood Formation and Social Networks," *Milbank Memorial Fund Quarterly* 42:82–97.
MacEwan, Grant. 1962. *Blazing the Old Cattle Trail*. Saskatoon, Sask.: Modern Press.
———. 1981. *Métis Makers of History*. Saskatoon, Sask.: Western Producer Prairie Books.
McGinnies, William G., and William A. Laycock. 1988. "The Great American Desert: Perceptions of Pioneers, the Dustbowl, and the New Sodbusters," in *Arid Lands: Today and Tomorrow*, ed. Emily Whitehead. Boulder CO: Westview Press.
MacGregor, J. G. 1968. *North-West of Sixteen*. Rutland VT: Charles E. Tuttle Co. Originally published as *Blankets and Beads: A History of the Saskatchewan River*, 1958.
McMurtry, Larry. 1985. *Lonesome Dove*. New York: Simon and Schuster.
Macoun, John. 1876. "Report of the Select Standing Committee on Agriculture and Colonization," *Journals of the House of Commons*, vol. 5.
———. 1880–81. "Report of Exploration by Professor John Macoun: Sessional Papers," *Journals of the House of Commons*, vol. 14, no. 3–4.
Madison County Publicity Club. 1907. *Madison County, Montana: Its Resources, Opportunities and Possibilities*. Virginia City MT: Madisonian Publishers.
Malin, James C. 1984. *History and Ecology: Studies of the Grasslands*, ed. Robert P. Swierenga. Lincoln: University of Nebraska Press.
Malone, Michael P., and Richard B. Roeder. 1976. *Montana: A History of Two Centuries*. Seattle: University of Washington Press.
Marchildon, R. G. 1985. "Improving the Quality of Rural Life in Saskatchewan: Some Activities of the Women's Section of the Saskatchewan Grain Growers, 1913–1920," in *Building Beyond the Homesteads*, ed. David C. Jones and Ian McPherson. Calgary: University of Calgary Press.
Marshall, James M. 1986. *Land Fever: Dispossession and the Frontier Myth*. Lexington: University Press of Kentucky.
Martin, Theodora Penny. 1987. *The Sound of Our Own Voices*. Boston: Beacon Press.
Mercier, Laurie K. 1988. "Women's Role in Montana Agriculture," *Montana: The Magazine of Western History* 38(3):50–61.
Milner, Clyde A., II. 1987. "The Shared Memory of Montana's Pioneers," *Montana: The Magazine of Western History*, 37(1):2–13.
Minifee, James. 1972. *A Prairie Boyhood Recalled*. Toronto: Macmillan of Canada.
Mitchell, Elizabeth B. 1981. *In Western Canada Before the War*. Saskatoon, Sask.: Western Producer Prairie Books.
Morton, A. S. 1938. *History of Prairie Settlement*. Vol. 2 in *Canadian Frontiers of Settlement*, ed. W. A. Mackintosh and W. L. G. Joerg. Toronto: Macmillan of Canada.
———. 1973. *A History of the Canadian West to 1870–71*. Toronto: University of Toronto Press.

Mullan, John. 1863. *Report on the Construction of a Military Road from Fort Walla Walla to Fort Benton.* Washington DC: Government Printing Office.

———. 1865. *Miners and Travellers Guide to Oregon, Washington, Idaho, Montana, Wyoming, and Colorado, via the Missouri and Columbia Rivers.* New York: W. M. Franklin.

Murphy, Robert F. 1983. *Half Interest in a Silver Dollar: The Saga of Charles E. Conrad.* Missoula MT: Mountain Press.

Myers, Rex C. 1990. "Homestead on the Range: The Emergence of Community in Eastern Montana, 1900–1925," *Great Plains Quarterly* 2:218–27.

Myres, Sandra L. 1982. *Westering Women and the Frontier Experience, 1800–1915.* Albuquerque: University of New Mexico Press.

———. 1983. "Women in the West," in *Historians and the American West,* ed. Michael P. Malone. Lincoln: University of Nebraska Press.

Myrick, Delbert C. 1941. *Climate: The Limiting Factor.* U.S. Dept. of Agriculture, Bureau of Agricultural Economics.

Nicholson, Barbara. 1974. "Feminism in the Prairie Provinces to 1916," Master's thesis, University of Calgary.

Northern Boundary Commission. 1872–76. *Reports Upon Survey of Boundary Between United States and Possessions of Great Britain from Lake of the Woods to Summit of the Rocky Mountains.* Separate editions published by the Commission and by the U.S. Congress. Washington DC.

Orser, Edward W. 1988. "Toward a New Local History: The Possibilities and Pitfalls of Personal Narrative," *Oral History Review* 16/1 (Spring):111–18.

Ostergren, Robert C. 1988. *A Community Transplanted: The Trans-Atlantic Experience of a Swedish Immigrant Settlement in the Upper Middle West, 1835–1915.* Madison: University of Wisconsin Press.

Overholser, Joel F. 1987. *Fort Benton: World's Innermost Port.* Helena MT: Falcon Press.

Palliser, John. 1859. *Papers Relative to the Exploration by Captain John Palliser of that Portion of British North America which Lies Between the Northern Branch of the River Saskatchewan and the Frontier of the United States; and Between the Red River and the Rocky Mountains.* Presented to both Houses of Parliament by Command of Her Majesty. June.

Palmer, Howard, and Tamara Palmer, eds. 1985. *Peoples of Alberta.* Saskatoon, Sask.: Western Producer Prairie Books.

Paradise, Viola I. 1919. *Maternity Care and the Welfare of Young Children in a Homesteading County in Montana.* Rural Child Welfare Series No. 3, Publication No. 34; U.S. Dept. of Labor, Children's Bureau.

Parson, Edna Tyson. 1981. *Land I Can Own.* Ottawa: Westboro Printers.

Patterson-Black, Sheryll, and Gene Patterson-Black. 1978. *Western Women in History and Literature.* Crawford NE: Cottonwood Press.

Paul, Rodman W. 1988. *The Far West and Great Plains in Transition: 1859–1900.* New York: Harper and Row.

Petersen, Keith. 1986. *Historical Celebrations: A Handbook for Organizers for Diamond Jubilees, Centennials and Other Community Anniversaries.* Boise: Idaho State Historical Society.

Peterson, Charles W. 1919. *Wake Up Canada: Reflections of Vital National Issues*. Toronto.

Peterson, Hans J. 1986. "The Cypress Hills Massacre." Paper presented to the Palliser Triangle Conference, May, at Medicine Hat College, Medicine Hat, Alta.

Peterson, Jacqueline, and Jennifer S. H. Brown, eds. 1985. *The New Peoples: Being and Becoming Métis in North America*. Lincoln: University of Nebraska Press.

Peterson, Robert L. 1969. "The Completion of the Northern Pacific Railroad System in Montana, 1883–1893," in *The Montana Past: An Anthology*, ed. Michael P. Malone and Richard B. Roeder. Missoula: University of Montana Press.

Petrik, Paula. 1987. *No Step Backward: Women and Family on the Rocky Mountain Mining Frontier: Helena, Montana 1865–1900*. Helena: Montana Historical Society Press.

Petryshyn, Jaroslav. 1985. *Peasants in the Promised Land: Canada and the Ukrainians, 1891–1914*. Toronto: James Lorimer and Co.

Pohorecky, Zenon. 1978. "The Changing Role of Ethnocultural Organizations in Saskatchewan: Case Studies with Statistical Data Cast in Historical Perspectives," in *Ethnic Canadians: Culture and Education*, ed. Martin L. Kovacs. Regina, Sask: Canadian Plains Research Center.

Pollack, Norman, ed. 1967. *The Populist Mind*. New York: Bobbs-Merrill.

Potrebenko, Helen. 1977. *No Streets of Gold: A Social History of Ukrainians in Alberta*. Vancouver: New Star Books.

Rasmussen, Linda, Lorna Rassmussen, Candace Savage, and Anne Wheeler. 1976. *A Harvest Yet to Reap*. Lincoln: University of Nebraska Press.

Raymer, Robert George, ed. 1930. *Montana: The Land and the People*, vol. 2. Chicago: Lewis Publishing Co.

Redfield, Robert. 1955. *The Little Community: Viewpoints for the Study of a Human Whole*. Chicago: University of Chicago Press.

Rich, E. E. 1960. *Hudson's Bay Company, 1670–1870*. 3 vols. Toronto: University of Toronto Press.

Rickard, Timothy J. 1979. "The Great Plains as Part of an Irrigated Western Empire, 1890–1914," in *The Great Plains: Environment and Culture*, ed. Brian W. Blouet and Frederick C. Luebke. Lincoln: University of Nebraska Press.

Ridge, Martin, ed. 1986. *Frederick Jackson Turner: Wisconsin's Historian of the Frontier*. Madison: State Historical Society of Wisconsin.

Riley, Glenda. 1988. *The Female Frontier: A Comparative View of Women on the Prairie and the Plains*. Lawrence: University of Kansas Press.

Roberts, Sarah. 1971. *Alberta Homestead: Chronicle of a Pioneer Family*, ed. Lathrop E. Roberts. Austin: University of Texas Press.

Rochlin, Harriet, and Fred Rochlin. 1984. *Pioneer Jews: A New Life in the Far West*. Boston: Houghton Mifflin.

Royal Commission on Agriculture and Rural Life. 1956. *The Home and Family in Rural Saskatchewan*. Report No. 10. Government of Saskatchewan. Regina: Queen's Printer.

———. 1957. *Service Centers*. Report No. 12. Government of Saskatchewan. Regina: Queen's Printer.
Rubin, David C., ed. 1987. *Autobiographical Memory*. Cambridge: Cambridge University Press.
Saarinen, Thomas Frederick. 1966. *Perception of the Drought Hazard on the Great Plains*. Chicago: University of Chicago Press.
Sallet, Richard. 1931. *Russian-German Settlements in the United States*. Fargo: North Dakota Institute for Regional Studies.
Saloutos, Theodore. 1945. "The Montana Society of Equity," *Pacific Historical Review* 14:393–408.
Saloutos, Theodore, and John D. Hicks. 1951. *Agricultural Discontent in the Middle West: 1900–1939*. Madison: University of Wisconsin Press.
Sanders, Helen Fitzgerald. 1913. *A History of Montana*, vol. 2. Chicago: Lewis Publishing Co.
Saveth, Edward N. 1965. *American Historians and European Immigrants, 1875–1925*. New York: Russell and Russell.
Schach, Paul, ed. 1980. *Languages in Conflict: Linguistic Acculturation on the Great Plains*. Lincoln: University of Nebraska Press.
Schlesier, Karl H., ed. 1993. *Plains Indians, A.D. 500: The Archaelogical Past of Historic Groups*. Norman: University of Oklahoma Press.
Schlissel, Lillian. 1982. *Women's Diaries of the Westward Journey*. New York: Schocken Books.
———. 1989. "Introduction," in Lillian Schlissel, Byrd Gibbons, and Elizabeth Hampsten, *Far From Home*. New York: Schocken Books.
Schwieder, Dorothy. 1986. "Education and Change in the Lives of Iowa Farm Women, 1900–1940," *Agricultural History* 60(2):200–215.
Sealey, D. Bruce, and Antoine S. Lussier. 1975. *The Métis: Canada's Forgotten People*. Winnipeg, Man.: Pemmican Publications.
Segalen, Martine. 1986. *Historical Anthropology of the Family*. Cambridge: Cambridge University Press.
Shannon, Fred A. 1945. *The Farmer's Last Frontier*. New York: Farrar and Rinehart.
Sharp, Paul S. 1948. *The Agrarian Revolt in Western Canada: A Survey Showing American Parallels*. Minneapolis: University of Minnesota Press.
———. 1955. *Whoop-Up Country: A History of the Canadian-American West*. Minneapolis: University of Minnesota Press.
Sherman, William C. 1983. *Prairie Mosaic: An Ethnic Atlas of Rural North Dakota*. Fargo: North Dakota Institute for Regional Studies.
Shortridge, James R. 1988. "The Heart of the Prairie: Culture Areas in the Central and Northern Great Plains," *Great Plains Quarterly* 8(4):206–21.
Silverman, Eliane Leslau. 1984. *The Last Best West Women on the Alberta Frontier, 1880–1930*. Montreal: Eden Press.
———. 1985. "Women's Perceptions of Marriage on the Alberta Frontier," in *Building Beyond the Homestead*, ed. David C. Jones and Ian MacPherson. Calgary: University of Calgary Press.
Sims, Newell Leroy. 1920. *The Rural Community: Ancient and Modern*. New York: Charles Scribner's Sons.

Smalley, E. V. 1883. *History of the Northern Pacific Railroad.* New York: G. P. Putnam's Sons.
Smith, Alson Jesse. 1948. *Brother Van: A Biography of the Rev. William Wesley Van Orsdel.* New York: Abingdon-Cokesbury.
Smith, Henry Nash. 1947. "Rain Follows the Plow: The Notions of Increased Rainfall for the Great Plains, 1844–1880," *Huntington Library Quarterly* 10:169–93.
———. 1950. *Virgin Land: The American West as Symbol and Myth.* Cambridge: Harvard University Press.
Smith-Rosenberg, Carroll, and Charles Rosenberg. 1973. "The Female Animal: Medical and Biological Views of Woman and Her Role in 19th-Century America," *Journal of American History* 60:332–56.
Smythe, William E. 1969. *The Conquest of Arid America.* 1899, 1905. Seattle: University of Washington Press.
Spry, I. M. 1963. *The Palliser Expedition: An Account of John Palliser's British North American Expedition: 1857–60.* Toronto: Macmillan of Canada.
Stanley, George F. 1960. *The Birth of Western Canada: A History of the Riel Rebellions.* 1936. Toronto: University of Toronto Press.
Stansell, Christine. 1976. "Women on the Great Plains, 1865–1890," *Women's Studies* 4:86–98.
Stegner, Wallace. 1962. *Wolf Willow.* New York: Viking Press.
Stephanow, Marlene. 1967. "Changing Bi- and Multi-Culturalism in the Canadian Prairie Provinces," in *Symposium on the Great Plains of North America,* ed. Carle C. Zimmerman and Seth Russell. Fargo: North Dakota Institute for Regional Studies.
Stratton, Joanna L. 1981. *Pioneer Women: Voices from the Kansas Frontier.* New York: Simon & Schuster.
Swanson, Bert E., Richard A. Cohen, and Edith P. Swanson. 1979. *Small Towns and Small Towners: A Framework for Survival and Growth.* Vol. 79, Sage Library of Social Research. Beverly Hills: Sage Publications.
Thomas, Lewis, ed. 1975. *The Prairie West to 1905: A Canadian Sourcebook.* Toronto: Oxford University Press.
Thompson, Larry. 1985. *Montana's Explorers: The Pioneer Naturalists, 1805–1864.* Helena: Montana Magazine.
Thwaites, Rueben G. 1959. *Montana: An Uncommon Land.* Norman: University of Oklahoma Press.
Tilley, Louise A., and Patricia Gurin, eds. 1992. Introduction to *Women, Politics and Change.* New York: Russell Sage Foundation.
Toole, K. Ross. 1950. "The Anaconda Copper Mining Co.: A Price War and a Copper Corner," *Pacific Northwest Quarterly* 41:312–29.
———. 1972. *Twentieth-Century Montana: A State of Extremes.* Norman: University of Oklahoma Press.
———. 1976. *The Rape of the Great Plains.* Boston: Little, Brown, and Co.
Tracie, Carl. 1976. "Ethnicity and the Prairie Environment: Patterns of Old Colony Mennonite and Doukhobor Settlement," in *Man and Nature on the Prairies,* ed. Richard Allen. Canadian Plains Studies No. 6. Regina: Canadian Plains Research Center.

Turner, Frederick Jackson. 1920. "The Significance of the Frontier in American History," in *The Frontier in American History*. New York: Henry Holt.
Turner, John P. 1950. *The North-West Mounted Police, 1873–1893*. 2 vols. Ottawa: Edmond Cloutier.
Tyre, Robert. 1962. *Douglas in Saskatchewan: The Story of a Socialist Experiment*. Vancouver: Mitchell Press.
Underwood, June O. 1984–85. "Civilizing Kansas: Women's Organizations, 1880–1920," *Kansas History* 7(4):291–306.
Van Kirk, Sylvia. 1980. *Many Tender Ties: Women in Fur Trade Society, 1670–1870*. Wyoming: Watson and Dwyer.
Vansina, Jan. 1985. *Oral Tradition as History*. Madison: University of Wisconsin Press.
Vincent, Joan. 1974. "The Structure of Ethnicity," *Human Organization* 33(4):375–79.
Voisey, Paul. 1985. "Rural History and the Prairie West," *Prairie Forum* 10:327–38.
———. 1988. *Vulcan: The Making of a Prairie Community*. Toronto: University of Toronto Press.
Walsh, Margaret. 1981. *The American Frontier Revisited*. Atlantic Highlands NJ: Humanities Press.
Walter, Dave. 1989. "Simon Pepin, a Quiet Capitalist," *Montana: the Magazine of Western History* 39(1):34–38.
Walters, Ronald, ed. 1974. *Primers for Prudery: Sexual Advice to Victorian America*. Englewood Cliffs NJ: Prentice-Hall.
Warren, Roland L. 1978. *The Community in America*. Chicago: Rand McNally College Publishing Co.
Weaver, J. E., and F. W. Albertson. 1956. *Grasslands of the Great Plains*. Lincoln NE: Johnson Publishing Co.
Webb, Walter Prescott. 1931. *The Great Plains*. New York: Grosset and Dunlap.
Wedel, Waldo. R. 1979. "Holocene Cultural Adaptations in the Republican River Basin," in *The Great Plains Environment and Culture*, ed. Brian Blouet and Frederick C. Luebke. Lincoln: University of Nebraska Press.
West, Elliot. 1989. *Growing Up with the Country*. Albuquerque: University of New Mexico Press.
West, Elliot, and Paula Petrik, eds. 1992. *Small Worlds: Children and Adolescents in America, 1850–1950*. Lawrence: University of Kansas Press.
White, M. C., ed. 1950. *David Thompson's Journals Relating to Montana and Adjacent Regions (1808–1812)*. Montana State University Studies, vol. 1. Bozeman: Montana State University.
Wieczynski, Joseph L. 1976. *The Russian Frontier: The Impact of Borderlands on the Course of Early Russian History*. Charlottesville: University Press of Virginia.
Wilson, Gary A. 1985. *Honky-Tonk Town: Havre's Bootlegging Days*. Havre: High Line Books.
Wilson, L. J. 1977. "Educational Roles of the United Farm Women of Alberta," *Alberta Historical Review* 25(2):28–36.

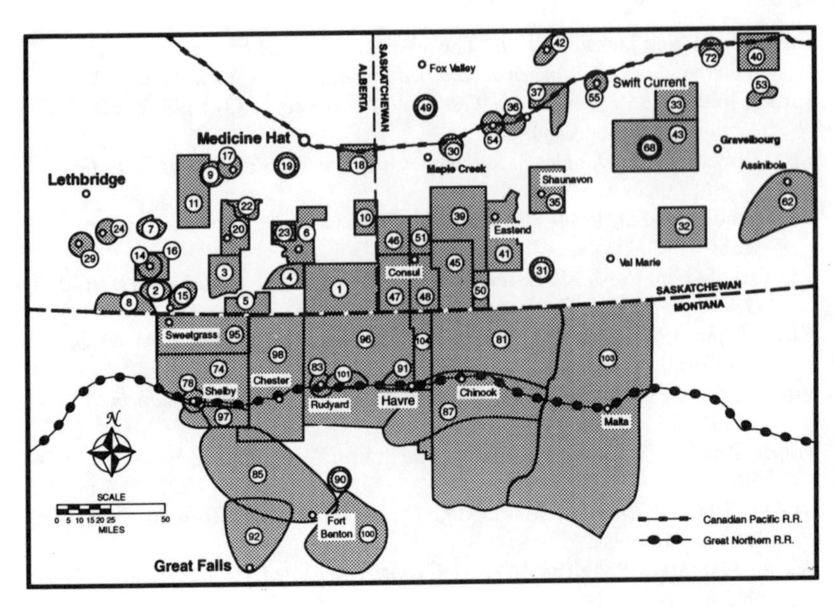

Figure 7. Geographical coverage of Heartland Collection of Local History Books. Numbers correspond to those of the community history books used as a source of quotations for the text. The selections were made to ensure representation from as many areas in the Heartland region as possible. The books are identified in the "Local History Books" section of the bibliography.

Woodcock, George. 1975. *Gabriel Dumont: The Métis Chief and His Lost World*. Edmonton: Hurtig Publishers.

Wyman, Walker D., and Clifton B. Kroeber. 1957. *The Frontier in Perspective*. Madison: University of Wisconsin Press.

Yans-McLaughlin, Virginia. 1990. "Metaphor of Self in History: Subjectivity, Oral Narrative, and Immigration Studies," in *Immigration Reconsidered*, ed. Virginia Yans-McLaughlin. New York: Oxford University Press.

Young, Walter D. 1969. *The Anatomy of a Party: the National CCF, 1932–61*. Toronto: University of Toronto Press.

Yuill, Clifford D., and Ellan R. Yuill. 1986. *Historic Homes of Montana*, vol. 1. Great Falls MT: VisYuill Enterprises.

Local History Books (LHB)

This bibliography consists of 109 numbered books, including the sources in our "Heartland Collection," keyed to the map in figure 7.

Except for the final four works, 106 to 109, which were added after the original sample had been compiled, the books are listed separately for Alberta, Saskatchewan, and Montana. For each book we have indicated its geographical region using the abbreviations SW (southwest), SE (southeast), NE (northeast),

SC (south-central), NC (north-central), IB (international boundary), and CPR (Canadian Pacific main line).

Alberta

1. *The Forgotten Corner: A History of the Communities of Comrey, Catchem, Hooper-Pendland, Onefour, and Wildhorse* (SE/IB). Ed. Olive Lanz and Beatrice Kusler. New Horizons Committee, 1981. 325 pp.
2. *Milk River Country* (SE). Ed. Alice A. Campbell. Milk River Old Timers' Association, 1959. 437 pp.
3. *Prairie Footprints: A History of the Community in Southern Alberta Known as Pendant d'Oreille* (SE). Ed. Helen Finstad. Pendant d'Oreille Lutheran Church, 1970. 264 pp.
4. *Long Shadows: A History of Shortgrass Country* (SE). Emma Dickson, Lylla Lagna, Jean Thompson, and Pauline Taylor. Commentator Pub. Co., 1974. 333 pp.
5. *The Hills of Home* (SE/IB). Hills of Home Historical Committee, 1975. 220 pp.
6. *Manyberries Chinook: A History of the Communities of Glassford, Manyberries, Minda, New Home, Orion, Ranchville* (SE). Manyberries Historical Society, 1980.
7. *Homestead Country: Wrentham and Area* (SE). Wrentham Historical Society, 1980. 740 pp.
8. *Heritage of the High Country: A History of Del Bonita and Surrounding Districts* (SC/IB). Del Bonita Historical Society, 1981. 604 pp.
9. *Burdett Prairie Trails* (SE). Ed. Jean Clark, Marie Dillenbeck, and Merle Thacker. Burdett History Book Committee, 1981. 580 pp.
10. *Down the Years at Elkwater* (SE). Ed. Hope Michael and Hope Johnson. Medicine Hat Museum and Art Gallery, 1981. 76 pp.
11. *Faded Trails: Grassy Lake and Purple Springs* (SE). Grassy Lake Historical Society, 1982. 557 pp.
12. "Fort Whoop-Up: America's First and Most Notorious Whiskey Fort" (SC). Georgia Green Fooks. Occasional Paper No. 11, Historical Society of Alberta, 1983. 64 pp.
13. *From Sandstone to Settlers: Writing on Stone District History, 1900–1983* (SE). Masinasin Historical Society, 1983. 788 pp.
14. *Wagons to Wings: Warner, Alberta* (SC). Warner District Historical Society, 1985. 939 pp.
15. *History of the Border Country of Coutts* (SC/IB). Ed. Sunshine Women's Institute History Committee. Women's Institute of Coutts, 1957 (rev. 1965). 541 pp.
16. *Warner Pioneers* (SC). Ed. M. McKenzie, B. Cassell, R. Graham, K. Pittman. Warner Old Timers' Association, 1962. 304 pp.
17. *Silver Sage* (SE). Ed. Bow Island History Book Committee. Lions Club of Bow Island, 1972. 703 pp.
18. *Memories of Early Walsh and Graburn* (SE/CPR). Ed. Margaret Fulton. Women's Institute of Alberta, 1980. 102 pp.
19. *Seven Persons: One Hundred Sixty Acres and a Dream* (SE). Ed. Lillian Ost. Seven Persons Historical Society, 1982. 144 pp.

20. *Shortgrass Country: A History of Foremost and Nemiskan* (SE). Ed. Alyce Butterwick and the Foremost Historical Society. Foremost Historical Society, 1975. 689 pp.
21. *Leaves from the Medicine Tree: A History of the Area Influenced by the Tree, and Biographies of Pioneers and Old Timers Who Came Under its Spell* (SC). High River Pioneers' and Old Timers' Association, 1960. 522 pp.
22. *Conquerville: A Growing Community* (SE). Conquerville Women's Institute, 1963. 180 pp.
23. *The Piegan Country* (SE). Martha Dragland, 1966. 196 pp.
24. *Roundup: 1902–1967* (SC). Ed. J.O. Hicken, K. Redd, and J. Evans, 1967. Pub. n.d. 700 pp.
25. *Early History of the Medicine Hat Country* (SE). James William Morrow. Medicine Hat and District Historical Society, 1978 (1923, repr. 1974). 96 pp.
26. *Lethbridge: A Centennial History* (SC). Ed. Alex Johnston and Andy den Otter. Historical Society of Alberta, Whoop-Up Chapter, 1985. 240 pp.
27. *Splintered Dreams: Sikhs in Southern Alberta* (SC). Jaswinder Gundara. Arusha International Development Resource Centre, 1985. 79 pp.
28. *Lethbridge Place Names* (SC). Alex Johnston and Barry R. Peat. Occasional Paper No. 14, Whoop-Up Country Chapter, Historical Society of Alberta, 1987. 80 pp.
29. *Irrigation Builders: McGrath and District History Association* (SC). McGrath and District History Association, 1974. 545 pp.

Saskatchewan

30. *Piapot Prairie Trails* (SW/CPR). Piapot History Group, 1979. 784 pp.
31. *Prairie Wool: A History of Climax and Surrounding School Districts* (SW). Ed. Stone Diggers History Book Committee. Stone Diggers Historical Society, 1980. 395 pp.
32. *Mankota: The First Fifty Years* (SC). Ed. Jim White. Mankota Book Committee, 1980. 248 pp.
33. *Hodgeville: Prairie, Pioneers, Progress* (SC). Ed. Maurice Jago. Hodgeville Celebrate Saskatchewan Committee, 1980. 167 pp.
34. *History of Ponteix* (SW). Ed. Rachel Lacoursiere-Stringer. Village of Ponteix, 1981. 368 pp.
35. *Quarter Stake Echoes: Area South of Shaunavon* (SW). South Shaunavon History Book Club, 1981. 494 pp.
36. *From Prairie Trails to Pavement* (SW/CPR). North Gull Lake Historical Association, 1982. 676 pp.
37. *Prairie Memories* (SW/CPR). Ed. Lloyd Carl. Webb History Book Committee, 1982. 1,290 pp.
38. *Life in the New Finland Woods: A History of New Finland, Saskatchewan* (SE). Ed. Nancy Mattson Schelstraete. New Finland Historical and Heritage Society, 1982. 308 pp.
39. *Between and Beyond the Benches: Ravenscrag* (SW). Ravenscrag History Book Committee, 1983. 630 pp.

40. *A Time to Remember: A History of Mortlach and District* (SC/CPR). Ed. Gail Bossence. Mortlach History Book Committee, 1983. 313 pp.
41. *Range Riders and "Sodbusters"* (SW). Ed. Lyle LaRose. Eastend History Society, 1984. 895 pp.
42. *River Hills to Sand Hills: A History of Pennant and District* (SW). Ed. Grace E. Rose. Pennant and District History Book Committee, 1984. 791 pp.
43. *A Place by the Notukeu: Vanguard* (SC). Vanguard Historical Society, 1984. 764 pp.
44. *Heritage '85: Town of Assiniboia* (SC). Ed. History Committee of Assiniboia. Focus Publishing, Regina, 1985. 390 pp.
45. *Robsart Pioneers Review the Years* (SW/IB). Ed. Robsart Committee. Privately published, 1955. 100 pp.
46. *Merryflat and District* (SW). Privately produced, 1960. 92 pp.
47. *Pioneer Days* (SW/IB). Local Committee, privately produced, 1961. 96 pp.
48. *Homesteading in the Consul District* (SW/IB). Privately produced, 1961. 64 pp.
49. *History of the Golden Prairie Community* (SW). Local committee, 1961. 148 pp.
50. *Filing for the Future* (SW/IB). Ed. Cecil Wright. Clay Centre Handicraft Club, 1967. 160 pp.
51. *West Plains Oxarat* (SW). Oxarat Ladies Club, 1965. 108 pp.
52. *Our Pioneers* (SW). Ed. Gwen Pollack. Cypress Hills Pioneer Association, 1970. 104 pp.
53. *Pioneer Memories: A Historical Account of Courval and Districts Since 1908* (SC). Ed. Joseph Henri Tremblay. D. W. Friesen & Sons, 1974. 132 pp.
54. *Tompkins: Our Hometown We Love* (SW/CPR). Pioneer History Group of Tompkins, 1976. 495 pp.
55. *Yesteryear: History of Our Pioneers* (SW/CPR). Yesteryear History Book Committee, 1977. 511 pp.
56. *Golden Furrows: An Historical Chronicle of Swift Current* (SW). Local Council of Women, 1954. 55 pp.
57. *Land I Can Own: A True Account of Homesteading and the Years That Followed at Neidpath, Saskatchewan* (SW). Edna Tyson Parson, 1981. 213 pp.
58. "School Project: Community History of Govenlock, Saskatchewan, 1905–1955" (SW/IB). Privately produced, 1955. 17 pp.
59. "School Project: Golden Jubilee Day, Senate, Saskatchewan, March 11, 1955" (SW/IB). Privately produced, 1955. 15 pp.
60. "Saskatchewan Jubilee Year" (SW). Students and Teachers of Pennant, SD. No. 3182, 1955. 20 pp.
61. "History of the Lacadena Community" (SW). Lacadena Women's Association, 1955. 15 pp.
62. *Golden Memories* (SC). Ed. D. B. Ferguson, D. G. Neil, R. E. Ludlow, and E. D. Pettem. District of Assiniboia, 1955. 88 pp.
63. *Historical Sketches of the Parishes of the Diocese of Gravelbourg, Saskatche-*

wan, on the Occasion of Its Silver Jubilee (SW). Diocese of Gravelbourg, 1955. 112 pp.
64. "History and Reminiscences of Eastend and District" (SW). Eastend Enterprise, 1955. 35 pp.
65. *A Wheatland Heritage* (SW). Ed. Edith Vernette Armstrong. Saskatoon: Modern Press, 1955. 275 pp.
66. *Fox Valley Echoes* (SW). Privately produced, 1965.
67. "Reston-Wolseley C.P.R., 1906–1961: The 'Peanut.'" Gilbert McKay. World Spectator Print Service, 1961. 24 pp.
68. "The Changing Years" (SC). Margaret Sonder. Village of Vanguard, 1967. 37 pp.
69. *History of South Central Saskatchewan* (SW). Clovis Rondeau. Canadian Publishers, 1970.
70. *Centennial of St. Ignace des Saules Parish, 1870–1970* (SW). Parish of Willow Bunch, 1970. 71 pp.
71. *Progress: Our First Year; the Frontier Recreation Centre* (SW). Carmyn L. Evenson. Frontier Recreation Board, 1979. 108 pp.
72. "Chaplin Homecoming: 1905–1980" (SC/CPR). Village of Chaplin, 1980. 37 pp.

Montana

73. "Local History of Valley County, Montana" (NE/IB). Ed. Vesta O. Robbins. Montana Historical Society Pamphlet 241. Montana Federation of Women's Clubs, 1925. 79 pp.
74. *Toole County Backgrounds* (NC). Shelby History Group, Montana Institute of the Arts, 1958. 110 pp.
75. "Railroads to Rockets: Diamond Jubilee, Phillips County Montana" (NC). Montana Historical Society Pamphlet 1056. Historical Book Committee, Phillips County, 1962. 70 pp.
76. *Culbertson Diamond Jubilee, 1887–1962: Seventy-Five Years of Progress* (NE). Ed. Belvina Bertino. Montana Historical Society. Diamond Jubilee Committee, 1962. 132 pp.
77. *From Buffalo Bones to Sonic Booms: Glasgow Diamond Jubilee, 1887–1962* (NE) Ed. Vivian A. Paladin. Glasgow Jubilee Committee, 1962. 102 pp.
78. *Shelby Backgrounds* (NC). Shelby History Group, Montana Institute of the Arts, 1965. 302 pp.
79. "A Brief Historical Review of Life and Times on the Northeastern Montana Prairies" (NE/IB). Montana Historical Society Pamphlet 78. Homesteaders Golden Jubilee Association, 1963. 96 pp.
80. "Golden Jubilee: Wolf Point, Montana, 1915–1965" (NE). Montana Historical Society Pamphlet 1749. Golden Jubilee History Committee, 1965. 76 pp.
81. *In Blaine: A Bicentennial Book* (NC/IB). Marie Snedecor, Arlene Williamson, Janet S. Allison, and Madeleine Gilmore, 1975. 121 pp.
82. *Outlook-Daleview Community Diamond Jubilee Book* (NE). Ed. Helen Wagnild Stoner. Privately produced, Outlook Community and School Club, 1985. 159 pp.

83. *Rudyard Images* (NC). Ed. Ruby Langel. Privately produced, 1985. 912 pp.
84. *One Hundred Years in Culbertson, 1887–1987* (NE). Ed. Lorretta Segars. Historical Committee, 1987. 204 pp.
85. *Trails, Trials, and Tributes* (NC). Montana Historical Society Pamphlet 119. Egly Country Club, 1958. 104 pp.
86. *Golden Book of Plentywood* (NE/IB). Privately published, 1962. 108 pp.
87. *Trial and Triumph* (NC). Ed. Janet Snedecor Allison. North Central Montana Cowbelles, 1968. 211 pp.
88. *Treasured Years* (NE). Ed. Leota Hoye. Roosevelt County Bicentennial Committee, 1976. 1,084 pp.
89. "Knees Community History, 1886–1955" (NC). Genevieve Rossmiller and Gladys Neyland. Montana Historical Society Pamphlet 1569. Triple-F Home Demonstration Club, 1955. 16 pp.
90. *Footprints through the Valley* (NC). Pleasant Valley Home Demonstration Club, 1957. 49 pp.
91. *In the Years Gone By* (NC). Ed. Ruth Morse and Mary Meland. Cottonwood Home Demonstration Club, 1965. 254 pp.
92. *Prairie Pioneers: A Narrative of Montana Homestead Days* (NC). Portage History Society, 1966. 182 pp.
93. *Sheridan's Daybreak: A Story of Sheridan County and Its Pioneers* (NE/IB). Ed. Magnus Aasheim. Sheridan County Historical Association, 1970. 1,007 pp.
94. Omitted from this collection
95. *Echoes from the Prairie* (NC/IB). Prairie Homemakers Extension Club and Jayhawker Ridge Home Extension Club, 1976. 668 pp.
96. *Grits, Guts and Gusto: A History of Hill County* (NC/IB). Hill County Bicentennial Commission, 1976. 505 pp.
97. *Grime, Grit and Gumption: Early History of South Marias* (NC). Ponde-Toole Extension Homemakers Club, 1976. 117 pp.
98. *Our Heritage in Liberty* (NC/IB). Ed. Iva Kolstad. Liberty County Museum, 1976. 511 pp.
99. *Pioneer Trails and Trials: Madison County 1863–1920* (SW). Madison County Historical Association, 1976. 1,017 pp.
100. *Spokes, Spurs and Cockleb158urs* (NC). Ed. Geraldine History Committee. River Press Pub. Co., Fort Benton, 1976. 309 pp.
101. *The Eagle* (NC). Ed. Lillie Hall. Griggs Printing and Publishing, Havre, 1976. 155 pp.
102. *Daniels County History* (NE/IB). Ed. Claire A. Hillstrom. Montana Historical Society. Daniels County Historical Committee, 1977. 1,014 pp.
103. *The Yesteryears* (NC/IB). Phillips County Historical Society, 1978. 578 pp.
104. *Always the Wind* (NC/IB). North Havre St. Joe Area Residents, 1979. 219 pp.
105. *Homesteading, Our Heritage* (NE/IB). North Valley County Bicentennial Committee, 1980. 844 pp.

Additional Books

106. *History of Glacier County Montana* (NW/IB). Ed. Joy MacCarter. Glacier County Historical Society, 1984. 297 pp.
107. *Montana: Sheridan's Daybreak II* (NE/IB). Ed. Magnus Aasheim. Montana Historical Society. Sheridan's Daybreak II Committee, 1984. 1,008 pp.
108. *Life as It Was* (NC). Lillie Hall Hollingshead, 1975. 96 pp.
109. *Speaking-Out on Sod-House Times* (North Dakota). Interviews by Pauline Neher Diede. Richardton ND: Abbey Press, 1985. 112 pp.

Archival Documents and Privately Produced Manuscripts

Copies of these documents are deposited in the library of the Medicine Hat Historical Museum and Gallery, Medicine Hat, Alberta.

Alberta Women's Institute. Committee on Legislation Suggestions for Year 1928–29. Edmonton: Alberta Provincial Archives, acc. no. 86.125.

Benson, Roy, and Verna Benson. "Letters from an American Homesteader, 1910–1926." Calgary: Glenbow Archives M87.

Chapman, Mrs. J. W. 1960. "A Time to Reminisce." Privately printed.

Christie, David. Christie Family Correspondence. St. Paul: Minnesota Historical Society, P1283, box D.

Diede, Pauline Neher. 1983. *Homesteading on the Knife River Prairies*. Bismarck ND: North Dakota Germans from Russia Heritage Society.

———. 1985. *Speaking-Out on Sod-House Times*. Richardton ND: Abbey Press.

———. 1986. *The Prairie Was Home*. Richardton ND: Abbey Press.

Dixon Brothers' Papers. 1884–1922. Regina: Saskatchewan Provincial Archives, G1255 E.J.-5.

Ever Ready Women's Institute, Coaldale, Alta. Minute Books 1919–25, 1925–30. Lethbridge, Alta.: Galt Archive, LA#P196623560000-GM.

Finnell, Eva Gorman, ed. 1980. *The Montana Years: Chouteau County, 1910–1926*. Helena: Montana Historical Society.

Flint Papers. 1915. Calgary: Glenbow Archives.

Floerchinger, Dorothy. n.d. "To Speak of Love Was Not Enough: A Biography of Daniel and Panayiota McCorkle." Privately printed.

Gorman Davis, Maggie. Letters. In Eva Gorman Finnell, ed., 1980, *The Montana Years: Chouteau County, 1910–1926*. Helena: Montana Historical Society.

Hansen-Horntvedt Letters. Northfield MN: Norwegian-American Historical Association.

Jacobsen, Carl and Averil. 1982. "Winding Trails." Privately published. Shaunavon: Saskatchewan Provincial Archives.

King, Annie Lacore. n.d. "Reminiscences." St. Paul: Minnesota Historical Society Archives.

Lea Park Women's Institute. Minutes, 1909–1911. Edmonton: Alberta Provincial Archives, acc. no 75.58/72.

Lind, Robert W. 1961. "From the Ground Up: The Story of 'Brother Van,' Montana Pioneer Minister, 1848–1919." Privately printed.

Miller, Lillian. n.d. "I Remember Montana." Helena: Montana Historical Society, sc1404.
Moorhouse, Myrtle G. n.d. *Buffalo Horn Valley.* Regina, Sask.: Banting Publishers.
Morehouse, Kent. Morehouse Papers, 1913, 1914. St. Paul: Minnesota Historical Society Archives.
Neil, Catherine. 1938. "Pioneer Days." Edmonton: Alberta Provincial Archives, acc. no 74.1/89.
Ouelette, Josie Olson. 1977. "As I Recall." Regina: Saskatchewan Provincial Archives.
Parson, Edna Tyson. 1981. *Land I Own.* Ottawa: Westboro Printers.
Rowley, Adelaide. n.d. In "Biographies Ros–Rz," p. 939. St. Paul: Minnesota Historical Society.
Slater, Barbara Alice. Letters, 1906–1918. Edmonton: Alberta Provincial Archives, acc. no. 78.79. These letters have been edited and published in Dryden and Myres (1987).
Turner, John P. n.d. "The Piapot-C.P.R. Episode." Regina: Saskatchewan Provincial Archives.
Weeks, Mary. n.d. "Forgotten Pioneers." Helena: Montana Historical Society Archives.
Wilkes, Bertha. n.d. Typewritten autobiography. Courtesy of Laura Wilkes Parsonage, Maple Creek, Saskatchewan.

Index

For the names of participants in the settlement process whose writings are cited or quoted in the text, see the relevant sections of the bibliography.